Images of America
Manhattan Beach
California

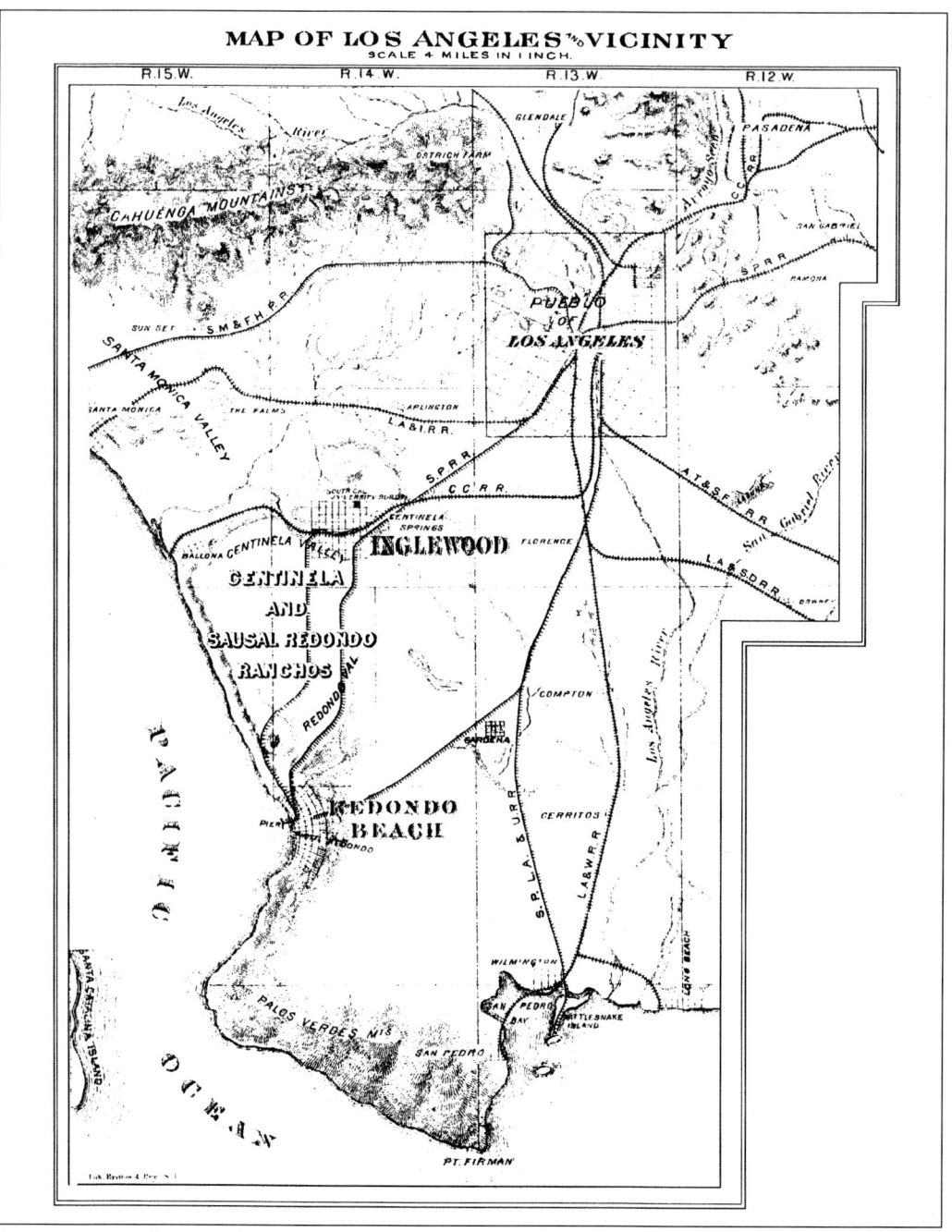

An 1889 map showing the Centinela and Sausal Redondo Ranch owned by Daniel Freeman, located in the Los Angeles vicinity.

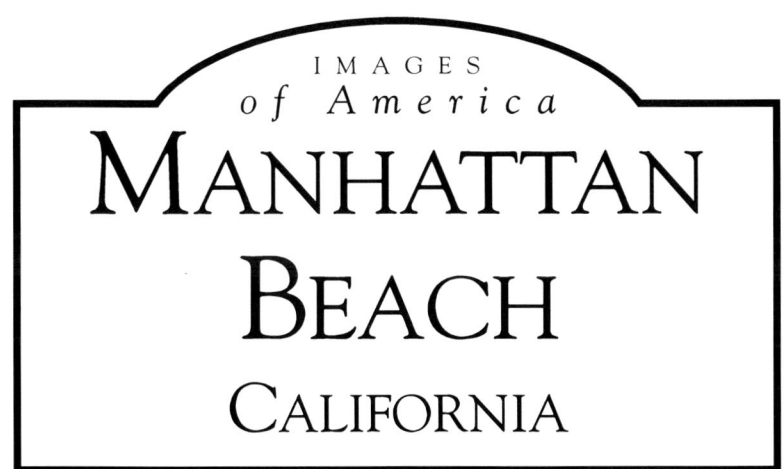

Images of America
Manhattan Beach
California

Jan Dennis

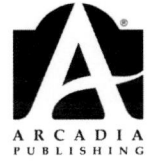

Copyright © 2001 by Jan Dennis
ISBN 978-0-7385-1911-1

Published by Arcadia Publishing
Charleston, South Carolina

Printed in the United States of America

Library of Congress Catalog Card Number: 2001093331

For all general information contact Arcadia Publishing at:
Telephone 843-853-2070
Fax 843-853-0044
E-mail sales@arcadiapublishing.com
For customer service and orders:
Toll-Free 1-888-313-2665

Visit us on the Internet at www.arcadiapublishing.com

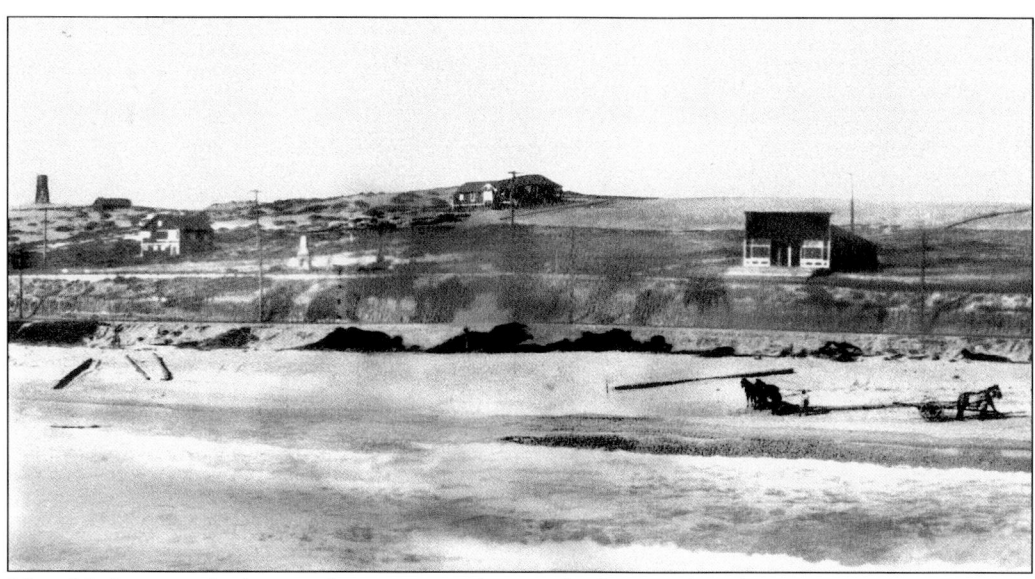

The old photograph above, taken in 1902, depicts the laying of track giving Manhattan Beach a public transportation link to the center of Los Angeles. This vital artery carried the crimson painted trolley known as the "Red Car." Running along the pristine surf, it ushered in the beginnings of a town by the seaside.

CONTENTS

Acknowledgments		6
Introduction		7
1.	Over the Sand	9
2.	Early Development	29
3.	Shifting Sand	55
4.	Rapid Growth	73
5.	End of an Era	91
6.	Preserving Character	111

Acknowledgments

Over the decades, old landmarks have disappeared and the image of the town has changed, but the one thing that has remained constant is a genuine fondness for the concept so proudly held by early residents: "A community that appreciated its independence and its rich heritage."

A pictorial review of this kind takes many hours of compiling, organizing, and researching from many sources. Appreciation and acknowledgments go to the many residents, old and new, who supplied photographs from their private collections; the publisher of *A Walk Beside the Sea* and *Shadows on the Dunes*; the City of Manhattan Beach; Don Stone; and Ernie Marquez.

I truly appreciate the interest and professional assistance of John Scott. Without his skill and dedication this volume would not have been possible. John reproduced many of the early pictures and graphics. Their clear and pristine restoration brought added life and visual strength to the project. Without his computer dexterity to enhance so many of these old and faded photographs, the images would not have been suitable for printing.

This acknowledgment would not be complete without my heartfelt thanks to my friend Esther Besbris, who read and edited the text and captions.

The text and photographs have been arranged in chronological order to give the reader the feeling of the city's creation. It is hoped the reader will enjoy the following pages and find a rekindling of interest in their community's heritage.

Jan Dennis
Researcher and writer
of Manhattan Beach History

Introduction

It was not until 1769 that the Spanish personally occupied California land. The colonization of California was started with an expedition made up of three groups: two groups came by land and the other by sea. Spain's method for colonization of foreign lands was the establishment of the mission: centers of shelter, education, and indoctrination. While converting the natives to Christianity and providing for their temporal needs, their aim was to transform them into loyal and industrious subjects obedient to the King of Spain. The Spaniards called the Indians of the Manhattan Beach region the Engnovangnas.

There is little evidence left that Indians actually lived on the land that is now Manhattan Beach; however, they no doubt passed through the area on their way to the salt flats that lay to the south.

As the expedition traveled north, presidios were established to house the soldiers and their families. The pueblo system was founded on land grants and essentially started when the King wished to reward those first explorer-soldiers for their service when they retired.

When Mexico gained its independence from Spain in 1822, it continued the land grant system with the only difference being that Mexican land grants gave title with the land. The Los Angeles area had many such grants; among them was Rancho Sausal Redondo, meaning "round clump of willows." Prior to the Civil War, in 1861, Sir Robert Burnett of Crathe's Castle, Scotland, purchased Centinela and Sausal Redondo Rancho from the heirs of Antonio Ygnacio Avila for $33,000. The two ranchos encompassed 24,678 acres.

By May of 1885, Daniel Freeman, who had been leasing the ranch from Burnett, acquired the deed to the property for the sum of $140,000. He had already paid $22,243 for a portion of the ranch on August 29, 1882. A few years later, due to unexpected financial problems, Freeman was force to sell much of the ranch. By May of 1887, the Redondo Land Company owned eight-and-one-half sections of the former Freeman ranch. The Land Company filed for an agreement of partition for the subdivision of those sections, five of which determined the boundaries of Manhattan Beach.

The city of Manhattan Beach was originally situated on a broad series of sand dunes on an elevated shoreline stretching from Playa del Rey in the north to Redondo Beach in the south. The true birthplace of the community, early in the 20th century, was along the Strand and in what is now its downtown area. Located on the shore of pristine Santa Monica Bay, the little town soon found itself being identified and promoted as one of the finest places to live.

As surrounding areas grew at a steady pace, Manhattan Beach remained a tranquil, sparsely populated area, inhabited only by those willing to challenge the sand dunes. Unlike much of Southern California the temperature does not vary as much as the rest of the surrounding areas due to the temperate effect of the ocean and the sea breeze, keeping the winter warmer and the summer cooler.

The rapid growth that took place in other South Bay areas did not occur in Manhattan Beach until the arrival of the Atchison, Topeka, and the Santa Fe Railroads in 1888. This was followed by the Pacific Electric "Red Car" in 1903. With better transportation, people could live near the shore yet work in Los Angeles or other areas in the Los Angeles basin. It would not be until after World War II, with returning GI's and the increase in air and space industries locating in the area, that the population in Manhattan Beach would swell once more.

Today the community of Manhattan Beach consists of 2,476.18 acres and is no longer a settlement of beach cottages on shifting sands, but a city with a population of 33,094 residents.

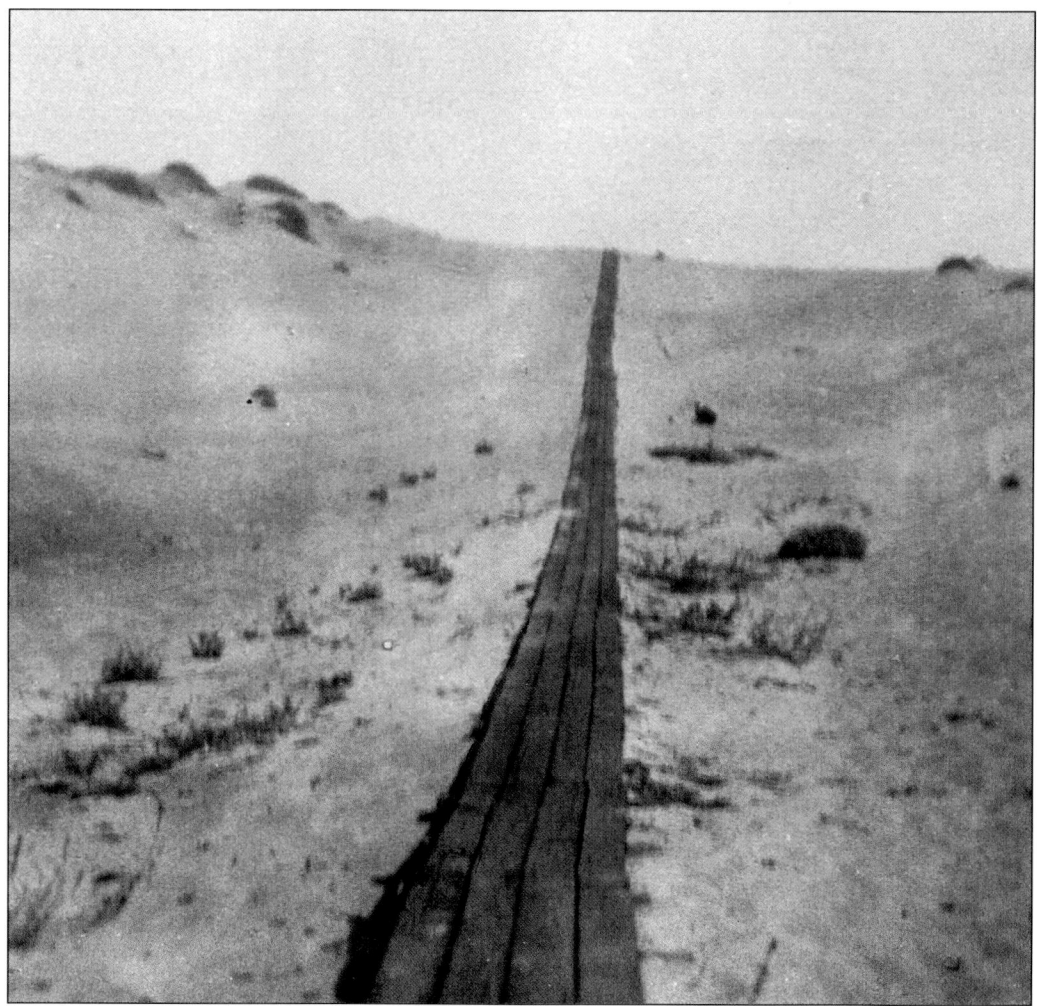

At road's end, the holiday visitor would take the wooden footpath leading over the sand dune to the beach, surf, and sea.

One
OVER THE SAND

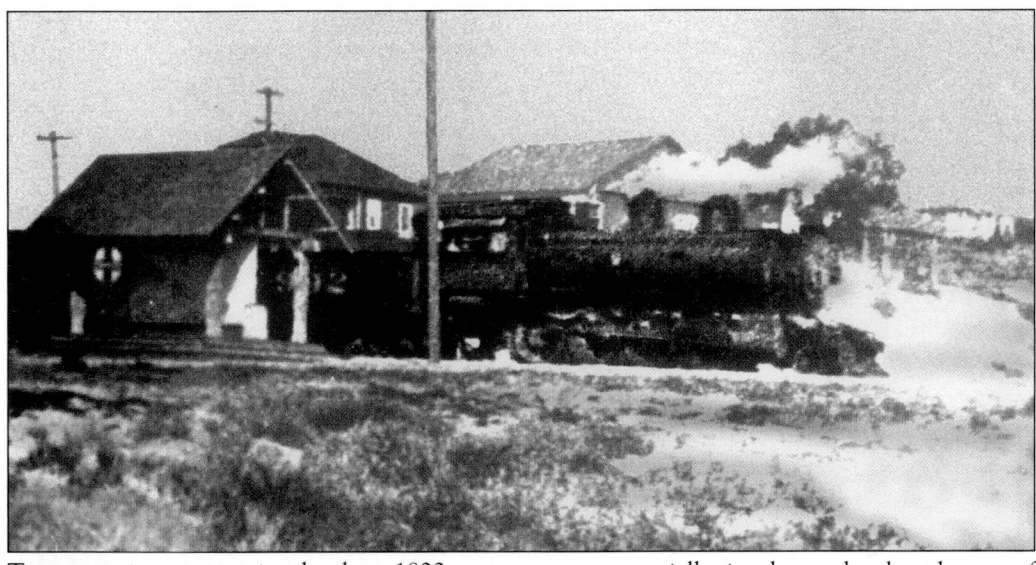

Transportation routes in the late 1800s were sparse especially in the undeveloped area of Manhattan Beach. Visitors came to the shore by foot or horseback. However, that was to change on October 24, 1888, with an agreement between Charles Silent, a major shareholder in the Redondo Land Company, and the Redondo Beach Railway Company. The land company gave the railway company a right-of-way for the construction, maintenance, and operation of a steam railroad line over their land. The strip of land, 10.77 miles long and 100 feet wide, ran from the nearby community of Inglewood to the harbor in Redondo Beach, California. In 1904, the rail line would be known as the Atchison, Topeka, and Santa Fe Railway Company.

The railroad played a vital part in the development of Manhattan Beach. Its main purpose was to carry freight, but it also provided a means for people to reach this coastal area. The tracks passed through the beach communities of Manhattan, Hermosa, and Redondo, bringing not only tourists, but the shipping trade dollar.

North of Center Street (now Manhattan Beach Blvd.), stood a small freight platform and two seats back-to-back covered by a small roof. This served as the station.

REDONDO JUNC., REDONDO AND SANTA MONICA.

THIRD DISTRICT.

TIME TABLE NO. 42 — October 23, 1897.

WESTWARD									EASTWARD		
Second Class	FIRST-CLASS		Siding Capacity	Telegraph Offices	Distance from Redondo Junc.	Ruling Grade Ascending	STATIONS	Ruling Grade Descending	Station Numbers	Telegraph Calls	Water and Fuel Stations	FIRST-CLASS		Second Class
161	145	141										140	144	162
Redondo and Santa Monica Freight	Redondo Accommodat'n	Seaside Special			MILES							Los Angeles Accommodat'n	Seaside Special	Los Angeles Freight
DAILY Except Sunday	DAILY	DAILY					Leave Arrive					DAILY	DAILY	DAILY Except Sunday
9.16 AM	4.51 PM	9.51 AM	27		0.0	0.0	REDONDO JUNC. 2.5		52.5	C 2		8.23 AM	4.19 PM	3.44 PM
f 9.25	f 4.55	f 9.56	47	D	2.5	1.1	NADEAU PARK 1.0	0.5	21.1	M 5	N I	f 8.18	f 4.14	f 3.37
f 9.27	f 4.57	f 9.58	11	D	3.6	10.6	CENTRAL AVENUE 1.0	18.5	M 6	O A	f 8.16	f 4.12	f 3.33
f 9.32	f 5.00	f 10.00			4.6	0.0	SLAUSON 1.5	15.6	M 7		f 8.14	f 4.10	f 3.29
f 9.37	f 5.03	f 10.02	8		6.1	44.8	WILDASIN 2.1	10.5	M 8		f 8.12	f 4.07	f 3.24
f 9.43	f 5.07	f 10.06			8.2	44.8	HYDE PARK 0.7	52.3	M 10		f 8.08	f 4.04	f 3.16
f 9.47	f 5.09	f 10.08	67		9.2	0.0	CENTINELA 0.7	52.3	M 11		f 8.06	f 4.02	f 3.12
s 9.50 12.01 PM	f 5.11	f 10.10	95	D	9.9	14.0	INGLEWOOD 3.8	22.4	M 12	W S	f 8.04	f 4.00	f 3.10
f 12.15	f 5.17	f 10.17	46		13.7	82.8	WISEBURN 3.5	42.2	B 4		f 7.57	f 3.53	f 2.55
f 12.27	f 5.24	f 10.24			17.2	6.0	POTENCIA 2.8	42.2	B 6		f 7.51	f 3.46	f 2.42
f 12.40 PM	f 5.30 PM	f 10.30 AM	285	D	20.5		REDONDO			B 11	D C	f 7.45 AM	f 3.40 PM	f 2.30 PM
10.12 AM			95	D	9.9	0.0	INGLEWOOD 2.6		52 3	M 12	W S			11.45 AM
f 10.21			12		12.5	0.5	MESMER 2.7		20.4	M 15				f 11.36
f 10.29			0		15.2	47.5	MACHADO 2.7		16.9	M 18				f 11.27
f 10.37			60		17.9	72.5	OCEAN PARK 0.7		0.0	M 20	Y			f 11.18
10.40 AM			40	D	18.6		SANTA MONICA			M 21	N I			11.15 AM
DAILY Except Sunday	DAILY	DAILY					Arrive Leave					DAILY	DAILY	DAILY Except Sunday

Between Inglewood and slow post, about one-half mile east of station, all trains must proceed under control, prepared to stop on short notice.

Do not exceed 15 miles per hour over any Railroad Crossing.

Yard Limits at Redondo and Santa Monica are shown by board bearing the words "Yard Limit." All freight and irregular trains while within yard limits must be under full control, expecting to find main track occupied.

Trainmen are forbidden from going between cars and high platforms of depots, warehouses, etc., for the purpose of coupling or uncoupling cars. Such work must be done only on the side opposite the platform.

Nos. 161 and 162 will carry passengers between Inglewood and Santa Monica.

SIDINGS BETWEEN STATIONS.

Corinto (B 2), 1.4 miles east of Wiseburn, connected east end, length 900 feet.
Pipe Works (M 6½), 0.5 mile west of Central Avenue, connected west end, length 2427 feet.

RAILROAD CROSSINGS AT GRADE.

L. A. & R. Ry.—0.5 mile east of Redondo, and 0.5 mile east of Wildasin; no targets at either crossing. All trains must know that crossings are clear before attempting to cross.
Southern Pacific—at Nadeau Park, inter-locking signals.

W. G. NEVIN, General Manager.   **A. G. WELLS,** General Superintendent.   **W. B. BEAMER,** Superintendent.

SOUTHERN CALIFORNIA RY.—REDONDO DISTRICT.

TIME TABLE No. 66. December 1, 1903.

WESTWARD							EASTWARD	
Second Class	First Class	Capacity of Sidings	Fuel, Water, Turning Facilities	STATIONS	Ruling Grade Ascending	Distance from Los Angeles	First Class	Second Class
161	141					Miles	144	162
Leave Daily Ex. Sunday	Leave Daily						Arrive Daily	Arrive Daily Ex. Sunday
AM 9.15	AM 10.17		Y	REDONDO JUNC. 2.5		52.8	PM 4.19	AM 8.00
f 9.25	f 10.22	89		NADEAU PARK (S.P. Co. Crossing.) 1.0		21.1	f 4.14	f 7.46
f 9.30	f 10.24	25		CENTRAL AVENUE 1.6	10.6	18.5	f 4.12	f 7.43
f 9.35	f 10.26			SLAUSON 0.3		15.6	f 4.10	f 7.38
				L. A. & S. Railway Crossing. 0.7		15.6		
f 9.45	f 10.27			WILDASIN 1.9	44.8	10.6	f 4.07	f 7.32
f 9.55	f 10.31	16		HYDE PARK 1.1	44.8	52.3	f 4.04	f 7.23
f 10.00	f 10.33	59		CENTINELA 0.8		52.3	f 4.02	f 7.18
f 10.10	f 10.35	46	Y	INGLEWOOD 3.8	14.0	22.4	f 4.00	f 7.15
f 10.23	f 10.41	51		WISEBURN 3.4	52.8	42.2	f 3.53	f 6.54
f 10.35	f 10.47	2		MANHATTAN BEACH 2.8		42.2	f 3.47	f 6.40
				L. A. & S. Railway Crossing. 0.5		21.1		
10.56 AM Arrive Daily Except Sunday	10.56 AM Arrive Daily	Yard	WT	REDONDO (20.4)		20	3.40 PM Leave Daily	6.30 PM Leave Daily Except Sunday
(12.2)	(22.2)						(21.4)	(12.6)

........Average speed per hour........

OLINDA DISTRICT.

TIME TABLE No. 66. December 1, 1903.

SOUTHWARD							NORTHWARD
Second Class		Capacity of Sidings	Fuel, Water, Turning Facilities	STATIONS	Ruling Grade Ascending	Distance from Los Angeles	Second Class
29							28
Leave Daily Ex. Sunday							Arrive Daily Ex. Sunday
AM 10.23		60	Y	RICHFIELD 4.2	111.4	122.9	AM 11.50
10.43 AM Arrive Daily Ex. Sunday			F	OLINDA (4.2)		127.1	11.30 AM Leave Daily Ex. Sunday

........Average speed per hour........

Nos. 741 and 744 will stop on signal at North Manhattan Beach one-half mile east of Manhattan Beach.

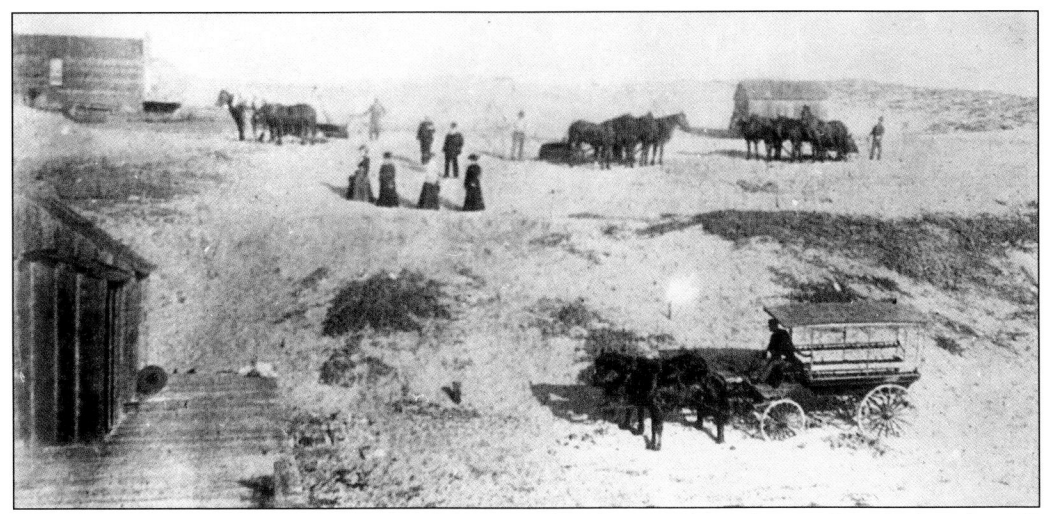

Late in 1901, John A. Merrill, one of the first developers of Manhattan Beach, bought 450 acres from the Redondo Land Company for $20,000. Later, he sold the northern 300 acres to George H. Peck Jr. for the original price of the 450 acres. Merrill and his newly formed Manhattan Beach Company would survey the remaining 150 acres in 1902, indicating the first development site. Merrill's office (upper left) was located just above the foot of the original pier (lower left).

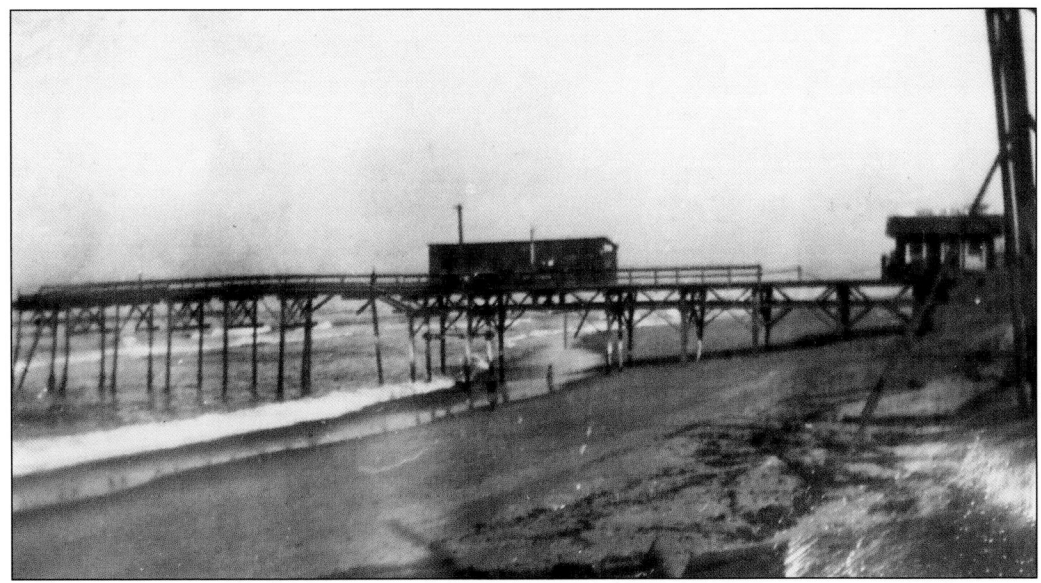

The first pier was 900 feet long and had an unusual construction. A narrow wooden deck was built on top of crisscrossed railroad ties that had been pounded into the sand. The 1902 survey map indicated an "Iron Pier" built at the end of Center Street (this would be renamed later as Manhattan Beach Blvd.). The pier was eventually destroyed in a winter storm of 1913–14.

(*opposite*) An 1897 timetable indicates the railway stop of a community called "Potencia." Later, in 1903, it was renamed "Manhattan Beach."

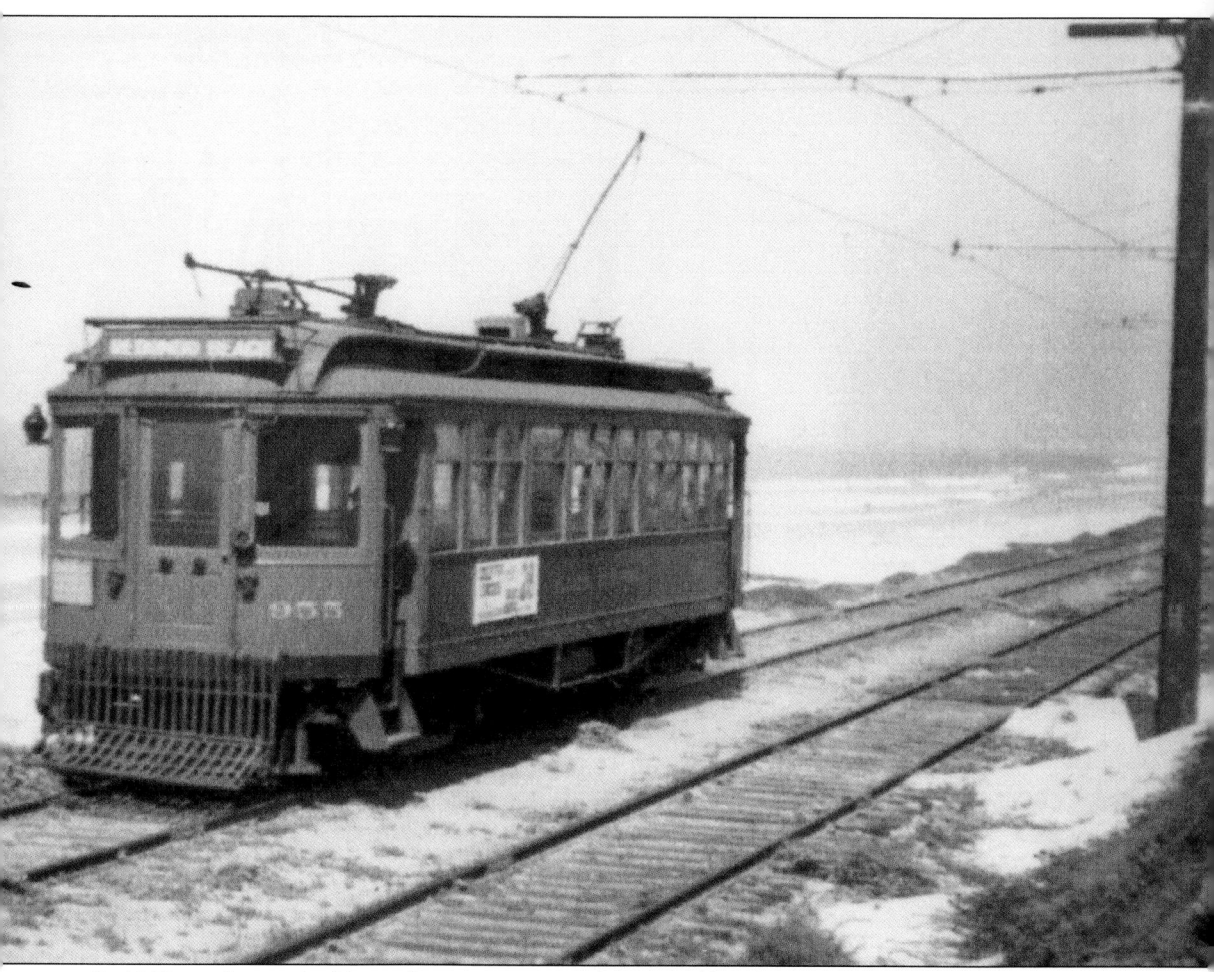

In 1902, work on a double track, narrow gauge, electric rail line began down the coast via Playa del Rey (a community just to the north of Manhattan Beach). The idea was that of Hazeltine Sherman and Eli P. Clark, who created one of the most innovative electrical railway systems ever seen. Sherman had already developed an electrified streetcar system in Phoenix, Arizona. By the end of the summer of 1903, tracks and ballasting were ready for a through train operating under the name of the Los Angeles Pacific Railroad Company. There were five stops established in Manhattan Beach. The tracks ran along the shoreline between the Strand walkway and the ocean.

The system, dubbed the "Red Car," brought sightseers as well as homebuyers. One could board the "Redondo Beach Line" at Hill Street in downtown Los Angeles and step off the train at Center Street in Manhattan, all within 53 minutes. The new transportation brought an atmosphere of excitement to the area. The "Big Red Car" service would stay intact for some 37 years. Though it was important to the community, the rumbling noises and the dimming of electric power each time the train passed was a definite annoyance to those living a few blocks from the tracks.

The line down the coast constituted the most spectacular bit of the company's trackage. It was a high speed line as well, for the sand gave it a good foundation, though storms would sometimes wash it away. This line ran from Ivy Junction on the Palms Division to Diamond Street in Redondo Beach, a distance of 1,440 miles, all double track and private right-of-way.

The most heavily used stations were at 22nd Street (now Marine Avenue) and Center Street (now Manhattan Beach Boulevard). The other stops were at Peck's Pier, Peck's Beach and Verano Beach (now the foot of 14th Street.)

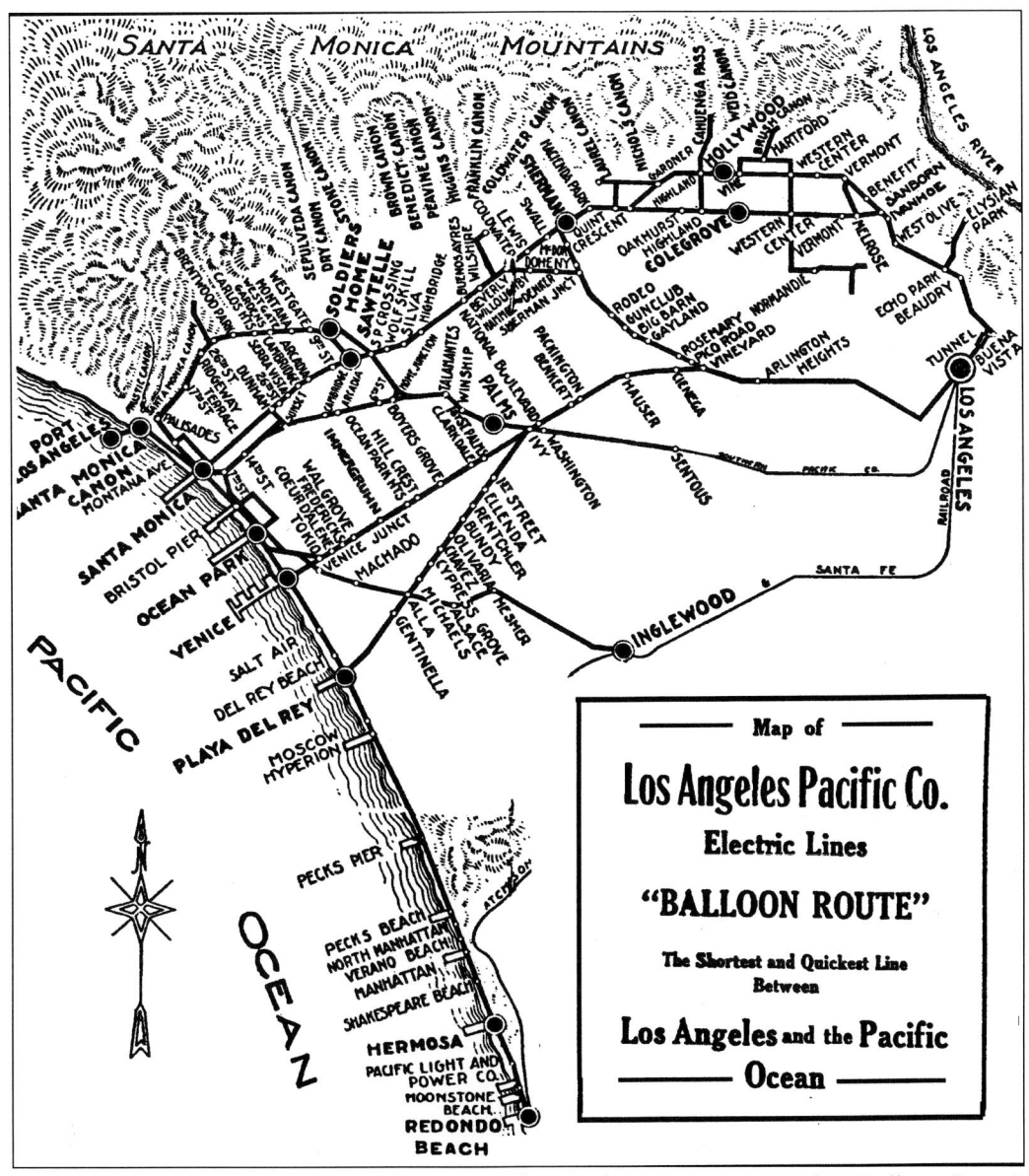

In 1909, one of the most popular features of the "Red Car" system was the "Balloon Route" Excursion Trip, which made one circle of the Los Angeles area without having to change trains.

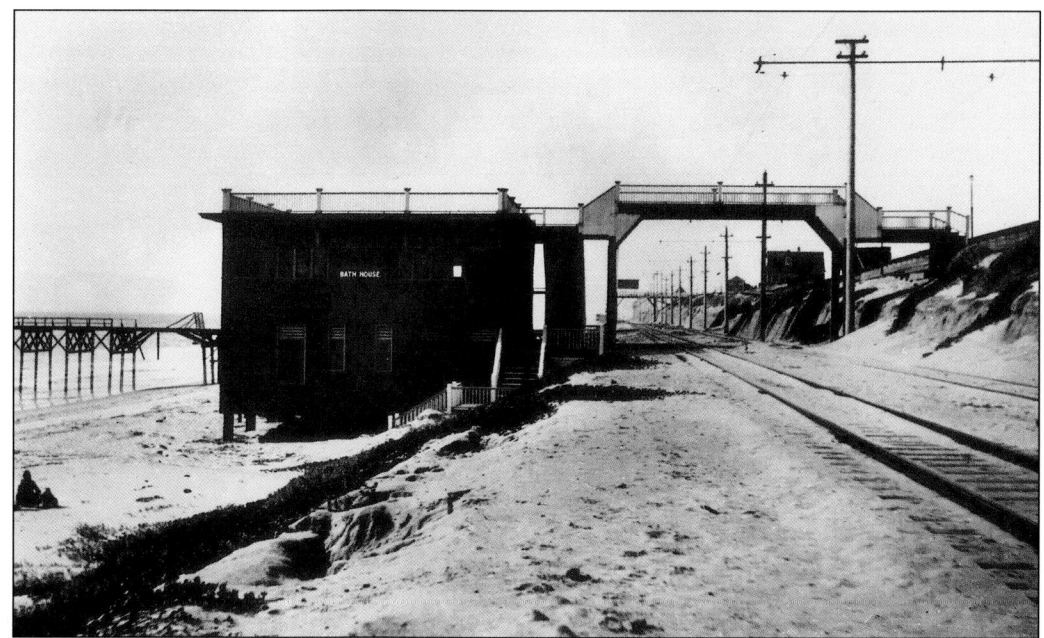

James G. Corteyou, a pioneer real estate developer in the beach cities, constructed this bathhouse at the foot of 11th Street in the spring of 1901. Built on the sand next to the "Red Car" tracks, it became a landmark as well as a favorite restaurant for tourists who enjoyed its famous clam chowder. However, in 1919 it was declared unsafe and was demolished in the same year.

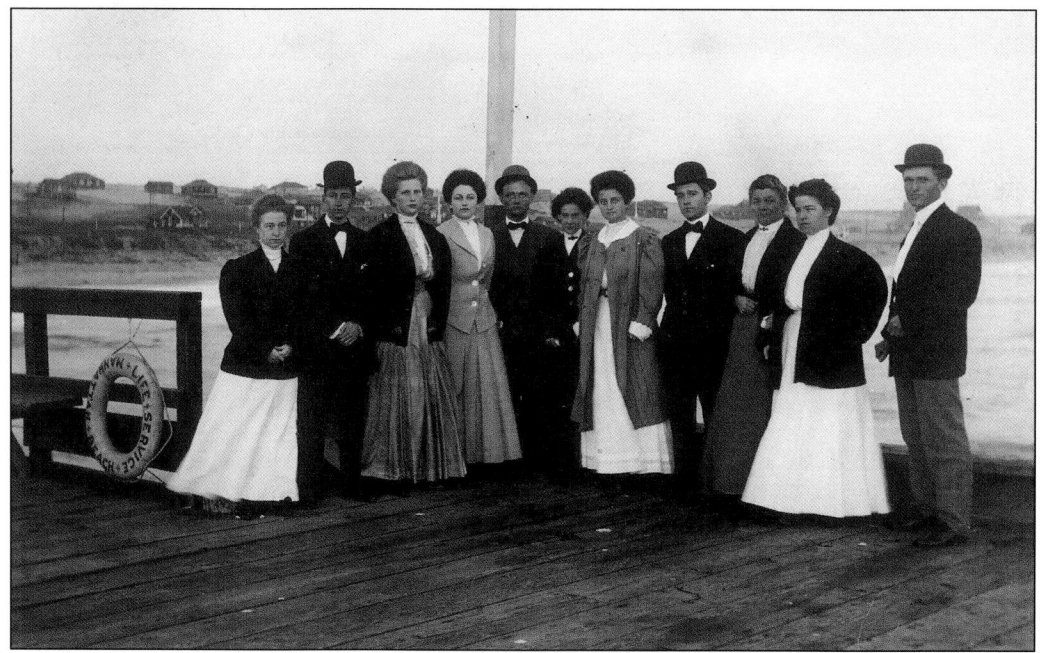

In 1908, visitors were often found having their picture taken at the end of the wooden pier. Tours took people past Manhattan, Shakespeare, and Hermosa beaches on their way to Redondo Beach. Shakespeare Beach was Sherman and Clark's effort to create a literary colony along the railway lines. Neither the name nor the colony really caught on.

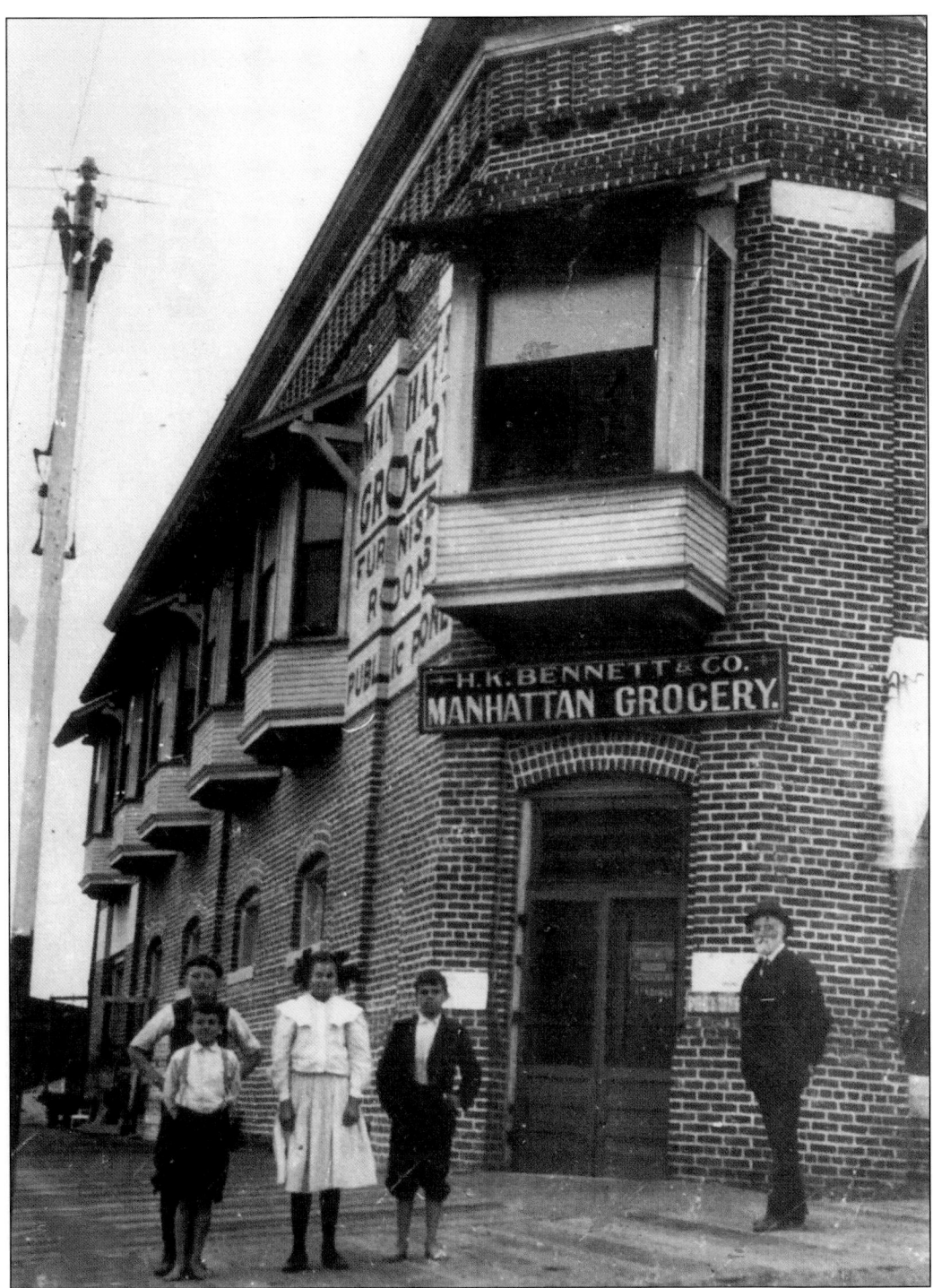

Standing in front of one of the earliest commercial structures in the downtown area built by the Merrill Brothers are the Kuhn children: Bob, Helen, Walter, and Marshall. The large two-story brick edifice housed the general store, post office, and a hotel on the second floor. The only telephone in town was also at the location, c. 1910.

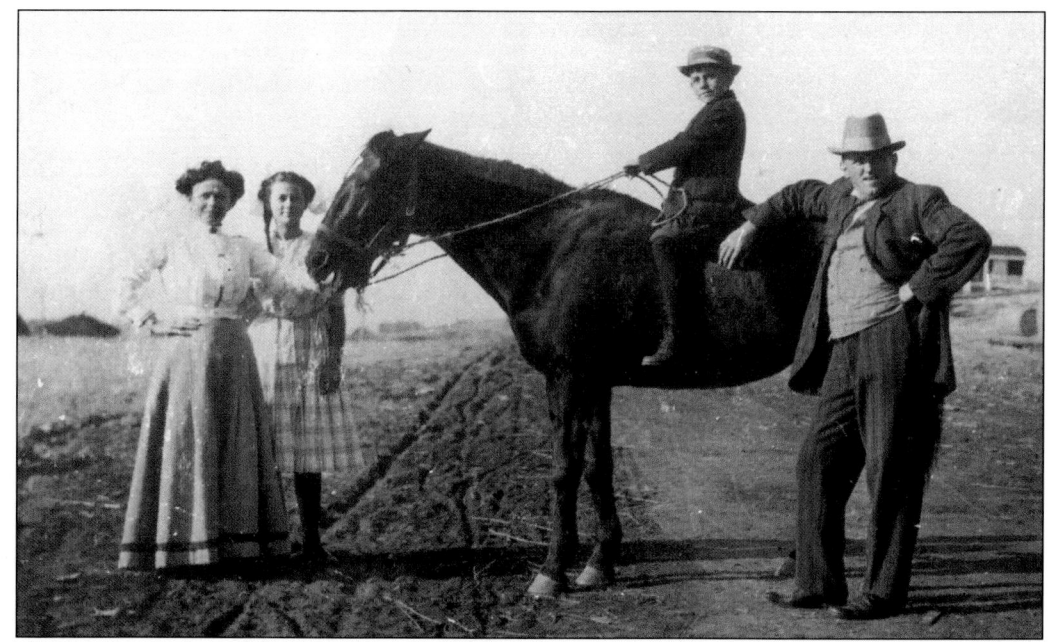

One family well acquainted with the trolley was the Kuhn family, seen here left to right: Mother Kuhn, Helen Kuhn, Marshall Kuhn, and Bob Kuhn. Bob was better known as "Dad" Kuhn (far right). A motorman on the "Red Car," he brought his family to Manhattan Beach in 1905. Bob "Dad" Kuhn later ran the grocery store and the post office. In 1914, he was the water superintendent, street superintendent, and the city Marshall. Young Bob, his son, was to become the city's first electric light tender. He was paid $3.00 per month for duties that included setting the master switch as well as replacing burned out bubble lamps.

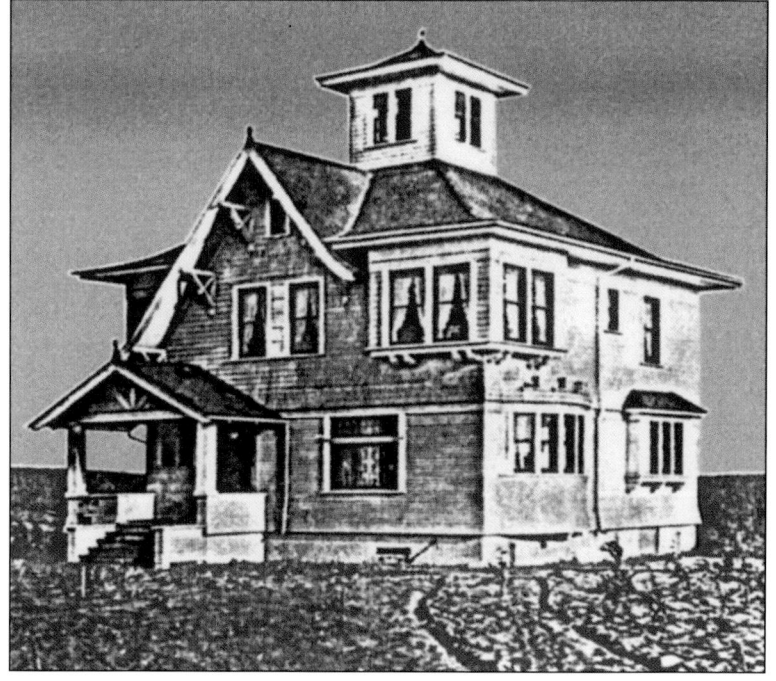

In 1906, an impressive "Prairie Box" style home was built for the Cardinell family. Their daughter, Ruth, married Marshall Kuhn and the couple lived across the road from the Cardinell home, located at 1230 Perry Avenue (later renamed 5th Street). Originally surrounded by sand, corn was planted in order to hold down the drifting sands. Later demolished, a sprawling home, tennis court, and swimming pool now cover the property.

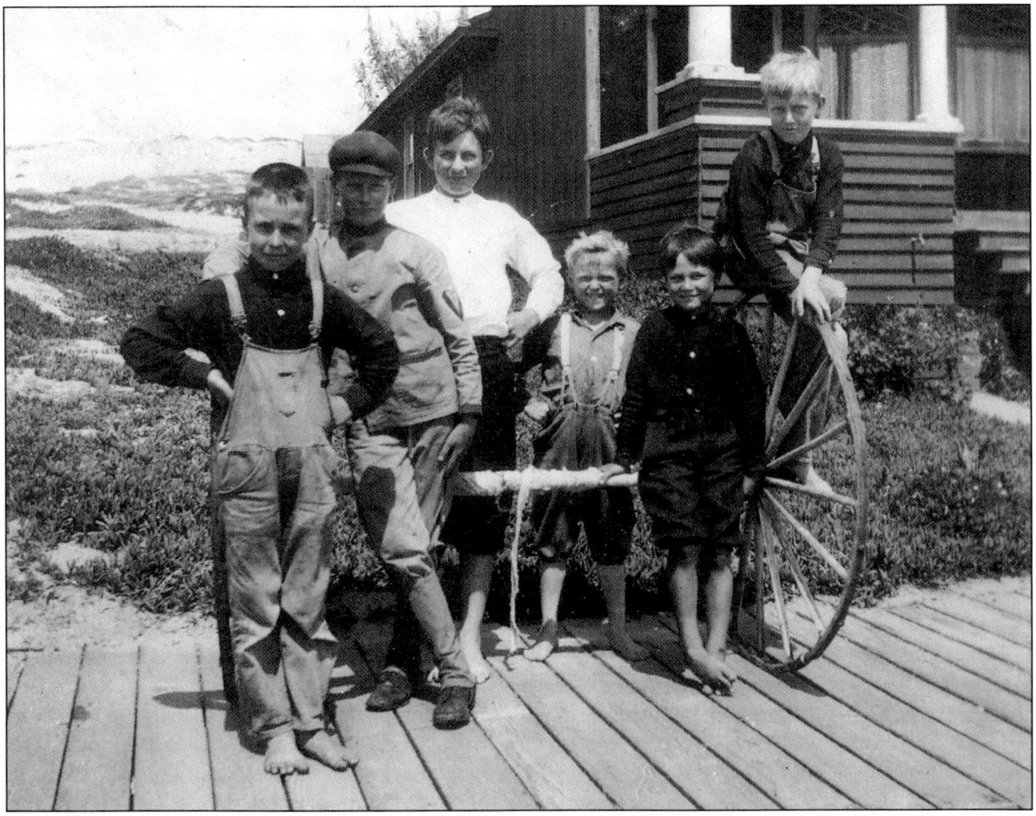

Ocean winds often buried streets under tons of sand while elsewhere beaches, road beds, and home sites were eroded. Boardwalks were utilized throughout the community as sidewalks over the soft sand. The boards were about 6 feet long and 6 to 8 inches wide. People not used to the sandy boardwalks along the Strand often fell when encountering sheets of sand. When out for a stroll, residents would carry a small pail of nails and a hammer to tack down any loose boards they might encounter. This was done to protect others from danger as they walked.

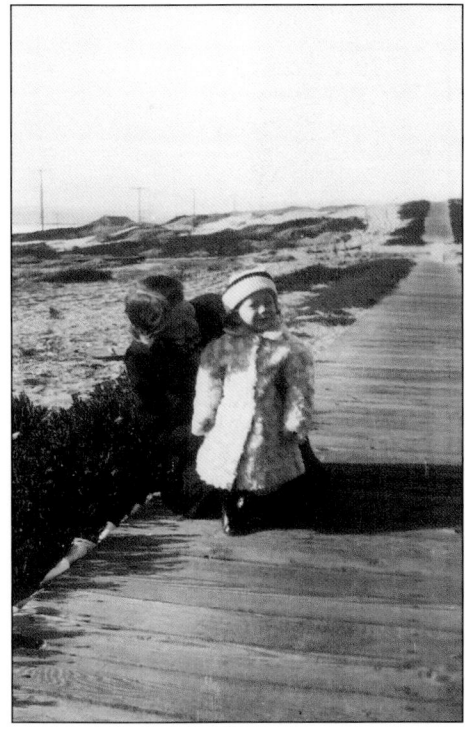

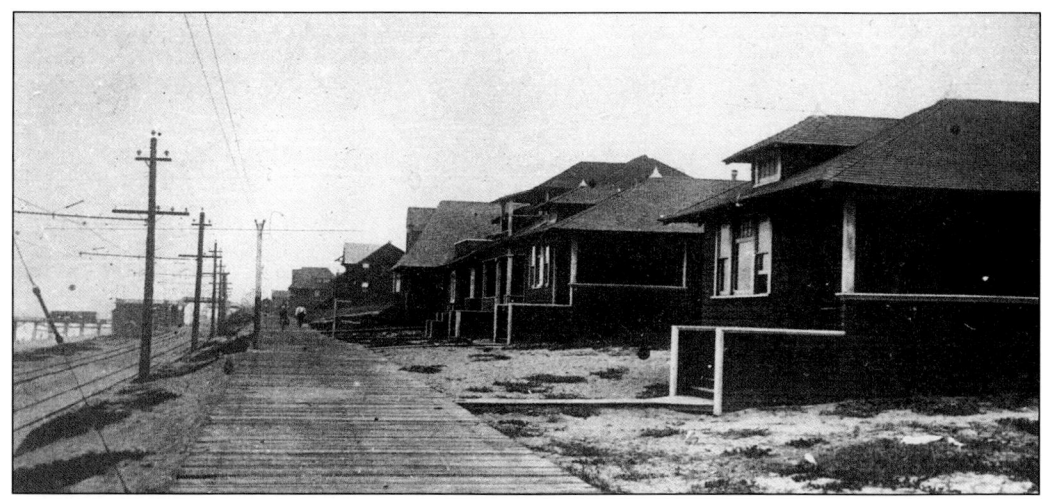

The wooden boardwalk along the Strand was one of the first to be developed. This area, with its unobstructed view of the ocean and pearly white beach, was highly sought after. It remains to this day the most desirable location within the community. The Manhattan Beach Company, which set conditions and restrictions on lots that they sold, developed the south portion of the Strand. One such condition was that the purchaser of a lot or lots fronting the Strand could not erect a building costing less than $750. Today, there is no such condition, and the homes cost millions of dollars.

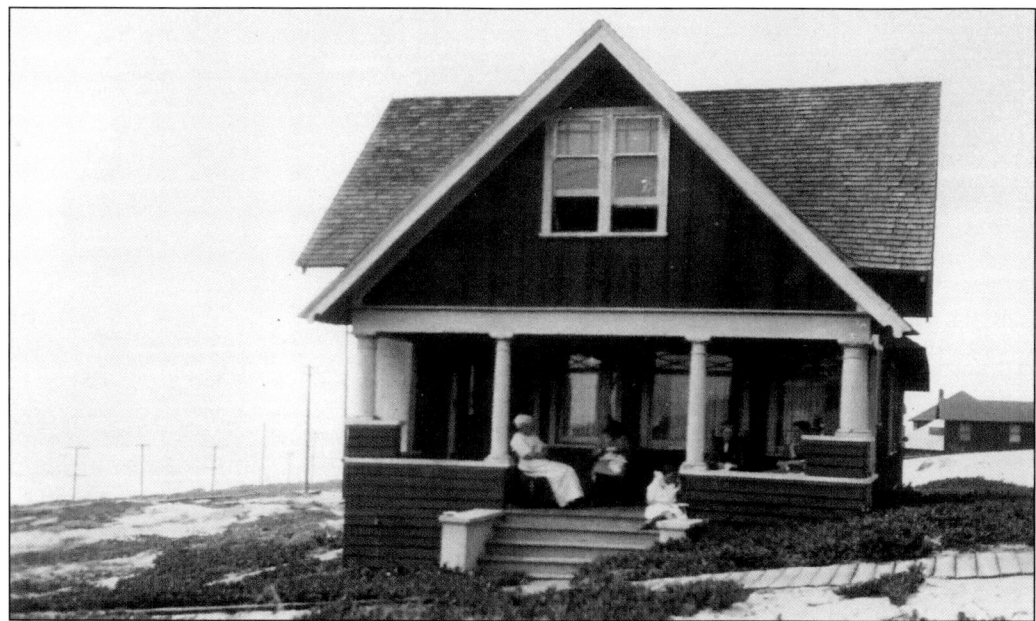

As more year round homes were being built during the late 1900s, the sand had to be dealt with. Several methods were tried in an effort to control this hazard. Barley was planted in hopes that this would hold the sand in place. Baled straw was cast over the sand and then mixed in. However, these methods were ineffective and great drifts continued to form. It was suggested that *mesembryanthemum*, commonly known as "ice plant," be planted. An abundant supply of this vegetation was readily available along the shoreline having been thrown overboard by sailing ships that used it as a coolant for cargo coming from Africa.

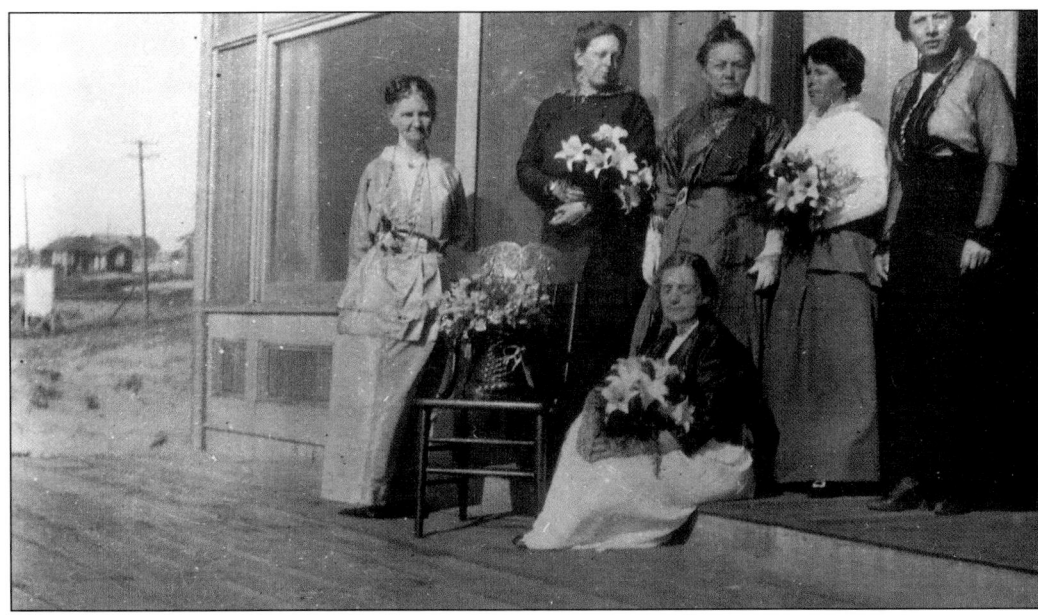

These six women of the original Neptunian Woman's Club of Manhattan Beach were members of one the community's first service organizations. The group was formed in 1909, and along with others in town, rolled up their sleeves and day after day trudged through the deep sand, planting the "ice plant" as a ground cover. The job done, the Club ladies joined forces with the Manhattan Improvement Association to bring about the incorporation of the town.

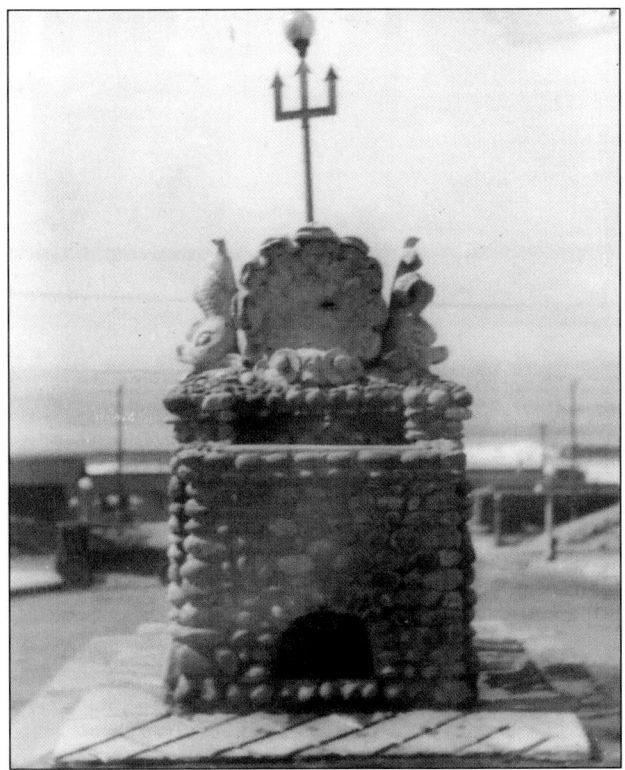

In 1915, a fountain was constructed in memory of Jessie Smith, founder of the Neptunian Woman's Club. The townspeople were encouraged to gather local cobblestones to be used in creating the imposing drinking fountain. It once stood at Center Street (now Manhattan Beach Blvd.) and Manhattan Avenue. Serving the thirsty needs of pedestrians on one level, it thoughtfully provided for pets from a trough at its base. Once admired as a landmark, it was later destroyed by an intoxicated automobile driver.

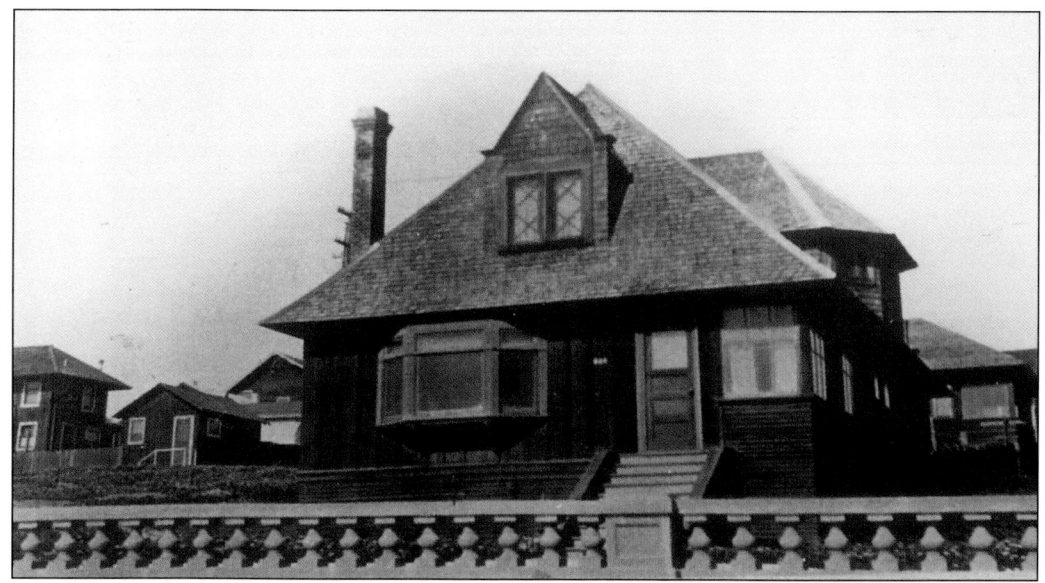

This is one of the homes erected by the Merrill, Manhattan Beach Company in 1902. Prior to the Manhattan Beach Community Church being built, Mr. and Mrs. Charlie Barker, owners of the well known Barker Brothers Furniture store in downtown Los Angeles, volunteered their home at the corner of Eighth Street and the Strand for Sunday afternoon church services.

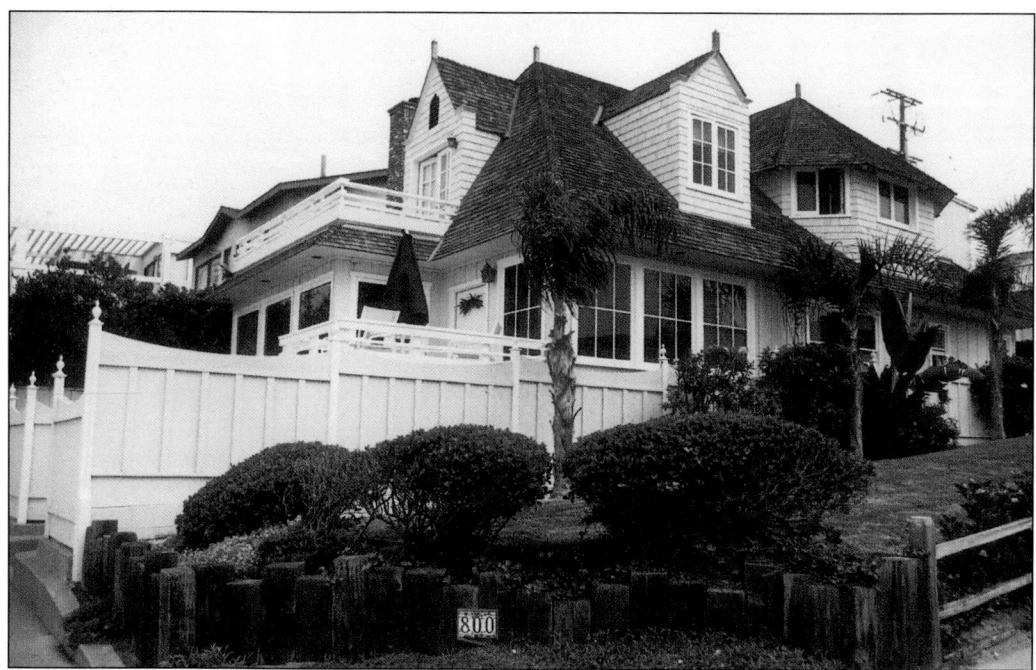

In later years, a porch was added to the front of the Barker house. Still more recently, this outstanding early beach cottage construction was refurbished by owner Dr. Robert Faries who kept much of the architectural style of the original 1902 home intact.

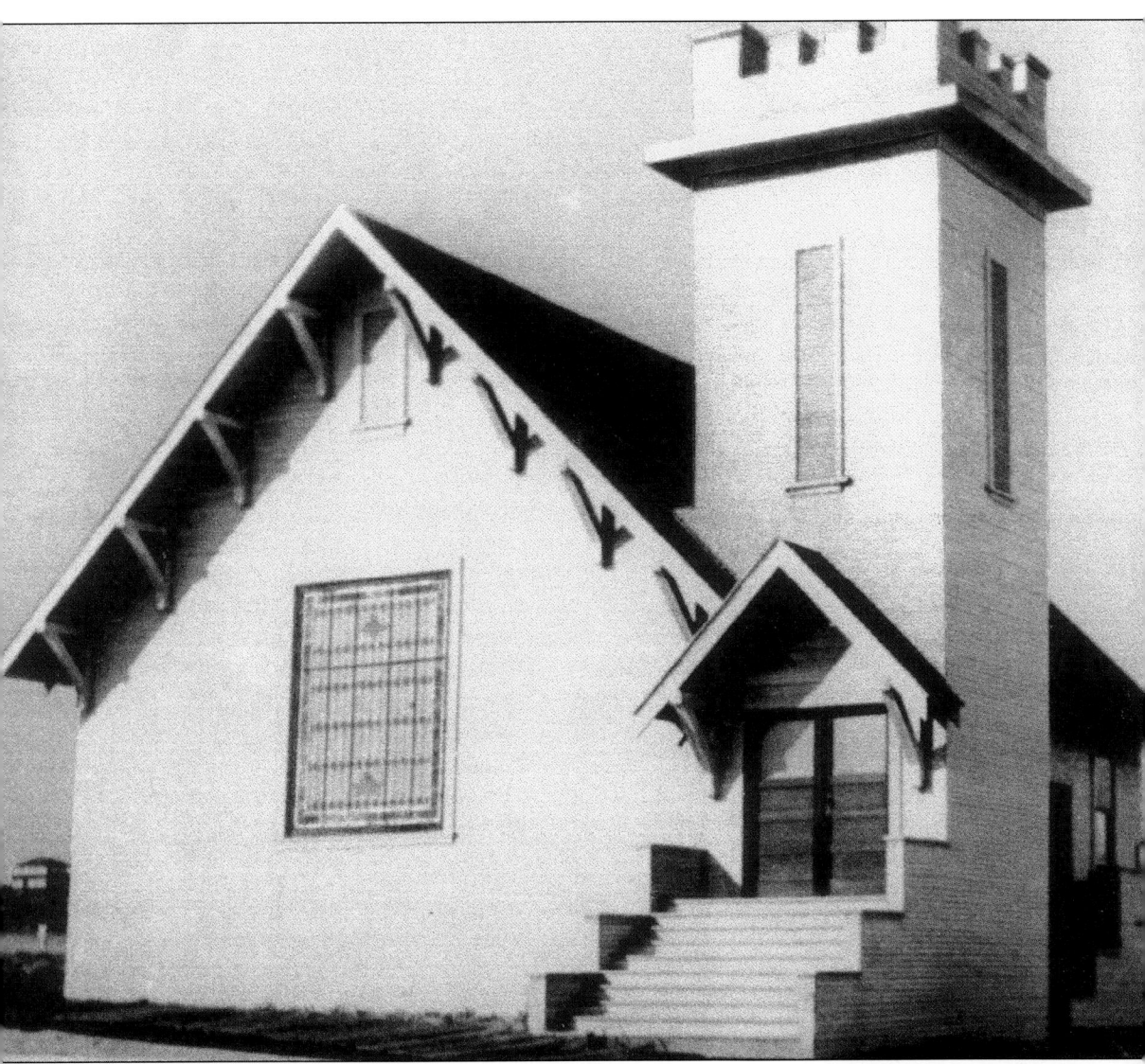

As more and more people moved into the sleepy town by the sea, it was determined that there was a need for formal religious services. Plans were set in motion to raise money to erect a church building. With a $600 loan from the Congregational Church Building Society of New York and community gifts, the redwood foundations were laid in the sand at the corner of Ninth Street and Highland Avenue on February 22, 1906. The lot, valued at $1,400, had been a gift to the members of the parish from the Manhattan Beach Company. An impressive feature of the church was the stained glass window; it was the first such window to be installed in town. The church always saw a much larger residential attendance during the summer months.

These summer attendees were also many of the strongest financial supporters. An affiliate membership was introduced so that the season al residents could hold membership in the Manhattan church as well as their "home" church.

Quoted in *The Cross in the Sand*: "In the early days the shifting sand raised considerable havoc with the church structure and the town in general. In 1916, the building was in danger of sliding downhill due to the dune formation which had left a 100 foot drop-off behind the church."

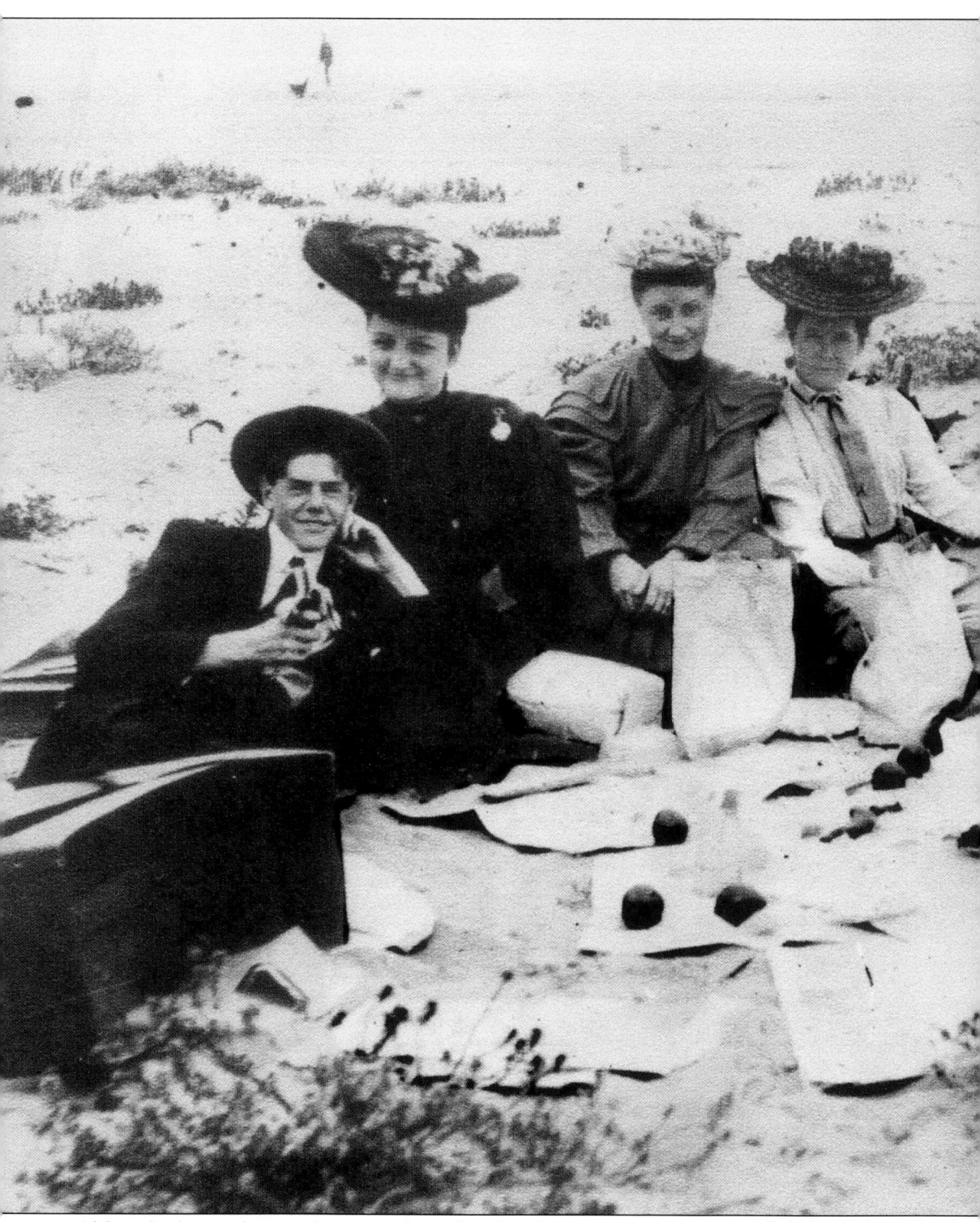
Although the sand was a hazard and trouble for the homeowners, it provided the holiday

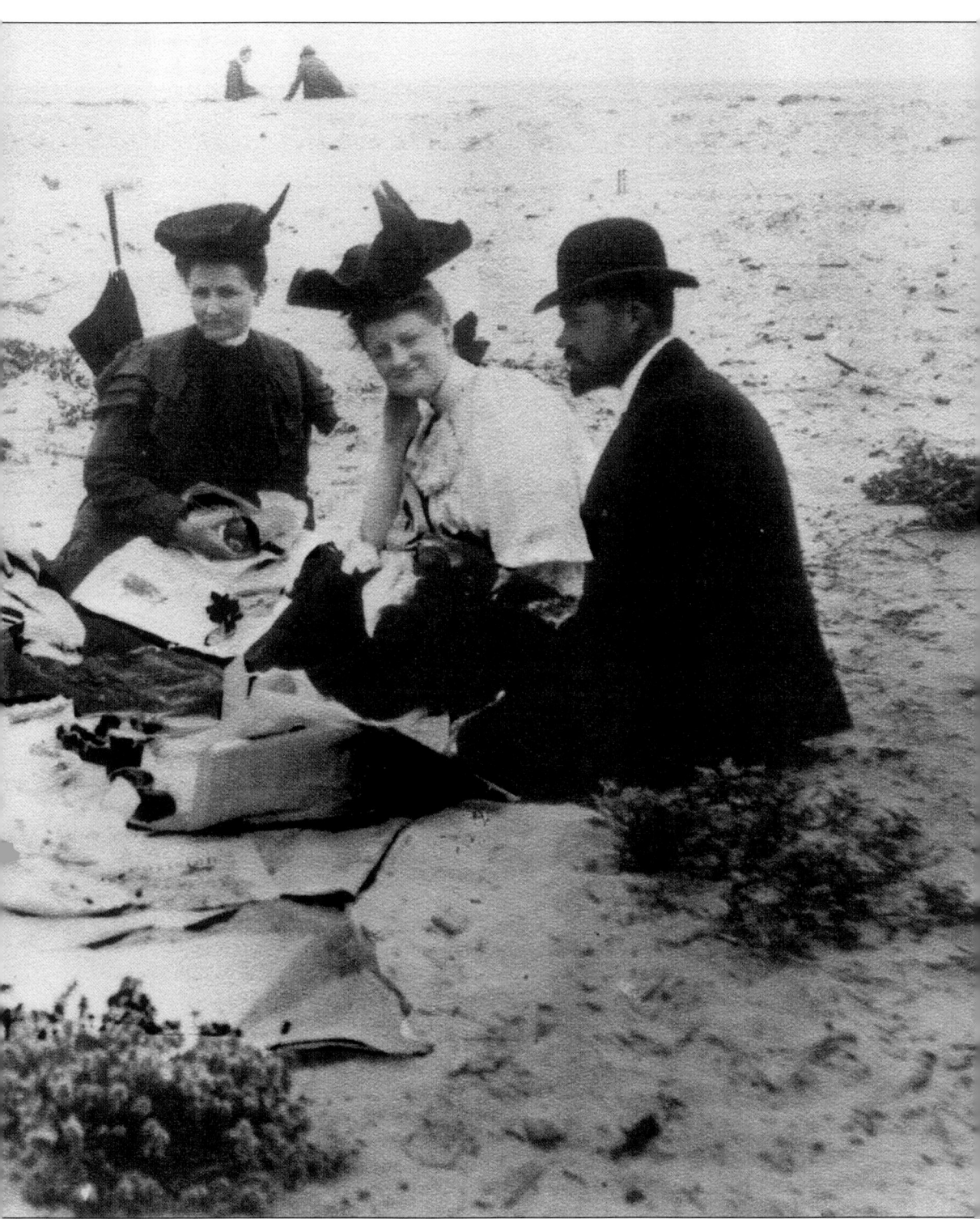
excursionist with a wonderful recreational venue. Picnicking along the pristine ocean side was no less popular then it is today.

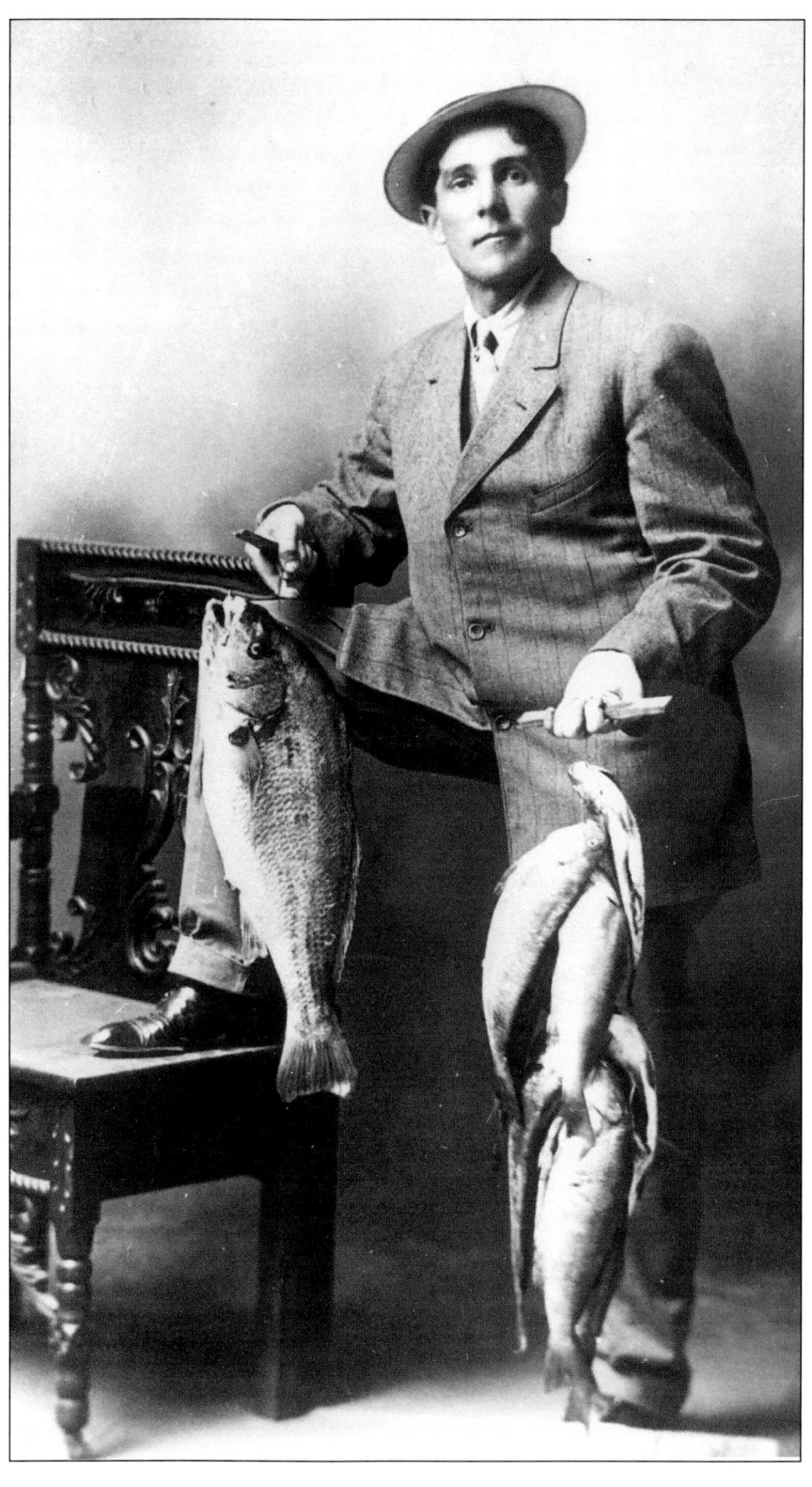

All the beach communities benefited from the variety of sea life offered by the Santa Monica Bay. "Uncle Fred," shown here in this photo, must have been truly pleased with his catch of the day. Both residents and visitors, via the "Red Car" trolley, could bring in a bounty of yellow fin, bonito, halibut, bass, sea trout, and shellfish from boat, pier, or surf.

When school vacation time came, the young of the community made a beeline for the beach. Aside from swimming, there were clams and sand crabs to gather from the surf. Of course, fishing was a major sport for both young and old. Here a young visitor displays his catch: a Yellow Fin caught from the pier.

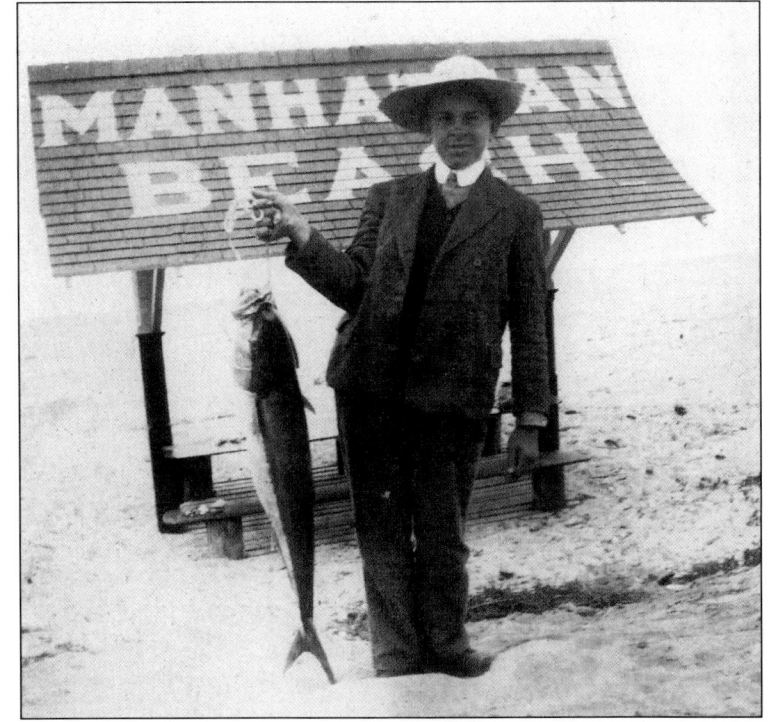

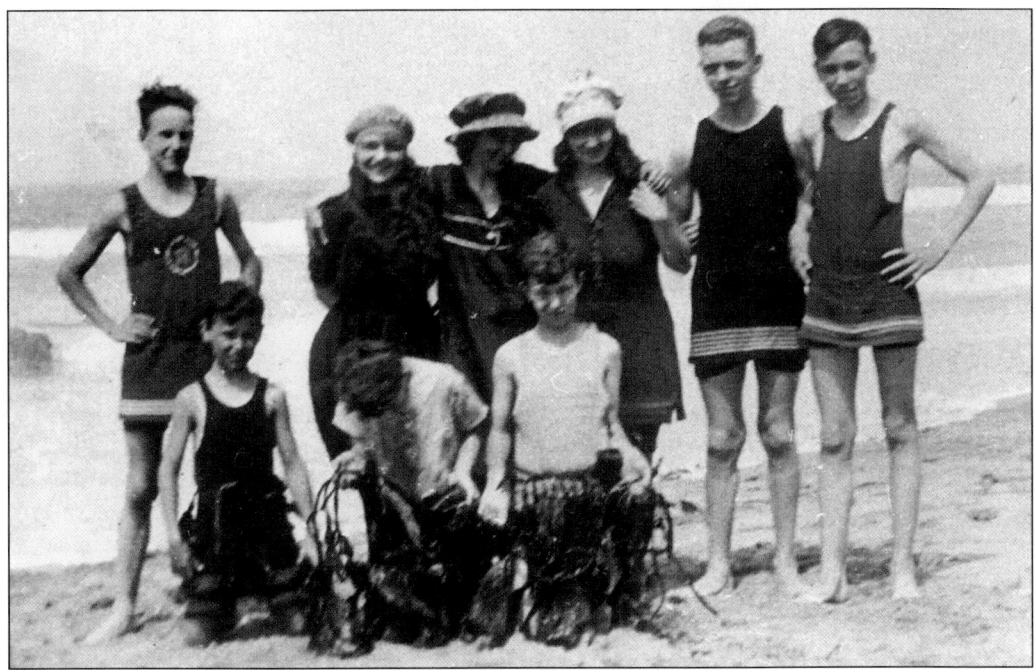

A group of sunbathers stands proudly before the camera with their display of seaweed collected along the shoreline. The dress code for both men and women was a far cry from today's standards. It would not be until 1933 that the dress ordinance would be modified. Men were then allowed to sport bathing trunks and women could wear two-piece bathing suits. However, everyone still had to cover up if they wanted to walk on the pier or the Strand.

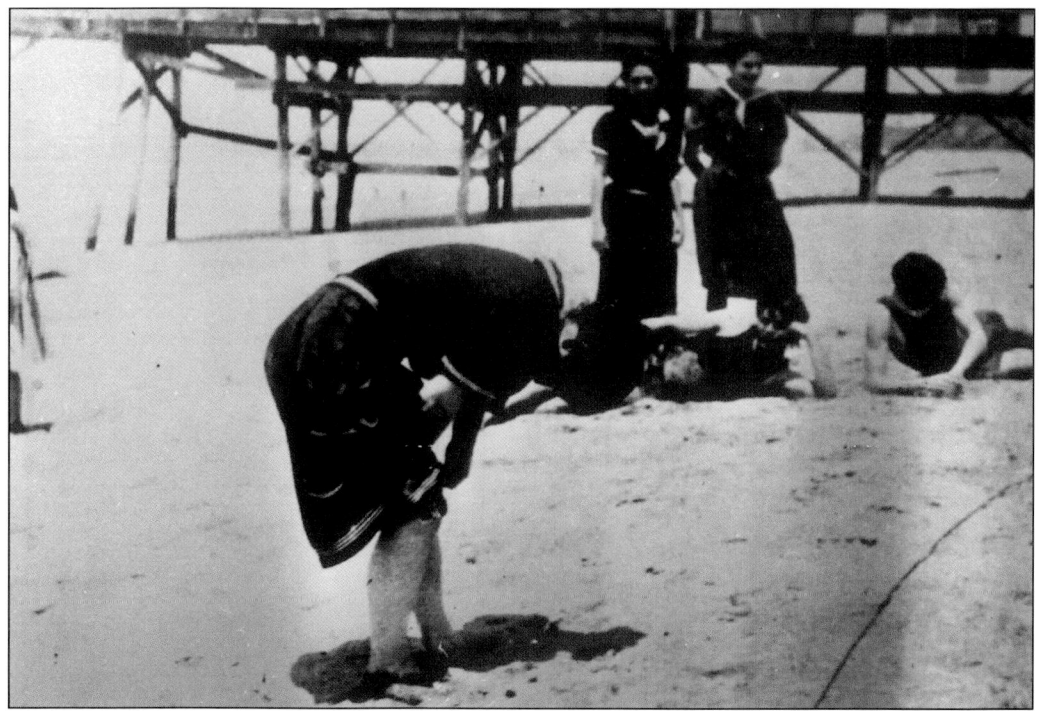

Here, a group of Neptunian Woman's Club ladies enjoys a day at the beach. The structure in the background is a section of the old iron pier.

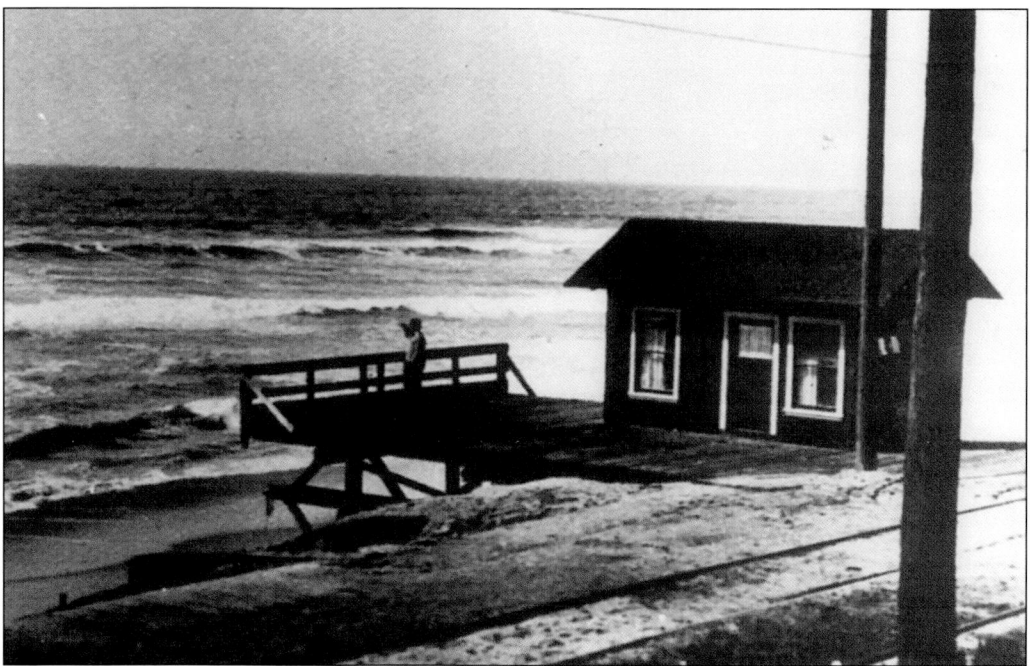

The storm of 1913–14 that destroyed the first pier also engulfed much of the beach as evidenced by this photograph. It would be many years before another municipal pier would be completed and the sand replenished.

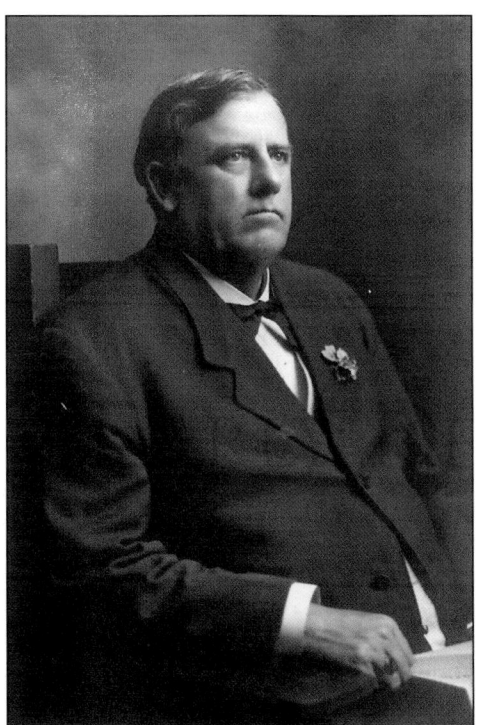

George H. Peck Jr.

As residents and visitors frolicked at the beach, developers like George H. Peck Jr. were promoting the town. Peck was born in San Francisco in 1857 and later moved to Los Angeles when his father became superintendent of the Los Angeles schools. Son George became legendary through his love for children and his dedication to creating a family oriented town. In 1897, he purchased 3 miles of ocean front property, better known as North Manhattan and El Porto.

The Finest Residence Ocean Beach in Southern California

Don't You Want to Make Some Money? Then Buy Ocean Beach Lots for $200 and Up

You May Build When You Make Your First Payment.

A part of this property was put on the market some years ago, some of which has been built up with good substantial homes; and every season sees a marked advance as it is coming more and more in favor as a beach for homes.

Experience has taught us that beach property is a good investment, and this part of **Manhattan Beach** has increased over 30% each season and we look for a greater advance in the future.

Main boulevard connecting all of the beaches passes through the heart of Manhattan.

Buy Now While They Are at Bargain Prices.

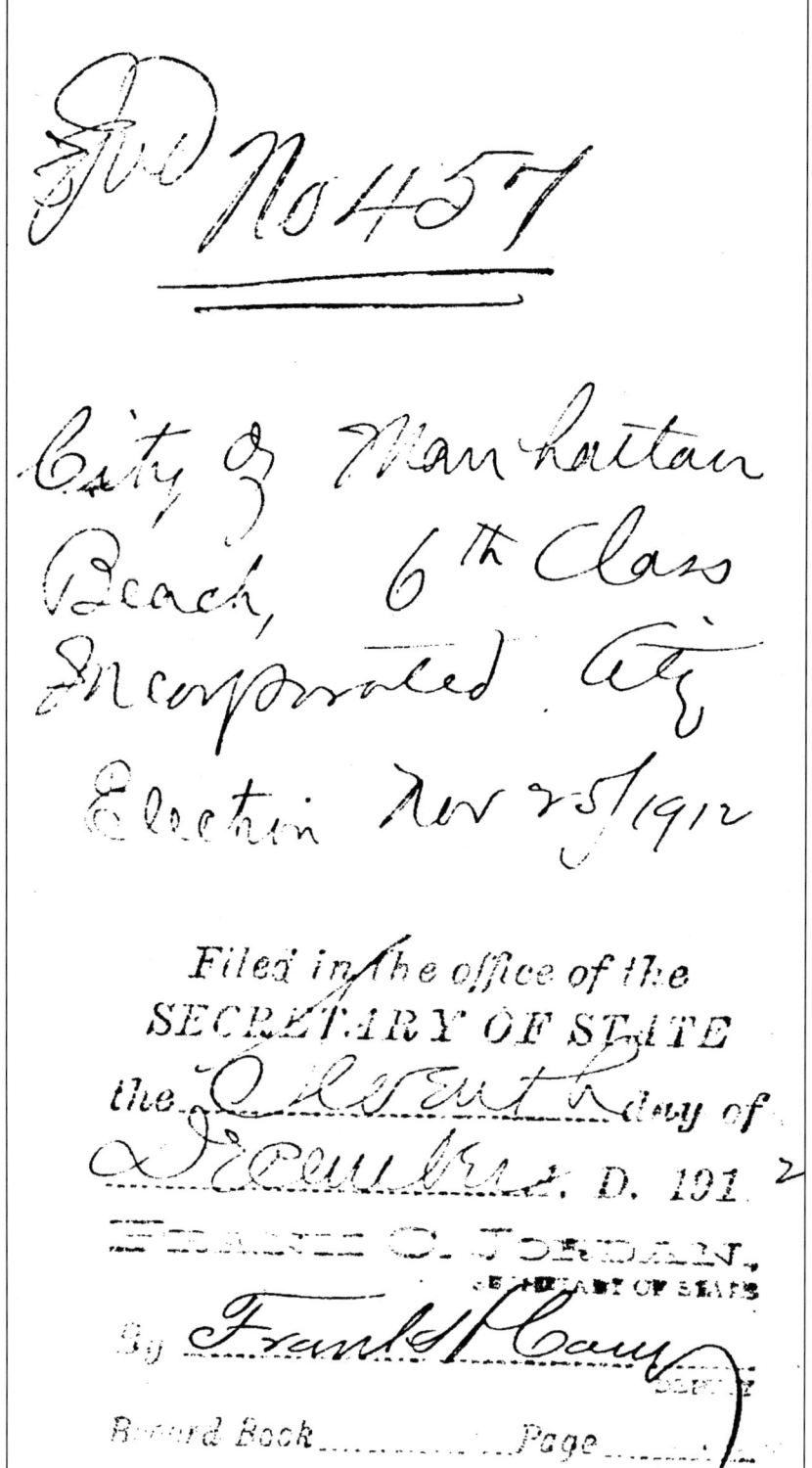

Incorporation papers signed by the secretary of state, December 7, 1912.

Two

EARLY DEVELOPMENT

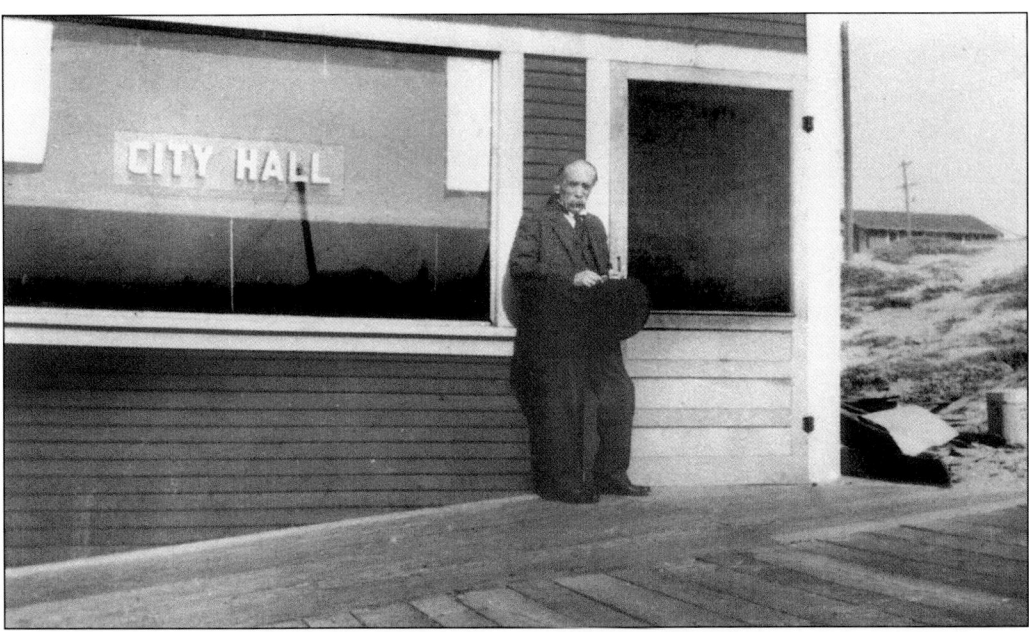

By 1912 there were approximately 600 inhabitants residing within the boundaries of Manhattan Beach. The local voters strongly felt that the area should become its own city and they decided to petition the county. After the necessary signatures were obtained, a petition was presented to the Los Angeles County Board of Supervisors on September 30, 1912. A date was set for an election on November 25, 1912, to determine whether the town had the necessary votes for incorporation. Returns were counted on December 2, with 95 voters in favor of incorporation and 32 against. With unanimous approval by the County Board of Supervisors, it was so ordered that all the territory situated within the boundaries described was a duly incorporated municipal corporation of the sixth class, under the name and style of "City of Manhattan Beach." The first city officers were elected for a four-year term. The first treasurer, Albert Clinton Conner, stands in front of the first City Hall, located in Meacham's Hall on Center Street (now Manhattan Beach Blvd.).

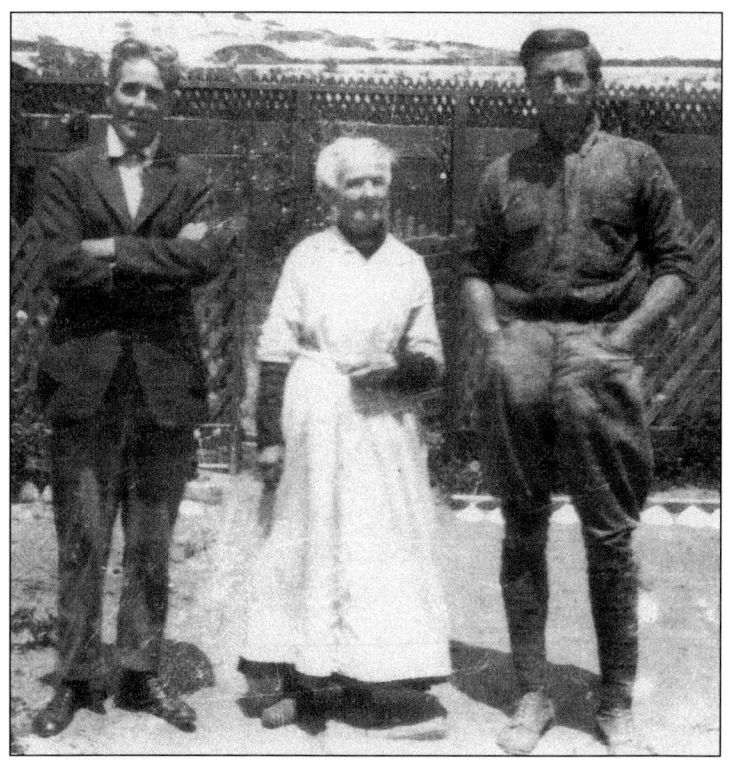

At the second Board meeting, held December 21, Fred A. Petway was appointed city marshal. Pictured here are Fred A. Petway; his mother, Mrs. Petway; and S.G. Davey, standing in front of the Petway home at 23rd Street and Manhattan Avenue, December 1912.

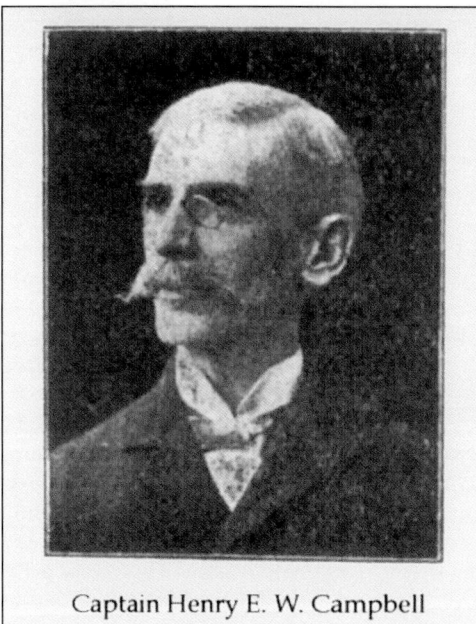

Captain Henry E. W. Campbell

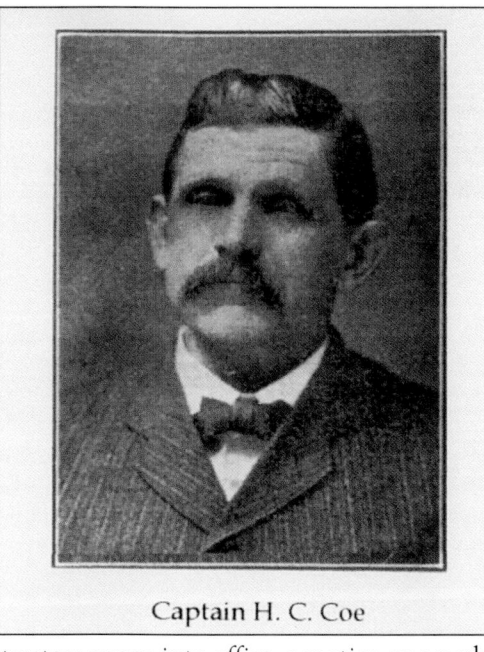

Captain H. C. Coe

Following the City's incorporation with all of the trustees sworn into office, a motion was made that resulted in the unanimous election of Captain Henry E. W. Campbell of the 150th Indian Volunteers as the city's first president to the Board of Trustees. Campbell did not survive his term. He died on March 22, 1914. Upon his death, Captain H. C. Coe, one of the founders of the Hood River Territory, was elected to the position on April 20, 1914.

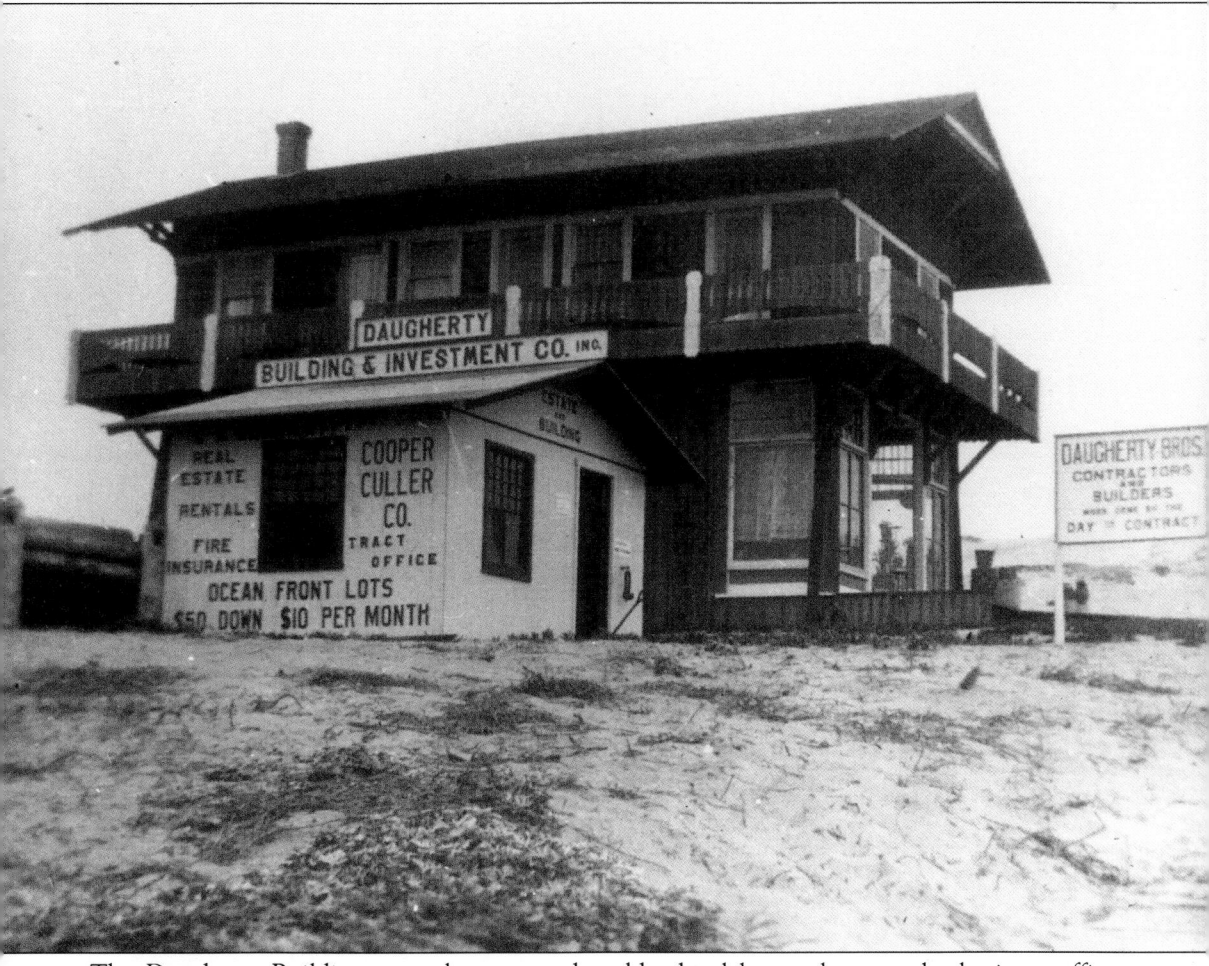

The Daugherty Building, once known as the old school house, became the business office of the Highland Beach Company directed by Frank S. Daugherty. He and five Los Angeles businessmen who purchased 20 acres in an area between Marine Avenue to 15th Street and Highland Avenue to the railroad tracks founded the company. They subdivided the land and made improvements, putting in sidewalks, water pipes, and developing building lots. The area is now known as North Manhattan Beach. Later this building was converted into apartments.

Frank Daugherty and his two brothers, Albert and Ammon, who had moved to Manhattan Beach in 1914 from Los Angeles, had great faith in the growth of the area and founded the Daugherty Bros. Contractors Co. They became a true part of the community through their work, as well as through their involvement in city affairs. Frank served the residents of the North-end as their representative on the city council for five years and later became the city's fourth mayor. It was through Daugherty's efforts that Ordinance 38 was granted to the Los Angeles Stone Company to construct, maintain, and operate a single railroad spur track on the Strand, between 25th and 29th Street. The line was to be used to haul materials and supplies for improvements to public streets.

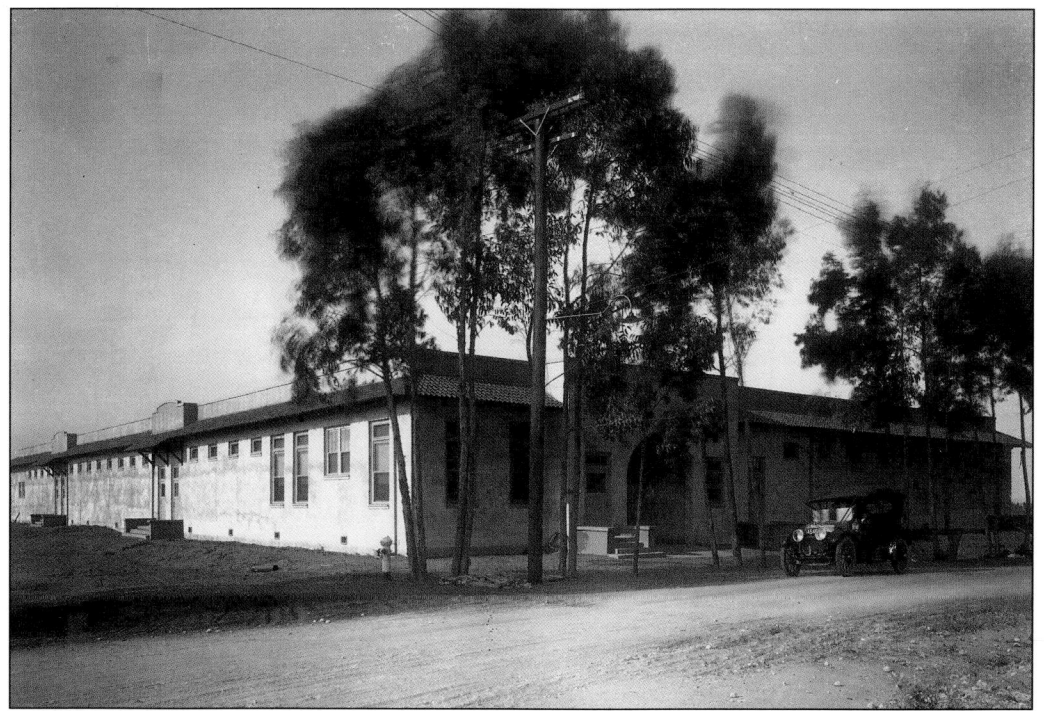

Education was a prime concern for the newly formed town. Prior to 1911, Manhattan Beach children attended classes in local area school districts. Many parents thought their children should go to school in their hometown and so began the city's first school, opening in what was to become known as the F.S. Daugherty Building, located on the northeast corner of Marine Avenue and Ocean Blvd. Later, youngsters attended classes in the back room of the Community Church. With the leadership of men like C.E. Jenkins and James Cortyou, a new district was formed February 13, 1913. By Easter Day, April 30, 1914, a new school on the corner of Center Street and Pacific Avenue was dedicated and ready for the local children.

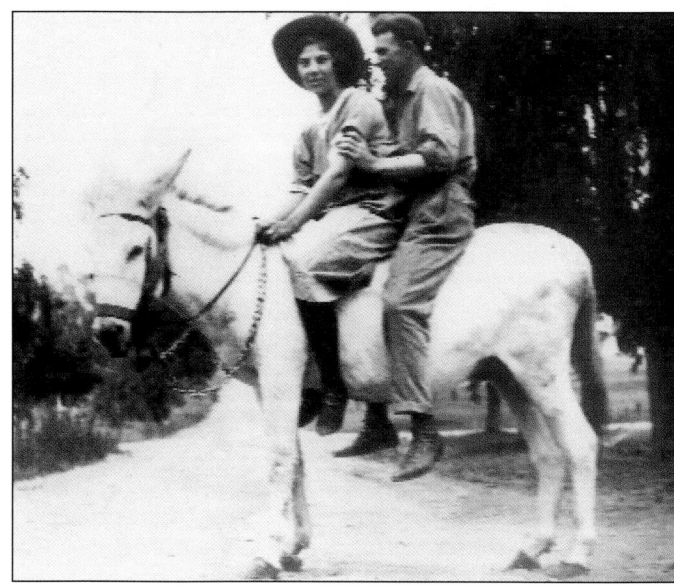

With the lack of transportation, school age children walked or rode horses to school. Here, two ride a donkey from the Tree Section at 17th Street and Pine Avenue.

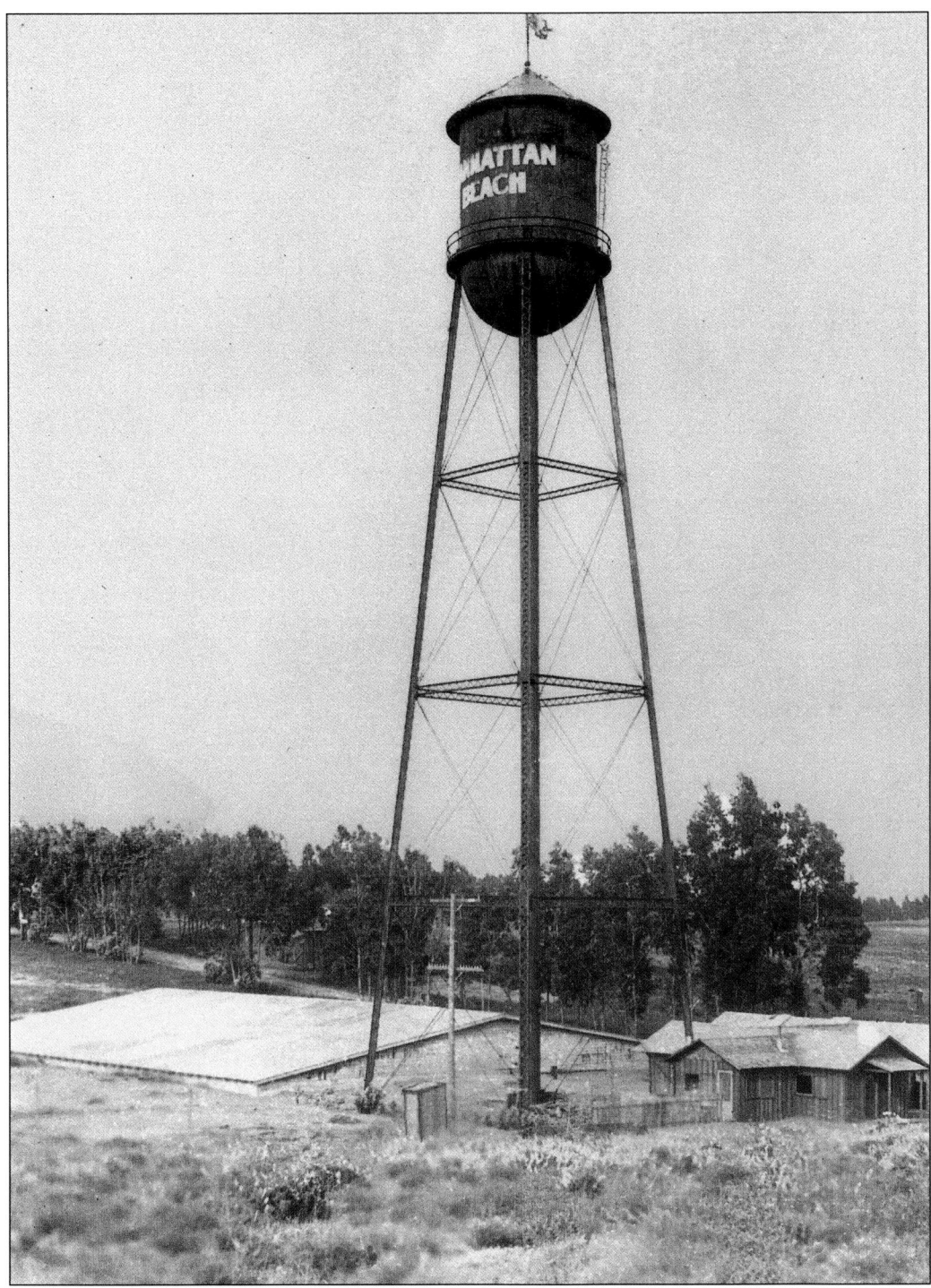

With progress going so well and more and more people coming down to the beach, the city was developing its public services. On February 7, 1914, with the passage of a voters $111,000 bond, the bids were opened for the construction of a municipal water system. The plant, with a 60,000-gallon water tank perched on the 145-foot high tower, was located between 6th and 8th Street.

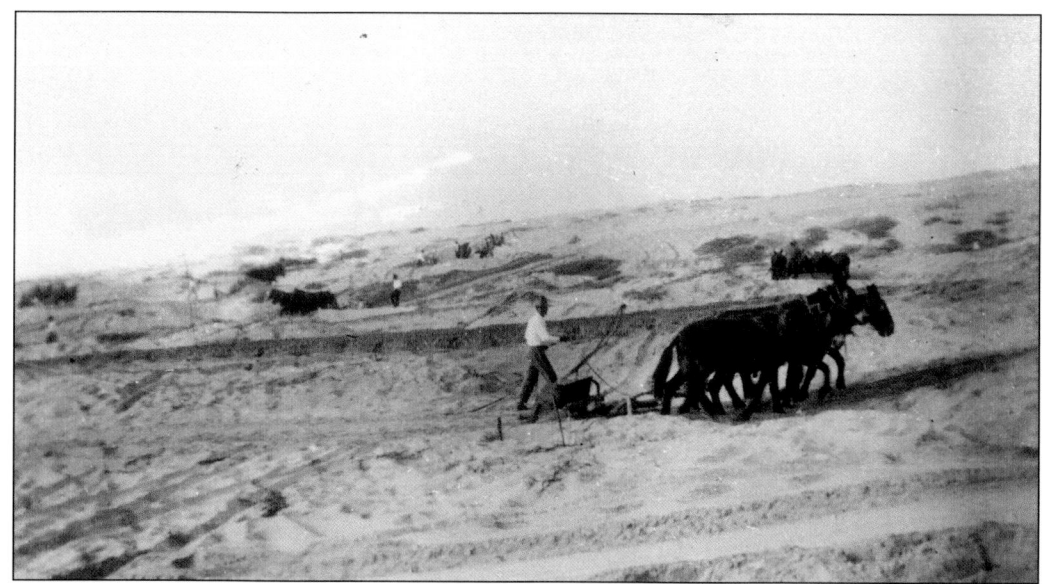

Developing the first roads was an immense task for both man and the horses and mules used to level and remove the mountains of sand. The city tried to get private contractors to take on the job, but no one would even offer a bid, so it was left to the developers. The Manhattan Beach Development Company and the Builders Material Company were the two main participants. Large tractors and other heavy equipment were brought in to level the city from Center (now Manhattan Beach Blvd.) to First Street. Men and machines worked 24 hours a day, every day for 2 years. They hauled out an estimated 1,300 yards of sand every 24 hours by way of the Santa Fe Railroad. Businessmen like N.R. Kuhn shipped sand for use in the Los Angeles Memorial Coliseum, highway construction, and as far away as Hawaii, creating the now famous Waikiki Beach. On the north end of town, George Peck spent $80,000 in seven months to grade the sand from 23rd to 37th Street.

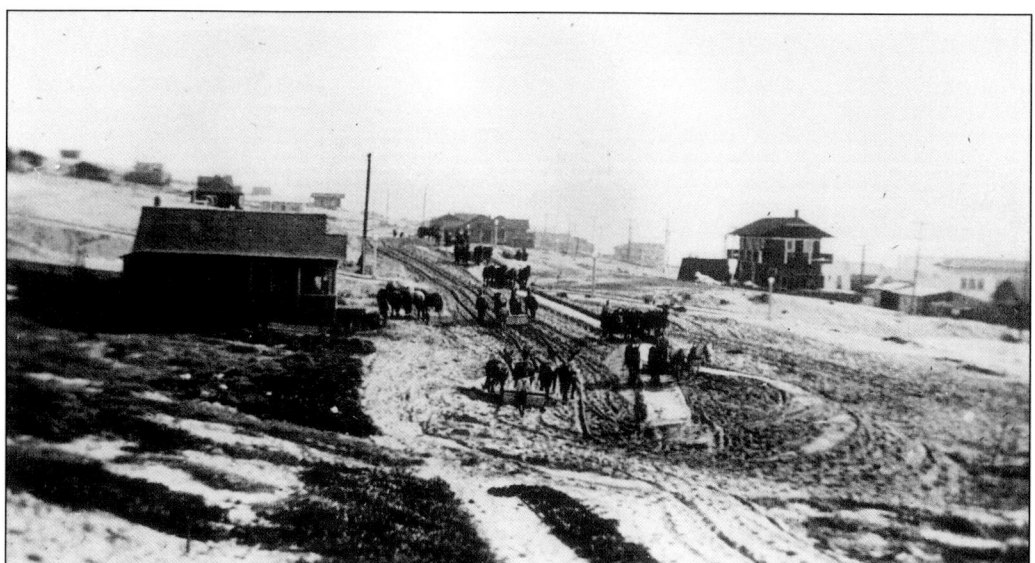

In 1914, main highways like Highland Avenue, which ended just beyond Marine Avenue, were excavated and improved later with paving.

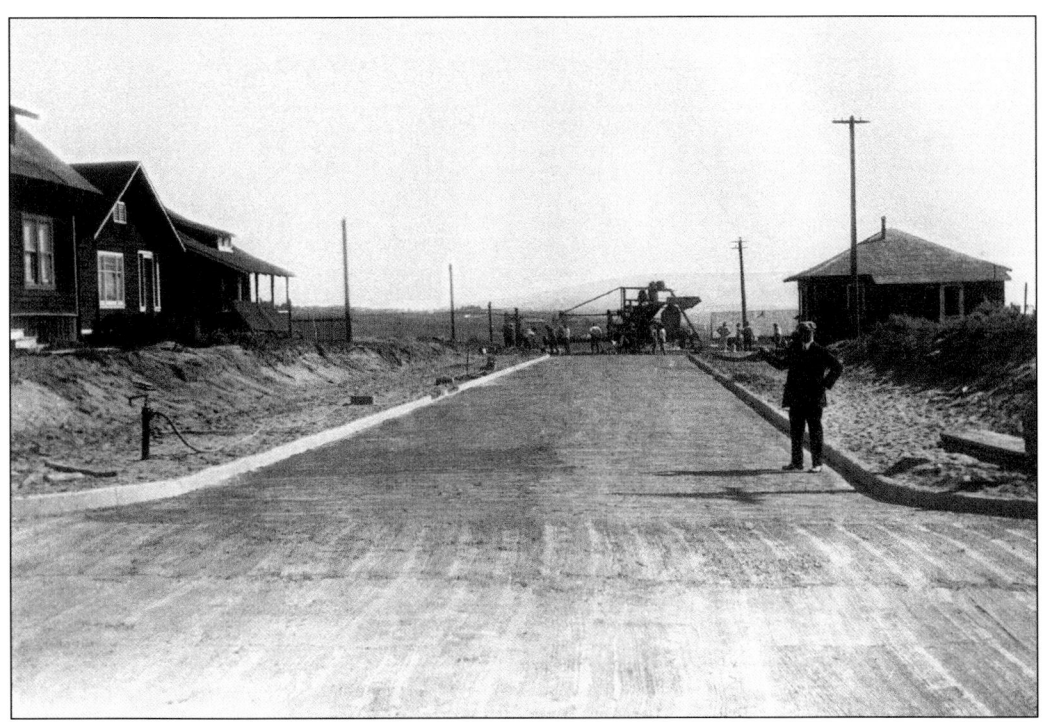
The year was 1915 and Highview Avenue at 13th Street was being paved. This was the section of town that would later be known as the Hill Section.

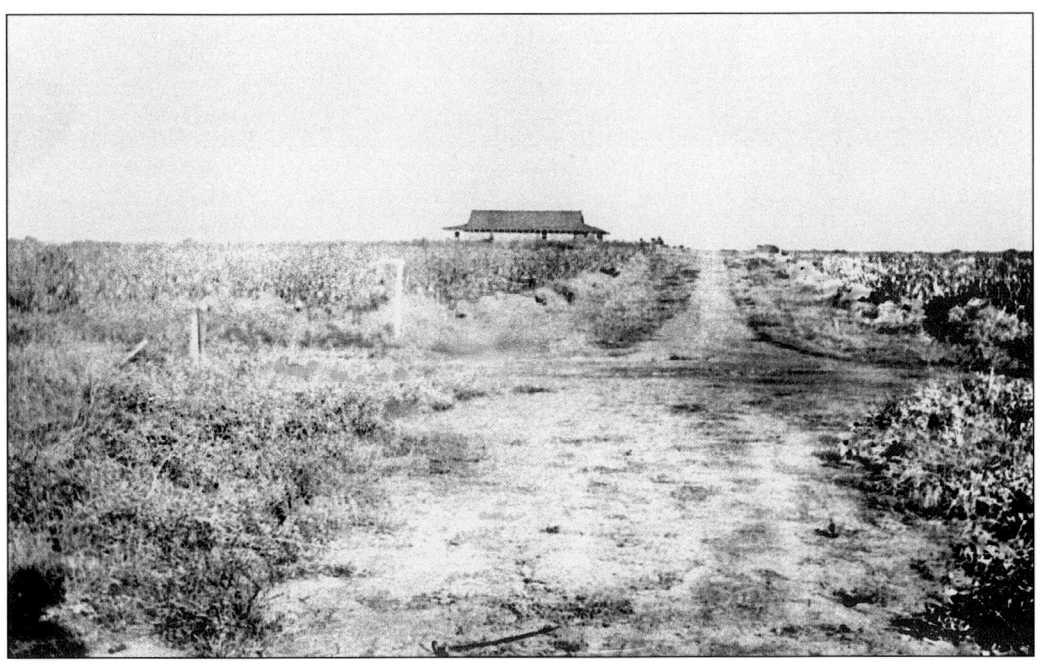
This area, known today by residents as the Tree Section, was once small truck farms growing acres of garbanzo beans. They operated with dirt roads and a limited water supply.

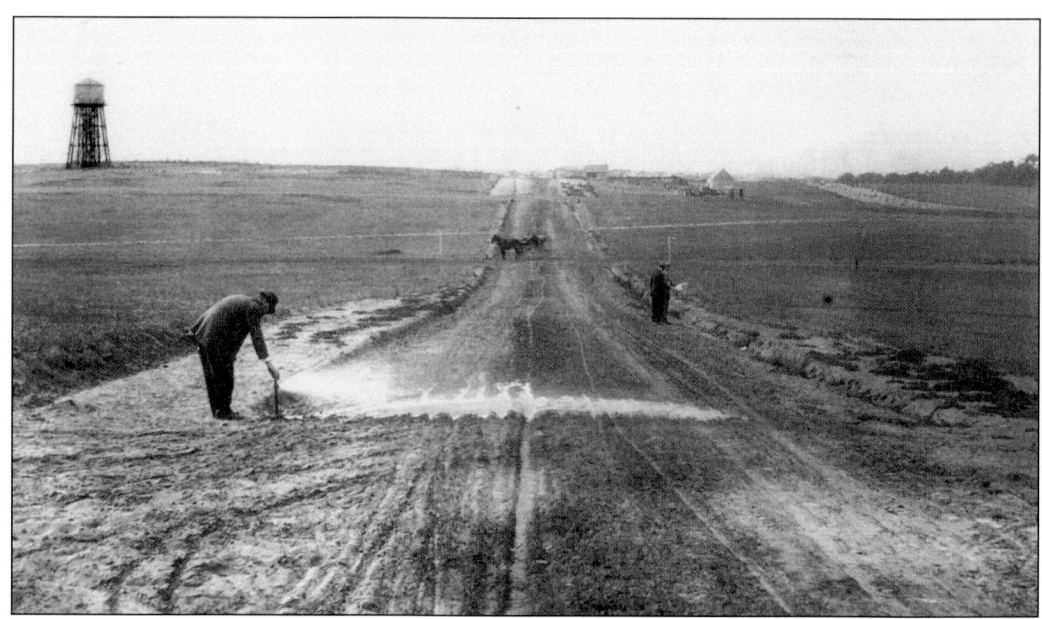

By 1914, the area north of the Santa Fe railroad tracks known as Standard Park at Pacific and Lefflor Avenue (later changed to 35th Street) was supplied with water. Trees could now be planted and lots could be sold. Today this intersection pictured above is in an area known as the Tree Section.

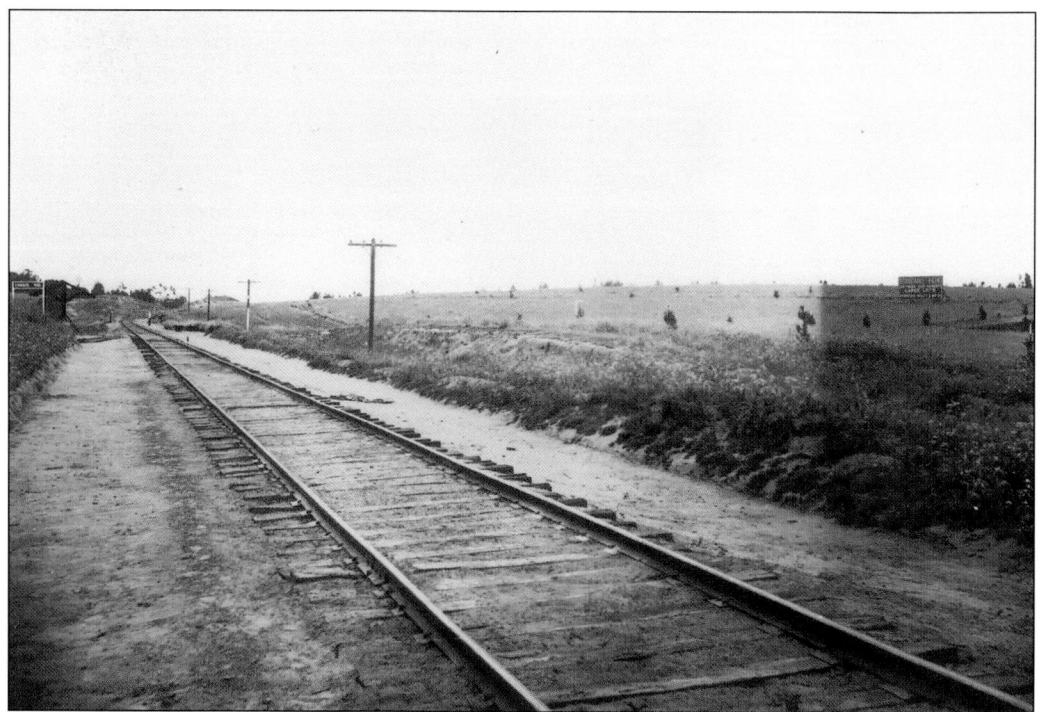

Looking east along the Santa Fe Railroad tracks that passed through the Standard Park Development, one could see the evidence of change. The land was reasonably flat with good soil. Each street was planted with a different tree species (i.e. Oak, Walnut, Palm, etc.).

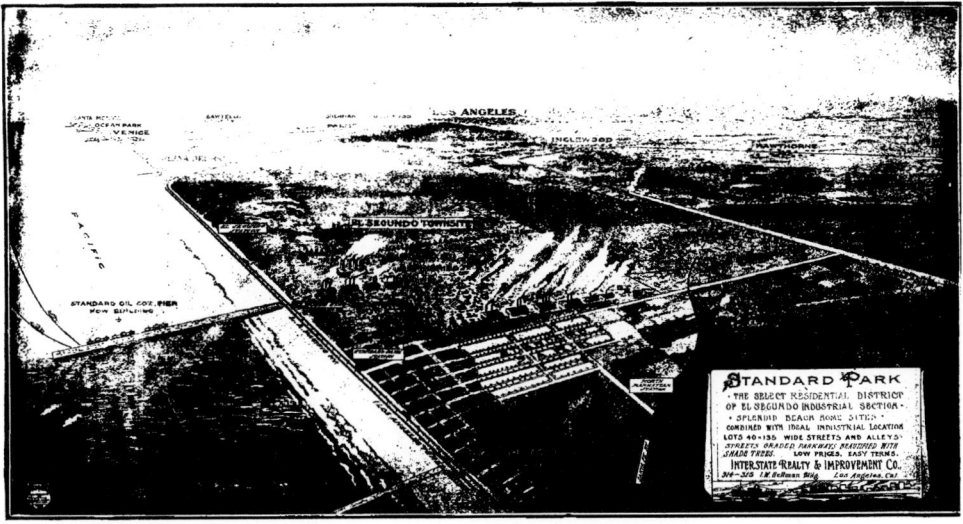

A Standard Park promotional flier.

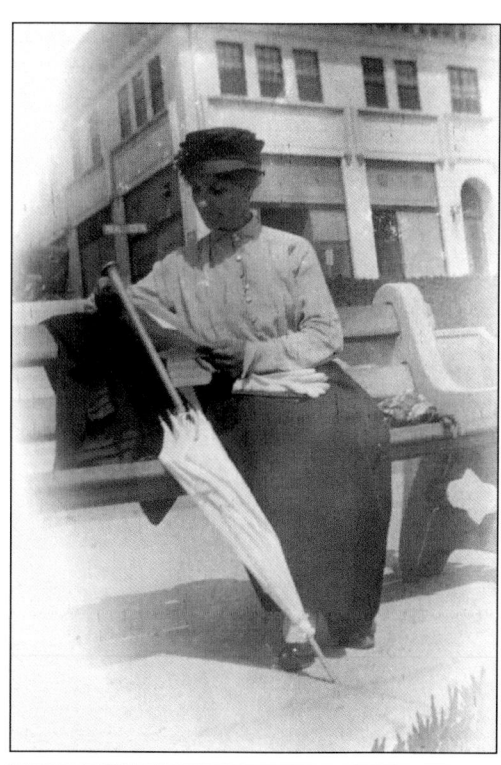

Mrs. Carrie Manlove (mother of Addie M. Pearson) waits at the foot of 22nd Street for the "Red Car."

In 1914, 22nd Street still retained its wooden sidewalk while work was being done on the Sadler building and road construction of what was to be known as Marine Avenue continued.

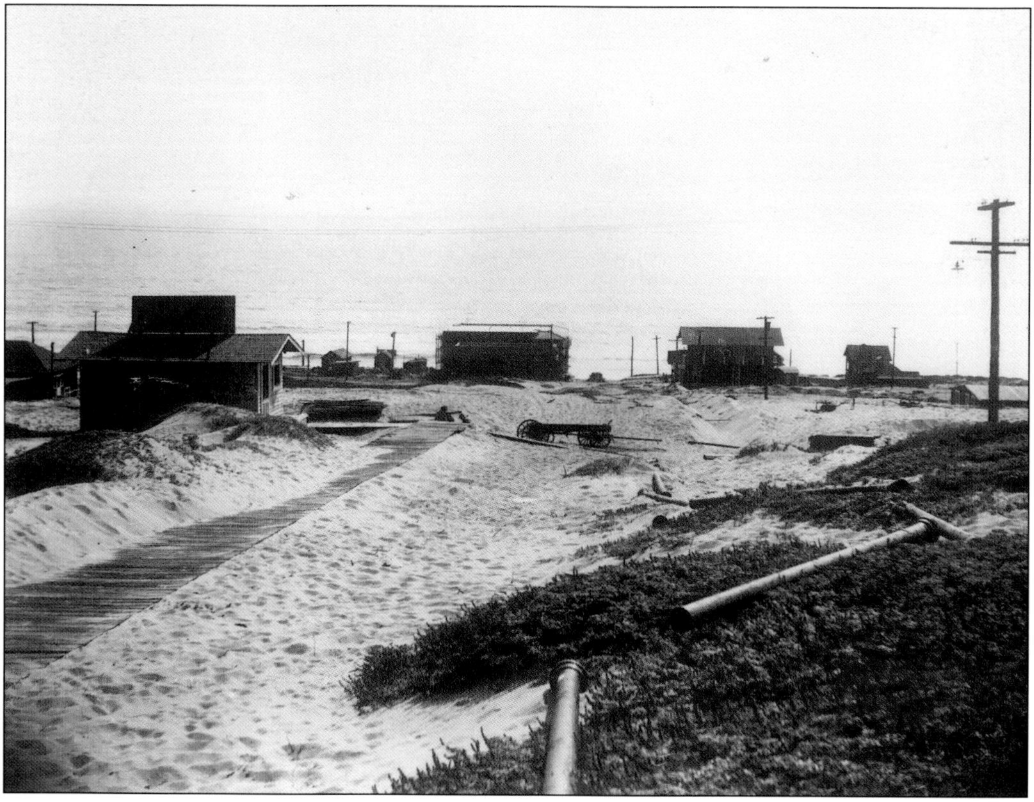

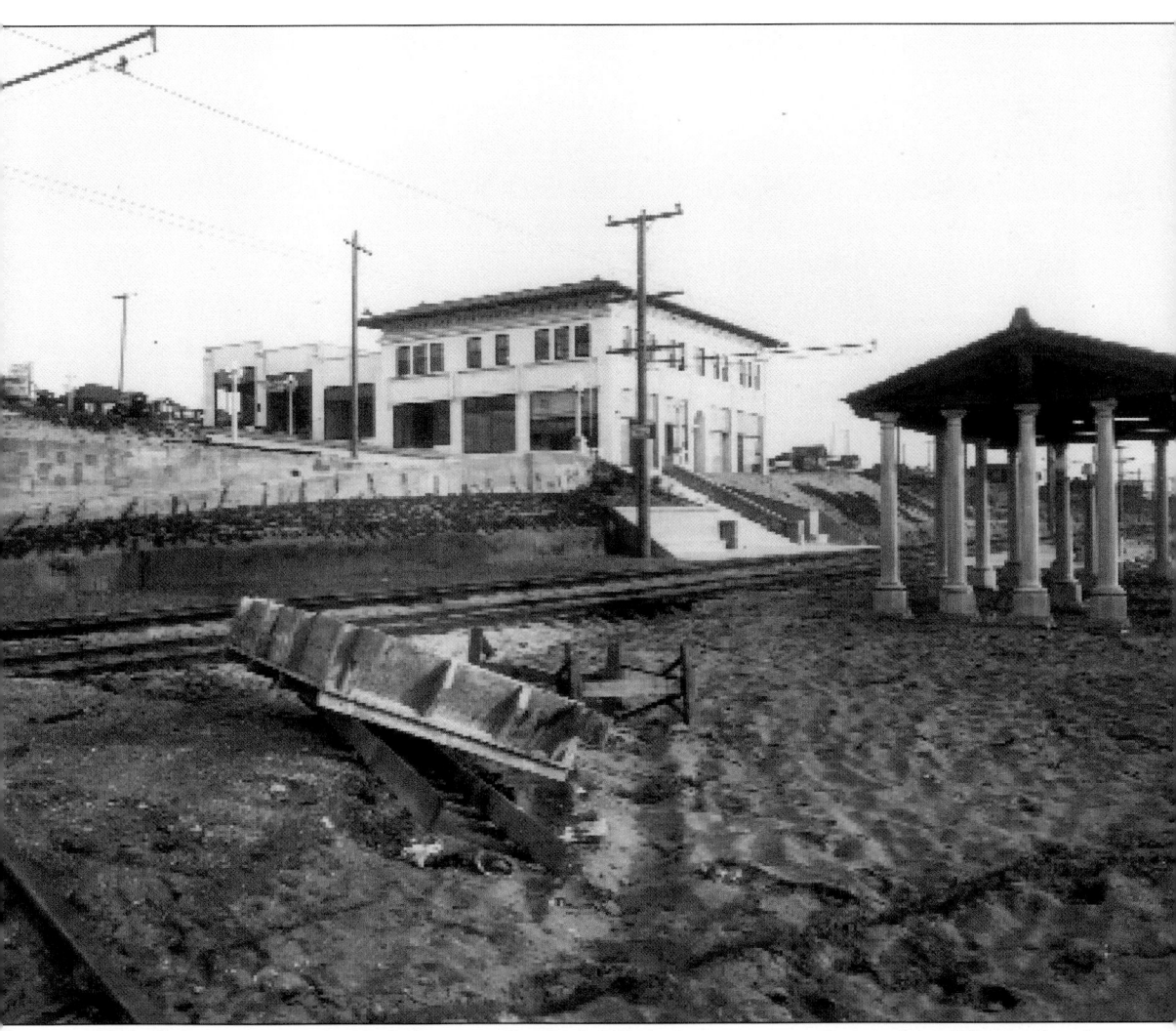

With the various sections of the town being developed, so too was the north end being freed of the ubiquitous sand. The Sadler building construction, beginning on March 21, 1914, was the first major building north of Center Street and consisted of eight stores and formed a two-story business block. A red tile roof accented the Spanish architecture and the cement walls on steel lath were finished with white plaster. The wrought iron grillwork and front plate glass with prism glass transoms finished in copper was truly an impressive addition to this area of town. The newly constructed "Red Car" depot at the foot of Marine Street was another added convenience for the residents of the area. Due to the growth of the town the city board of trustees located their offices on the second floor of the Sadler Building and remained there until 1916 when a new City Hall was built.

    A. Howard Sadler, originally from Pasadena, was another realtor/developer who built many homes in the Marine Avenue area and took advantage of the "Red Car" service. As George Peck had done, he brought prospective land and home buyers to the shore to show the value of investing in this community. The town site had been promoted in the past as a unique place in the South Bay, but it was Sadler who raised promotion to a new height. In his 1913 promotion piece, *Manhattan Beach Worth While, Where the Pacific Ebbs & Flows*, he elaborated on the splendid town of the future.

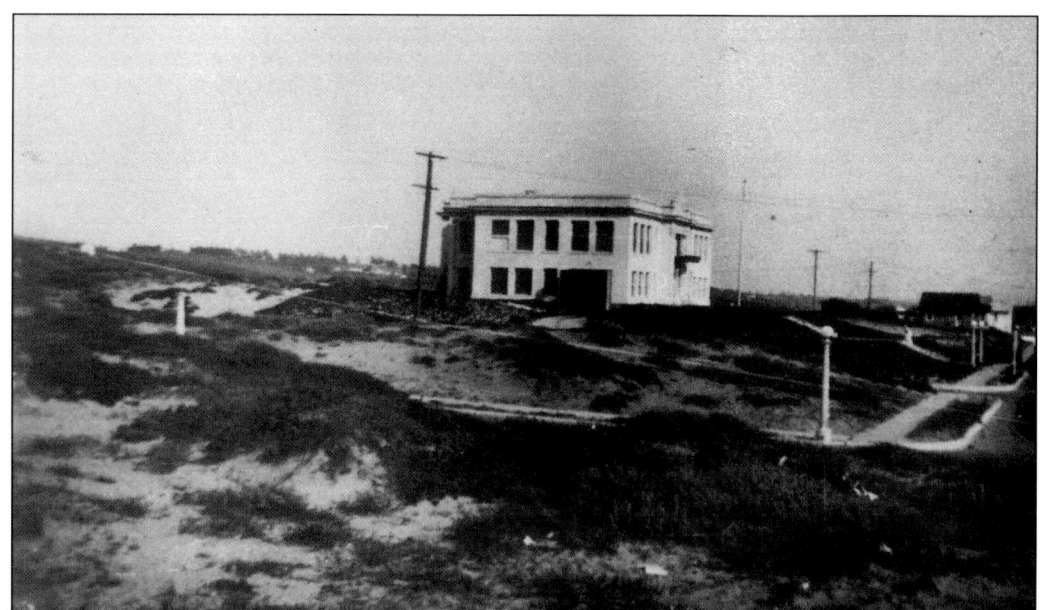

At the corner of 15th Street and Highland Avenue, the new City Hall is seen shortly after its completion in 1916. Financed by a $20,000 bond and a $220,000 mortgage, the new building contained city offices, a jail, and a large hall where dancing parties were held. Architects Train and Williams drew the plans for the building. Venerable and Morrell was contracted for the grading of the site at a price of 19.5¢ per cubic yard.

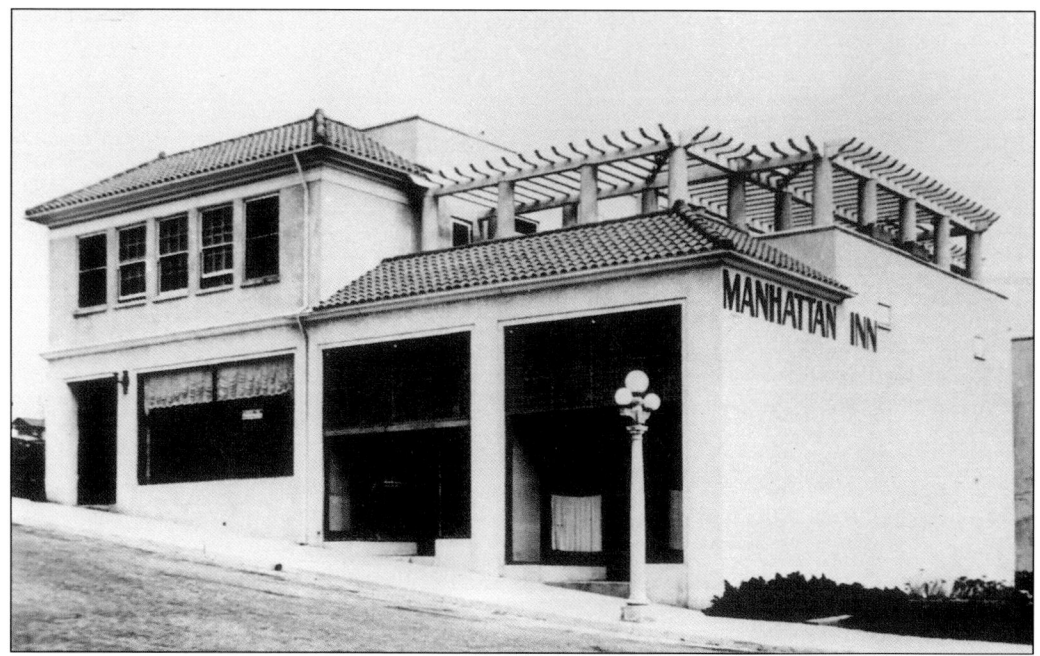

Construction of a 14 room, 3-story with roof top garden, Manhattan Inn was located south of Manhattan Avenue on Marine Avenue. It opened August 1, 1915. In the late 1930s, a restaurant called "Little Bavarian" occupied this structure. The cafe's garden patio was a scene of many weddings and parties. During the war years it was a popular place for military personnel to gather.

In 1914 with construction prevalent around town, there was still the ability to live on the beach and enjoy the cool summer breezes. Here, Lucey Caley is hanging her Monday wash on a nice summer day.

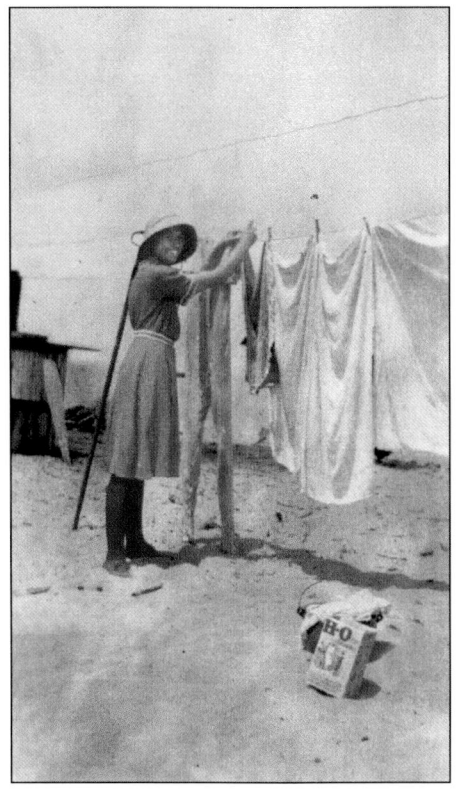

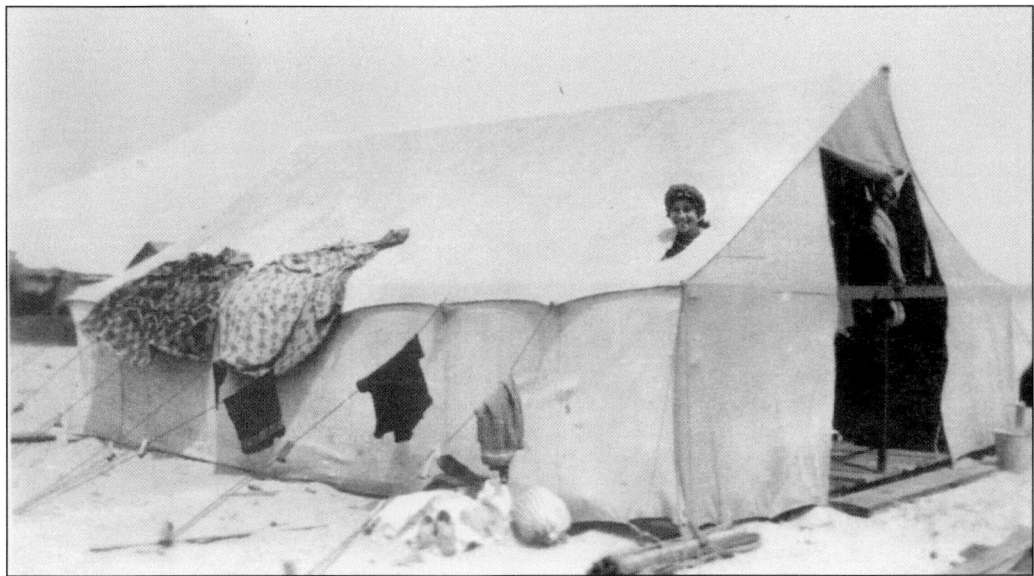

Lucey also hung bathing suits and dresses on the tent supports. It would not be until May 17, 1928, when Ordinance 320 outlawed any person to erect, maintain, or occupy a tent on any part of the ocean beach lying west of the Strand. If the law was not followed it constituted a $300 dollar fine or three months in jail.

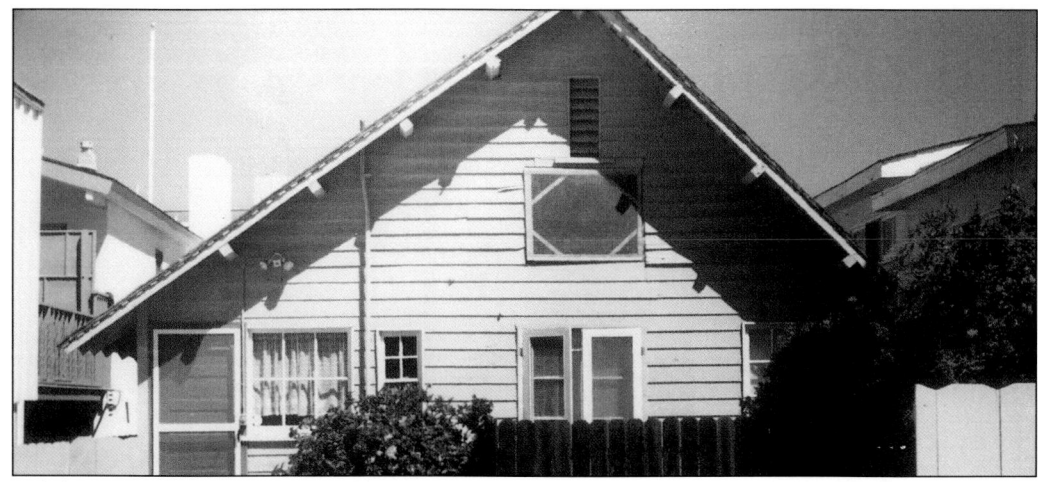

While people were enjoying life on the beach, there were many homes being built in all parts of the town. This type of bungalow with its off-centered roof was being constructed in the Sand Section. The roof's design gave the side to the west less chance of collecting sand during heavy windstorms.

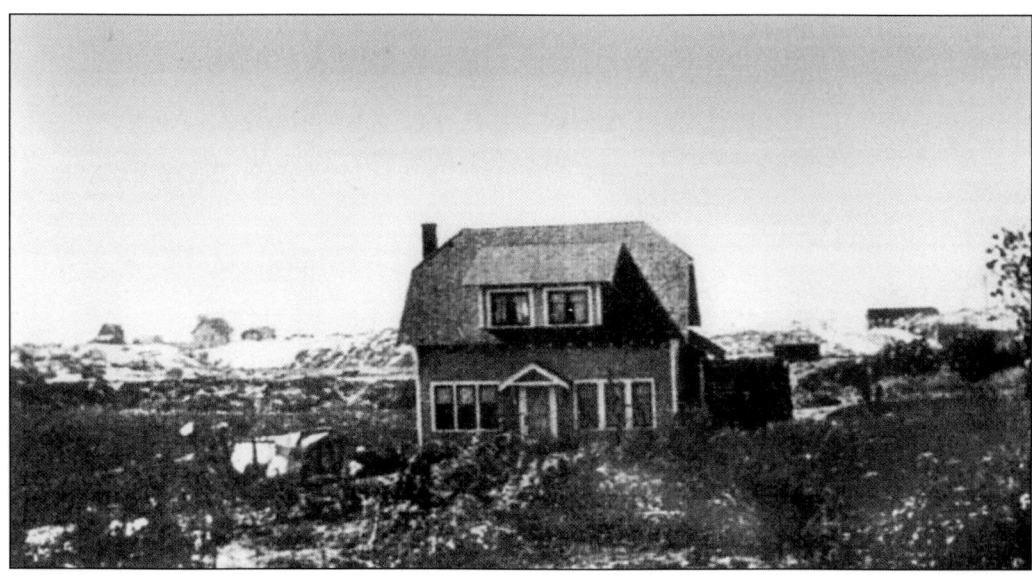

In 1916, more and more homeowners were living in the area year-round, and different architectural styles were appearing. Mrs. Harriet Rebecca Gower Gumbrella had this Dutch colonial revival style home built at the corner of Center Street (now Manhattan Beach Blvd.) and Highview Avenue, in the Hill Section. The home remains to this day.

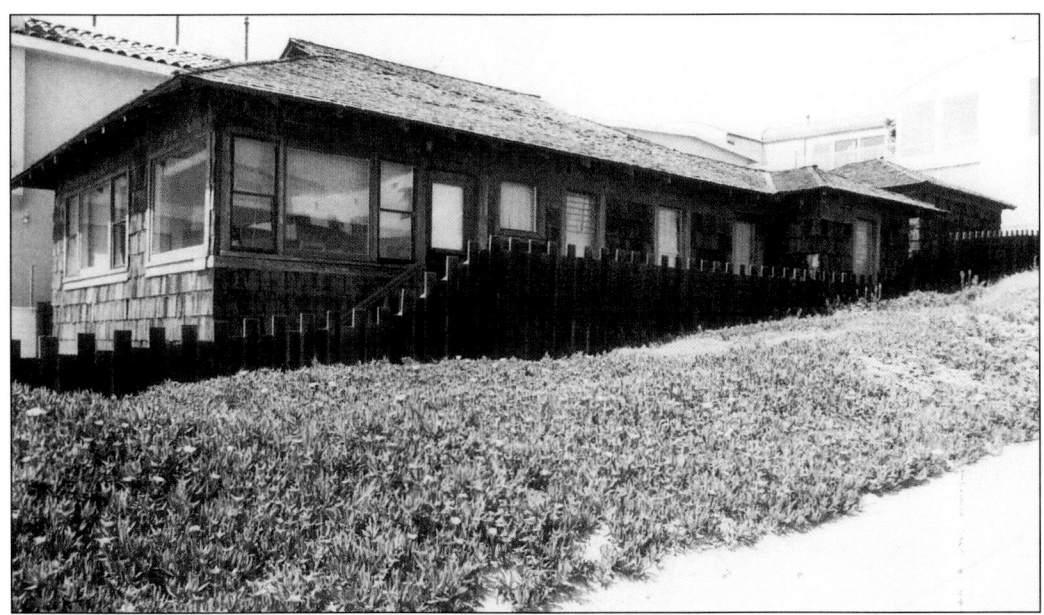

The shingled beach cottage style continued to be built. Still standing today, one of the last original cottages is located at the northwest corner of 3rd Street between the Strand and Ocean Drive. In 1915, Peter Orban from Pasadena, California, purchased the property from M/M Allie F. Hart. He had George Helfman (who charged $5.00 per day with the job taking 36 days) construct the brown-shingled beach cottage in 1916 for the grand sum of $774.47, plus $56.89 for paint.

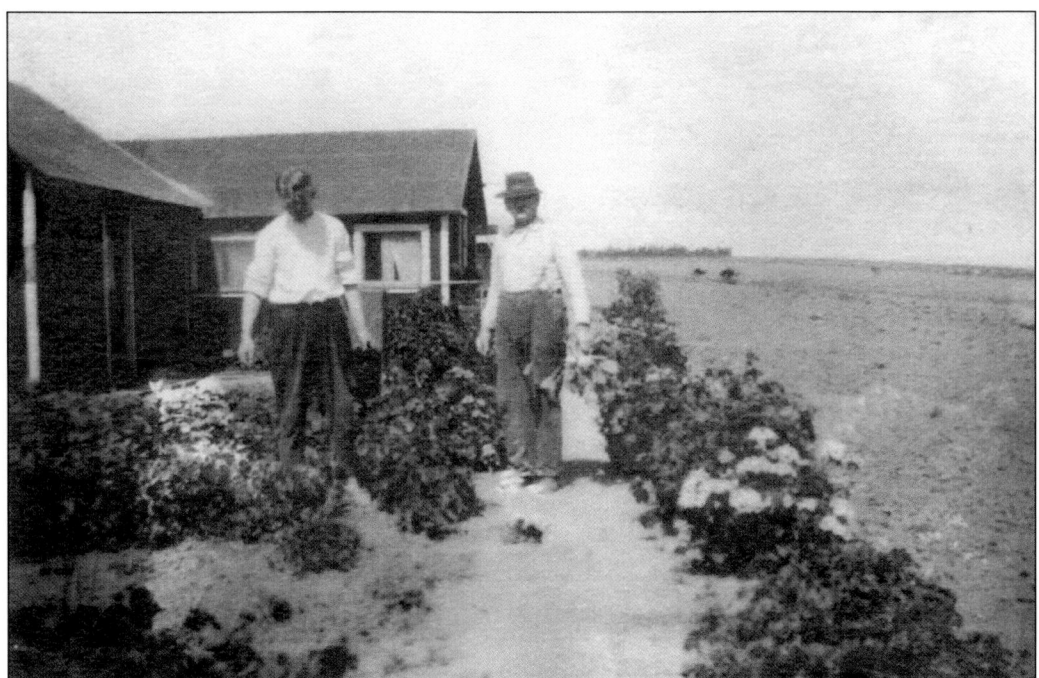

In 1916, the area, which much later would be designated as the Tree Section, north of Center Street (now Manhattan Beach Blvd.) was extremely fertile. As homes were built, vegetable gardens were planted. The Marshall home, located at 1921 Pine Avenue, was no exception.

Peck's Manhattan Beach
Splendid View Of Pacific Ocean, Catalina Island,

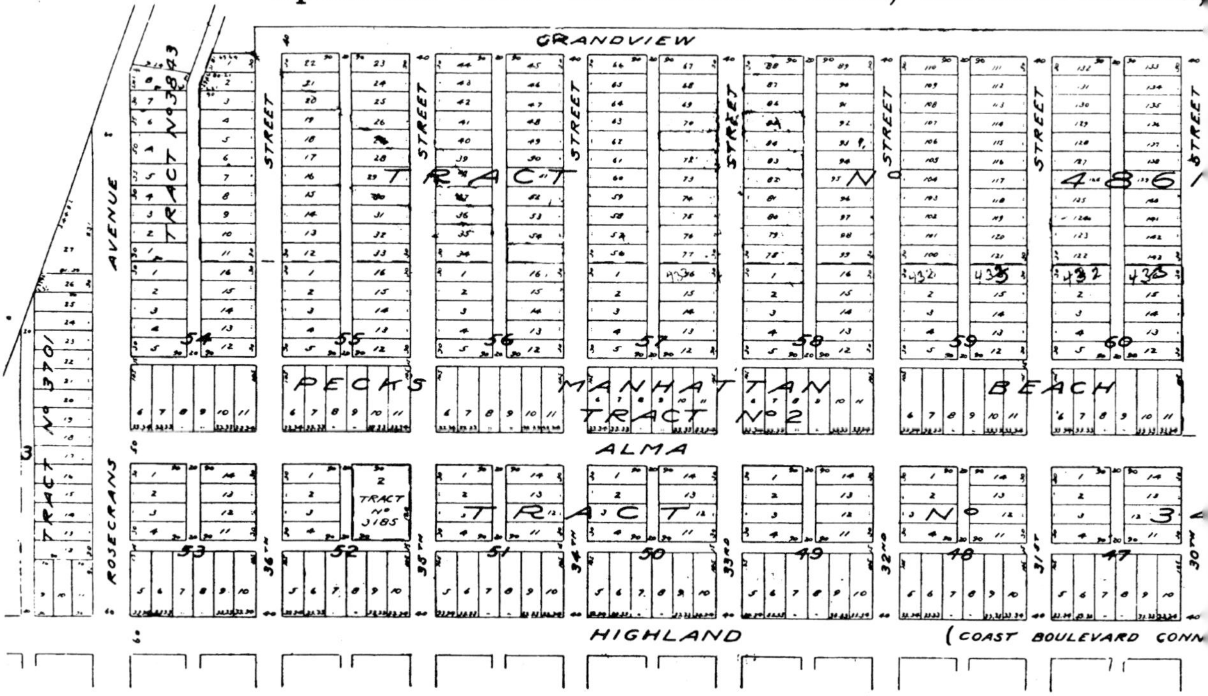

The Los Angeles Herald says, "*Every foot of Beach front will be occupied. GET YOURS NOW! Seize it NOW before prices go beyond your reach and while the getting is easy.*"

Los Angeles grows towards the beach. Be there when it arrives!

BUY Manhattan BEACH LOTS NOW!

There is only so much Close-in Beach, so get yours now! Beach lots at Venice and Long Beach made fortunes for investors. 3 Sand lot corners in Venice recently brought $170,000.00 cash.

Beach lots will never be cheaper. Buy now!

This is a 1916 ad used to promote George Peck's North Manhattan Beach housing track.

The Beach Worth While

Palos Verdes Hills And Santa Monica Mountains

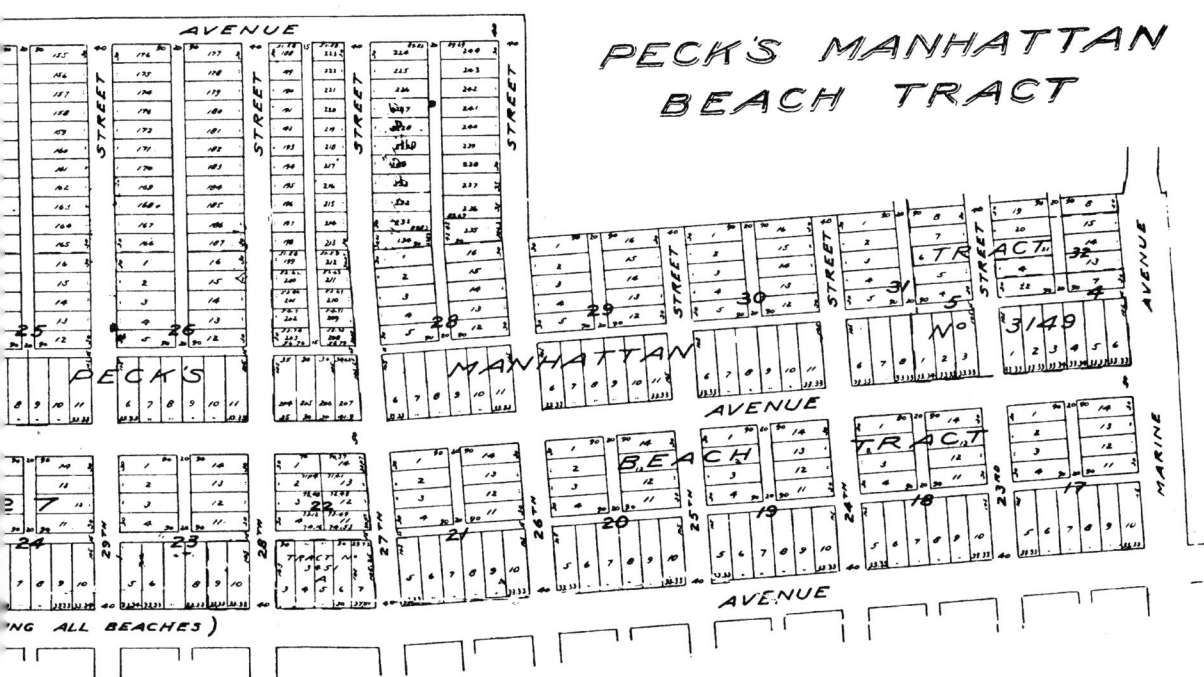

Buy Beach Lots now!   They will never be cheaper!

LIMITED AREA MAKES HIGH VALUES and Beach within easy reach of Los Angeles is less in area than the downtown and suburban business district or the industrial section or the exclusive residential section. Compare the prices.

$10 Monthly Buys a Beach Lot!

If you want to make money, buy Beach Lots now!
Can you afford NOT to buy?

Free Trip Daily [Except Monday] at 10.30 A. M.

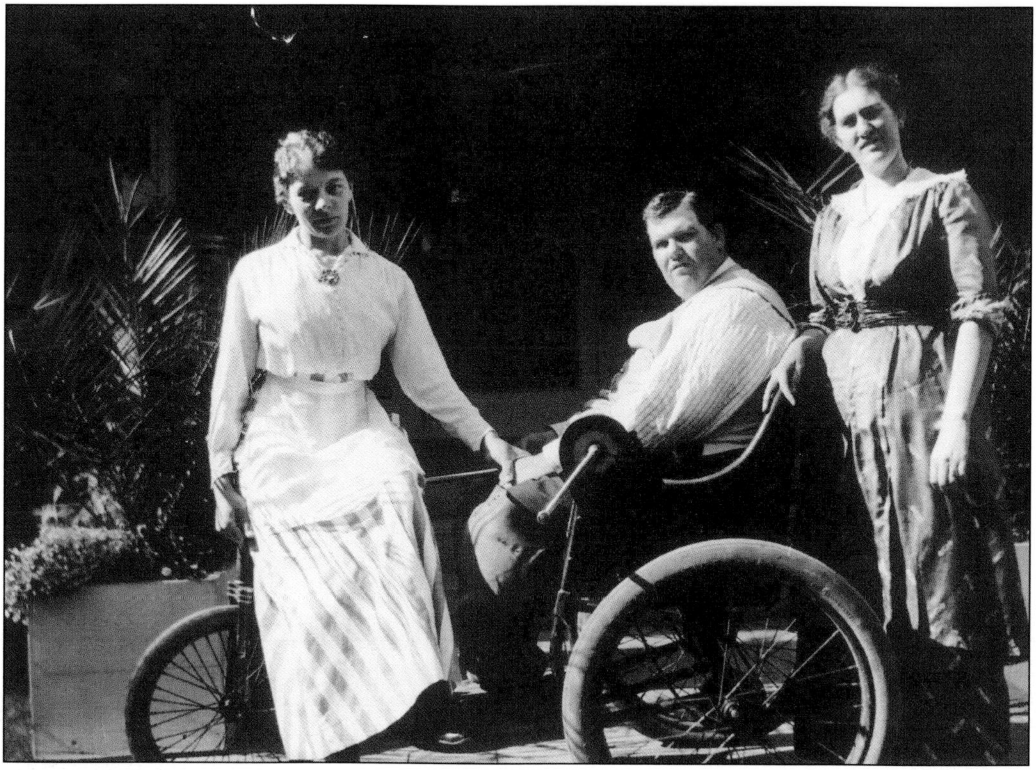

In 1916, George Peck Jr. was extremely busy with his many developments and land sales, yet his three children, Rena, Leland, and Alma, did not want for love and attention from him. He arranged for a cook, chauffeur, and around-the-clock nursing care for Alma and Leland. Both were born with physical handicaps for which no cure could be found. The Peck Manhattan Beach home was at 2620 Alma Avenue (the street was named after his daughter).

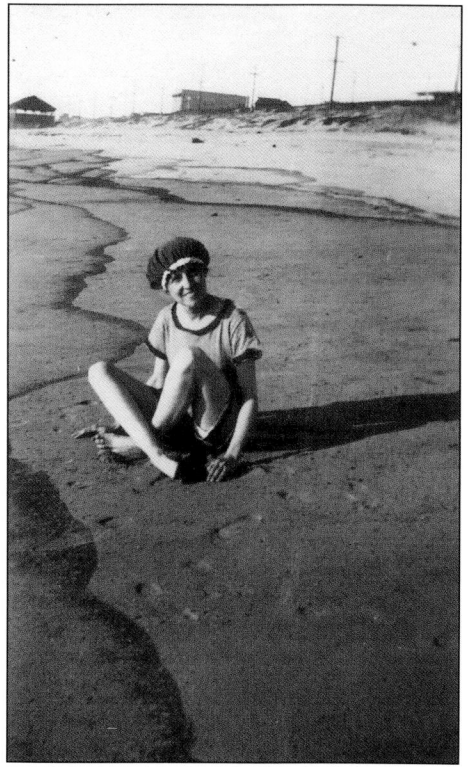

In 1917, Ms. Macbelle Pritchett enjoyed the ocean side in the late afternoon. In the background the Peck Pavilion can be seen.

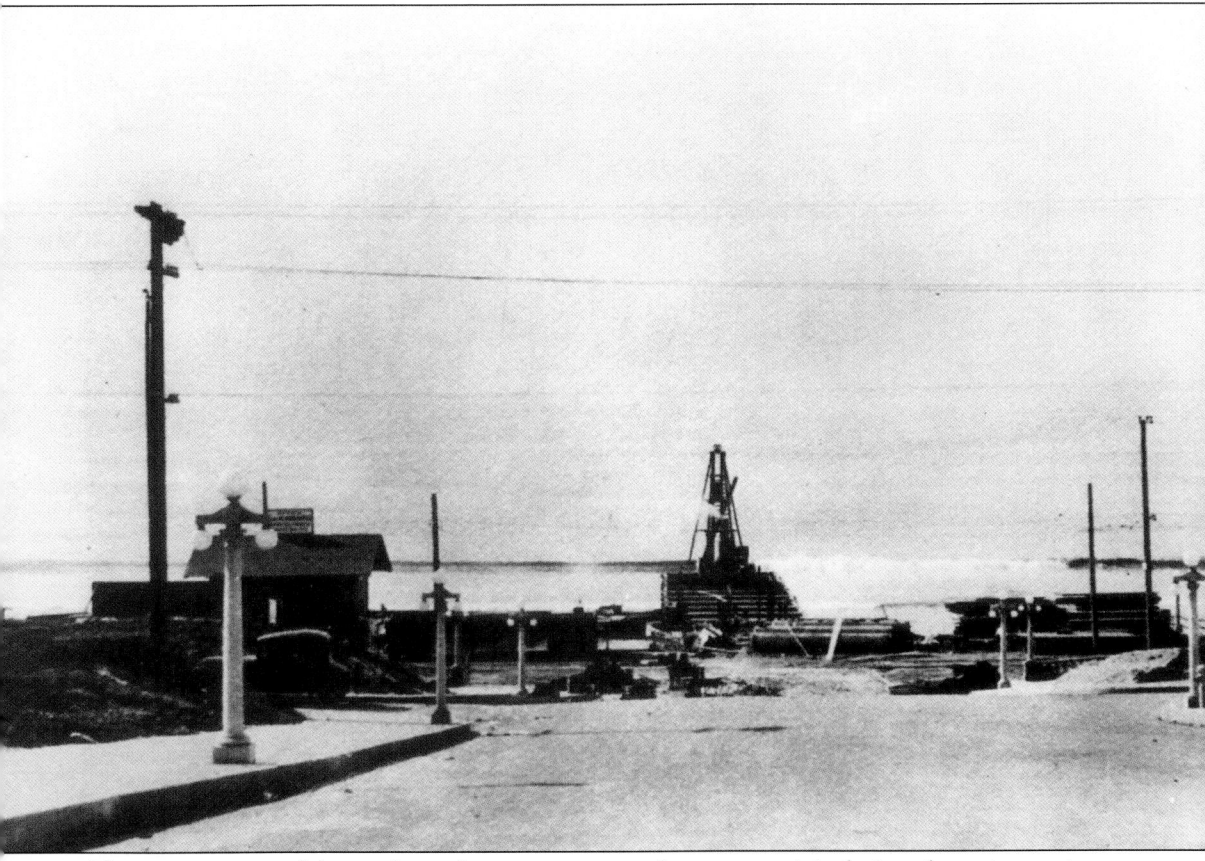

There were many debates about the construction of a new municipal pier when city engineer A.L. Harris submitted his plan on June 17, 1916. His proposal contained the idea of having a round-ended pier, a feature that had not been used on the California coast. He felt having the circular end made the pier much stronger against the action of the waves—the fewer piles the better and there was less opportunity for the water to take hold. Another reason for decreasing the number of piles was to save funds in order to have adequate dollars to spend on such items as the railings and a roundhouse on the seaward section of the pier. The plans for the pier were finally approved and the contract was awarded in 1917 to George Harding, who bid $61,000 to construct a 922-foot pier with four sun parlors at the land's end. After working on the pier for over a year, Harding abandoned the project. With the rising cost of materials caused by World War I, he could not stay within budget. The trustees turned the job over to city engineer A.L. Harris, only to have $8,000 worth of damage done to the pier by a heavy storm two weeks later. The entire project came to a sudden standstill when the United States entered the War.

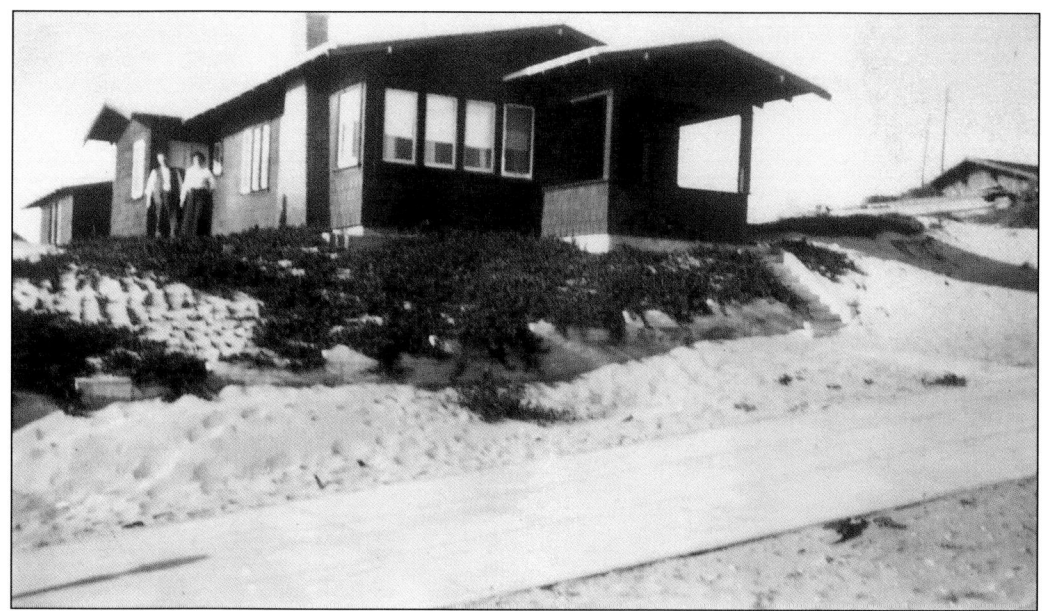

The Harold Cashin home was located on 16th Street a few blocks east of the Strand. Mr. J. Cashin's son, John "Jack" Cashin, served in many city and community organizations. Service to the city included a term as a planning commissioner, two terms as the city clerk, and a four-year-term on the City Council, from 1972 to 1976, where he held the ceremonial office of mayor. In the business world Cashin had a career as an educator and author writing *Foundations of Free Choice*, a political science textbook.

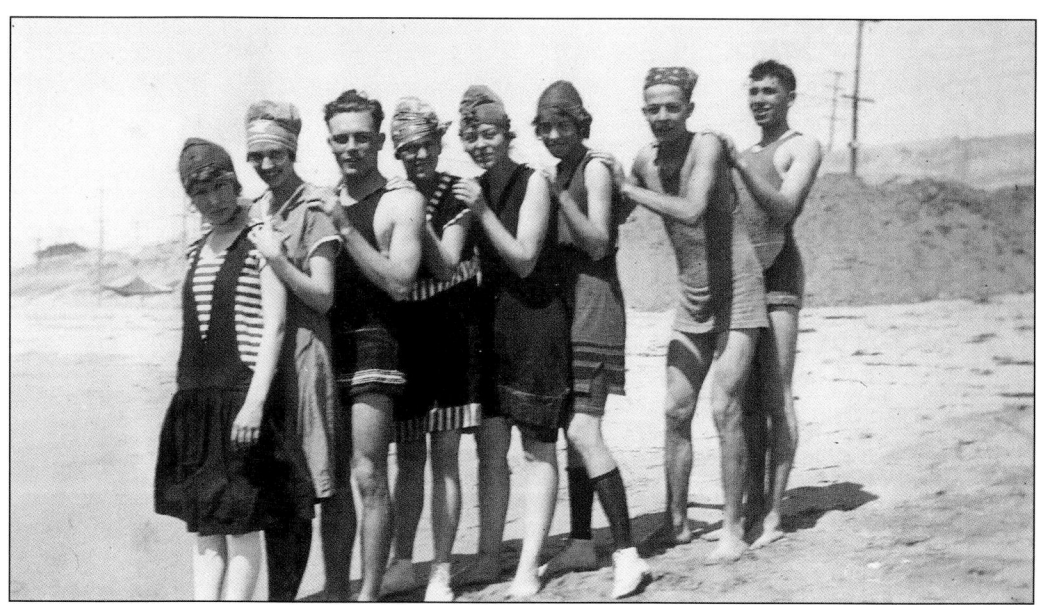

Here the Cashin family, with a group of friends, poses for the camera wearing the latest in bathing suit attire. Descendants of that family still reside in Manhattan Beach.

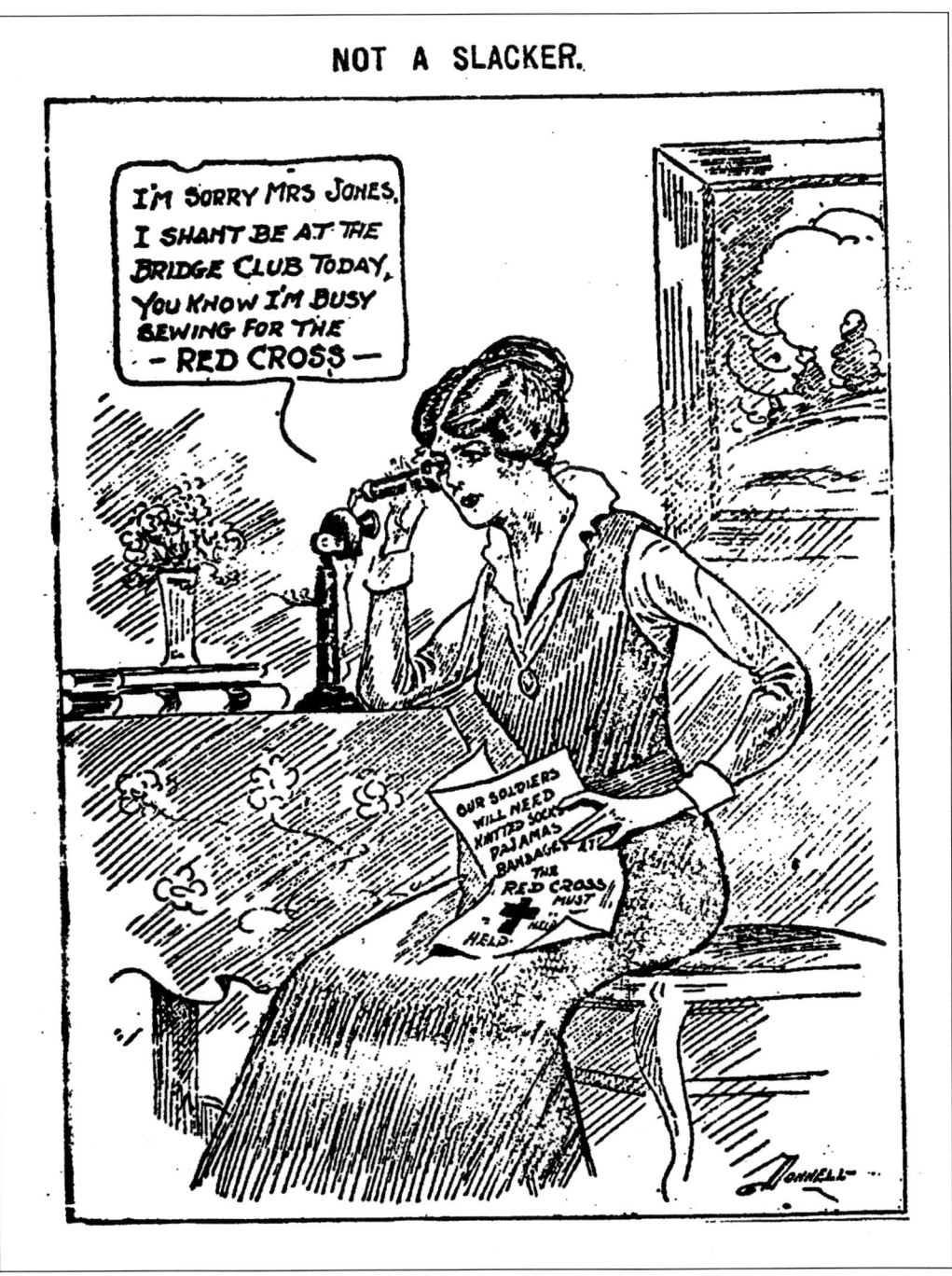

ACCEPTING THE CHALLENGE IN WORLD WAR I. Reprinted in the Manhattan Beach News, VI 1917. Like communities large and small across the nation, the First World War prompted everyone to pitch in.

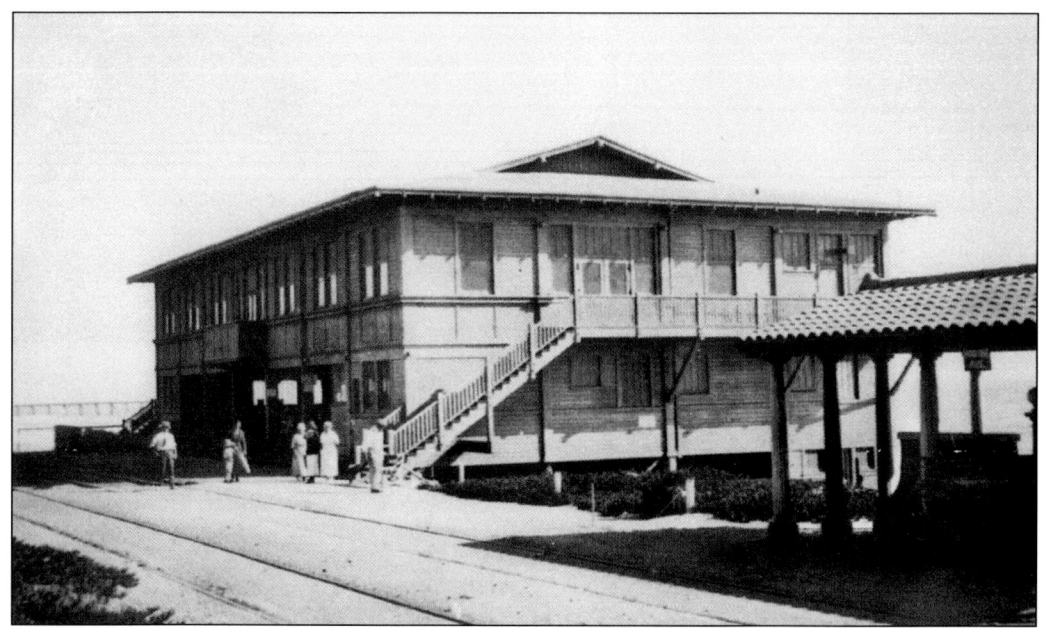

The pavilion, located at the foot of Marine Avenue, celebrated its grand opening with a Red Cross benefit ball on April 6, 1918. The benefit featured the best musicians from the submarine base in San Pedro and professional movie people from Hollywood. The pavilion was considered the grandest building in town. It offered a 5,600 square foot dance floor, 22 large picnic tables, a soda fountain, and lunchroom and concession area. The Red Cross opened a refreshment booth in the building with all proceeds going to the organization's treasury.

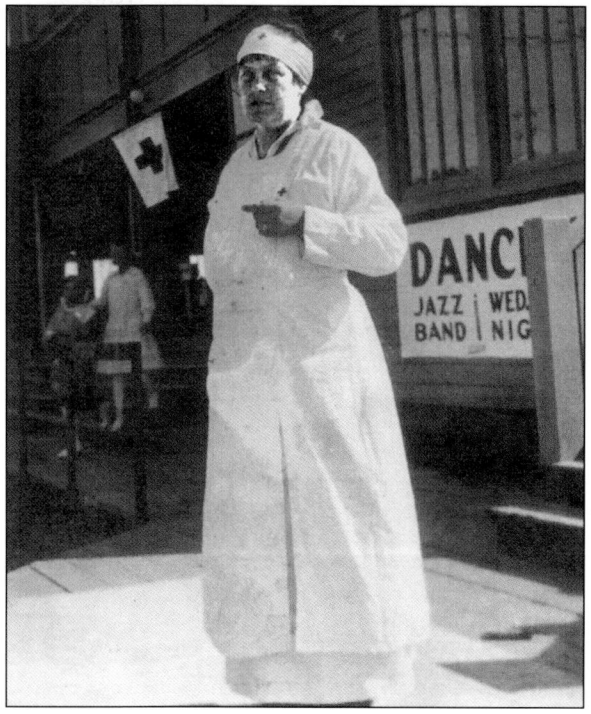

When the United States entered World War I, people in town were deeply involved as they sent their boys off to the battlefields in the summer of 1917. The ladies of the community volunteered in the Red Cross. Photographed in 1918, Mrs. William Simkins, standing here in front of the Marine Pavilion, was one such volunteer.

Mr. and Mrs. William Simkins and their son, George, home on leave at 233 7th Street.

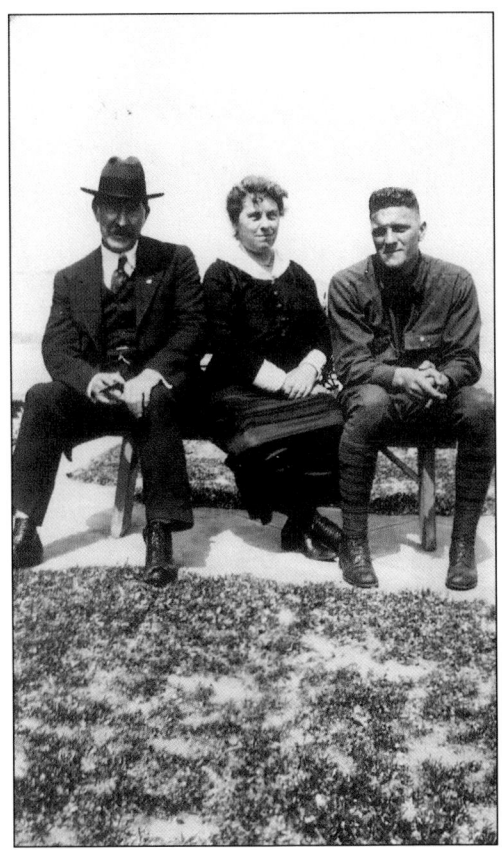

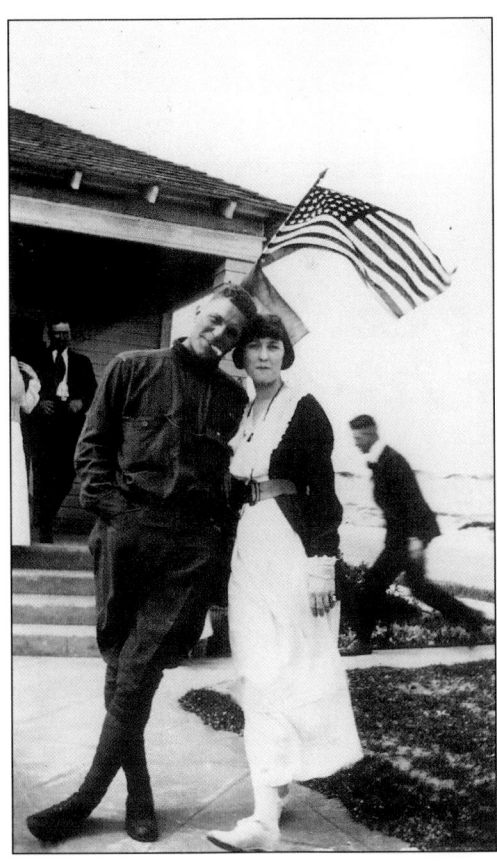

In August 1918, George Simkins, home on leave from the army, celebrated a visit with his family and sister, Mary.

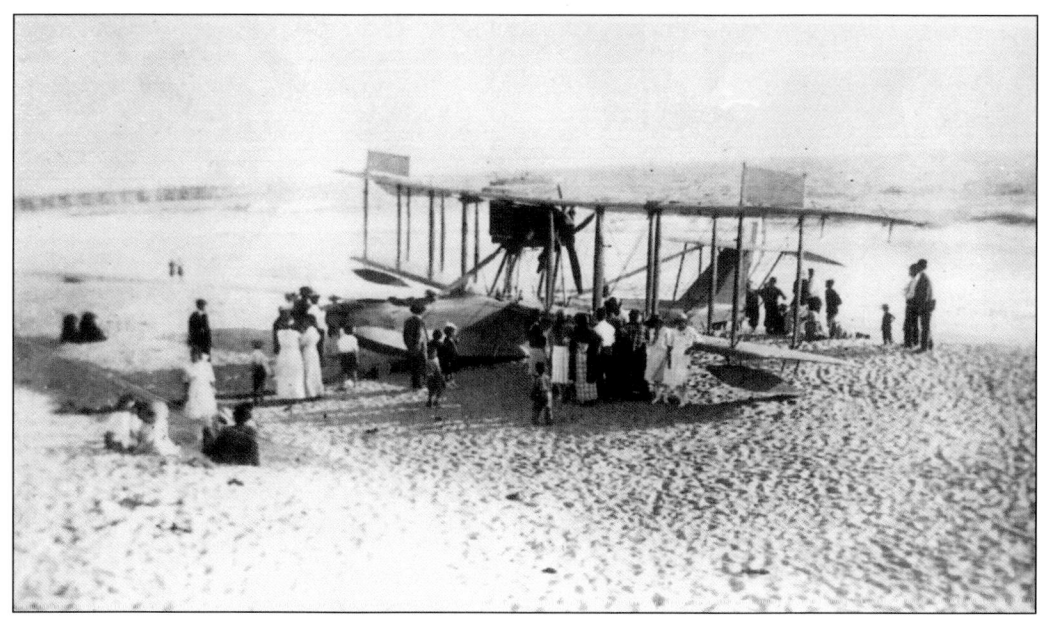

In August of 1919, a navy hydroplane was forced to land in the surf at the foot of 17th Street when the timing gear went down. The plane arrived safely home to base in San Diego after repairs and help from the local residents.

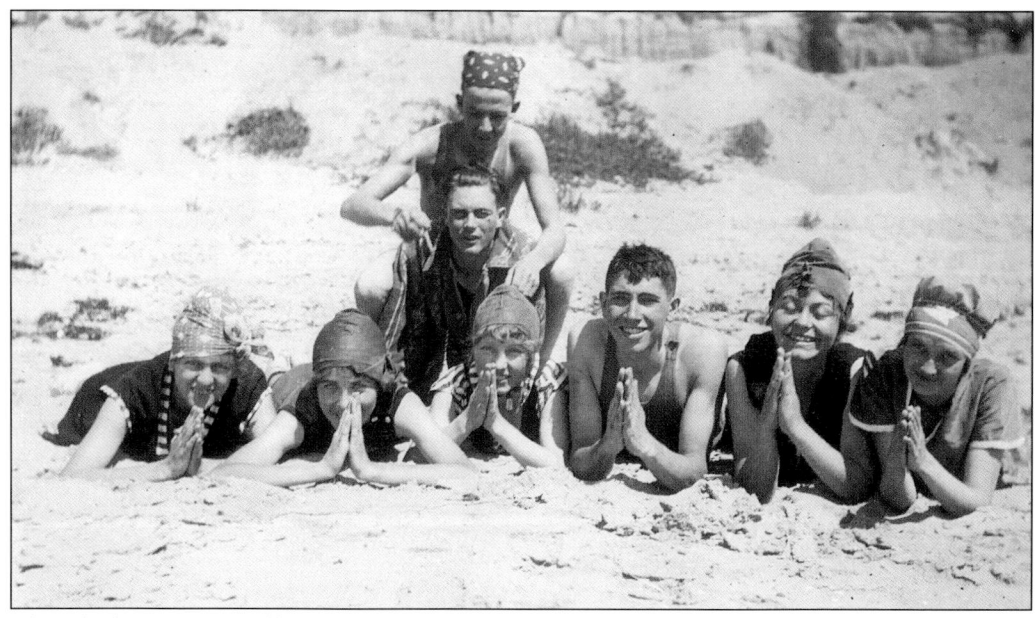

Though the war was still going on and all were involved with collecting scrap metal, rubber tires, inner tubes, and newspaper for the war effort, there was still time for the young people of the Cashin family to spend an afternoon at the beach.

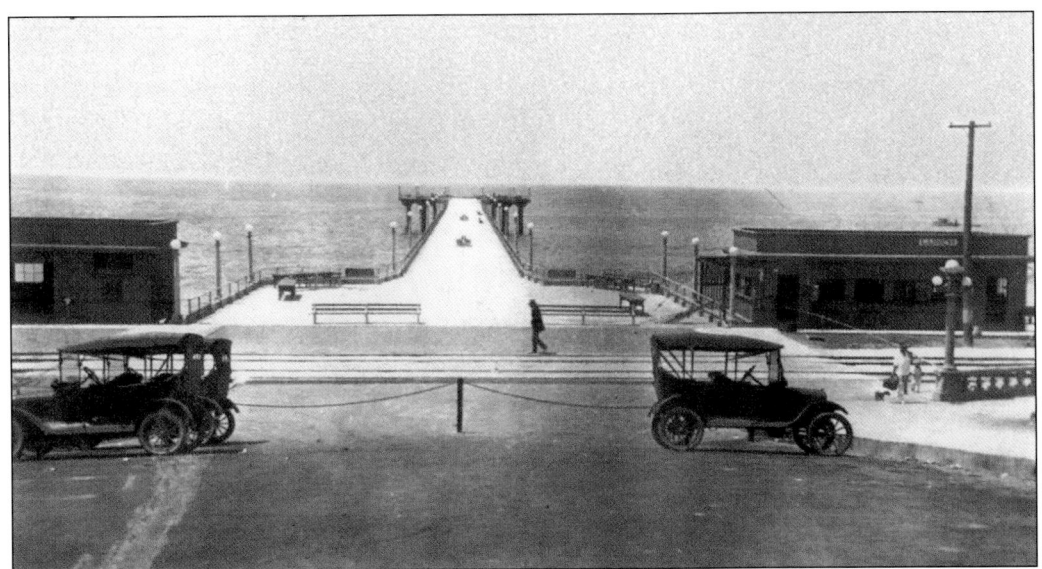

At last, the war was over, but the pier construction was still stalled by the Pacific Electric workers' strike. By the second week of the strike, freight hauling had been resumed. Realizing the need to finish the pier and that it would cost more money, the city issued a $45,000 bond on May of 1919. By July of that year, the Foundation Company of San Francisco agreed to complete the job. The engineer, A.L. Harris, was replaced by H.W. McGee and work resumed. A small railroad was constructed to the end of the pier in order to carry the piles and other materials.

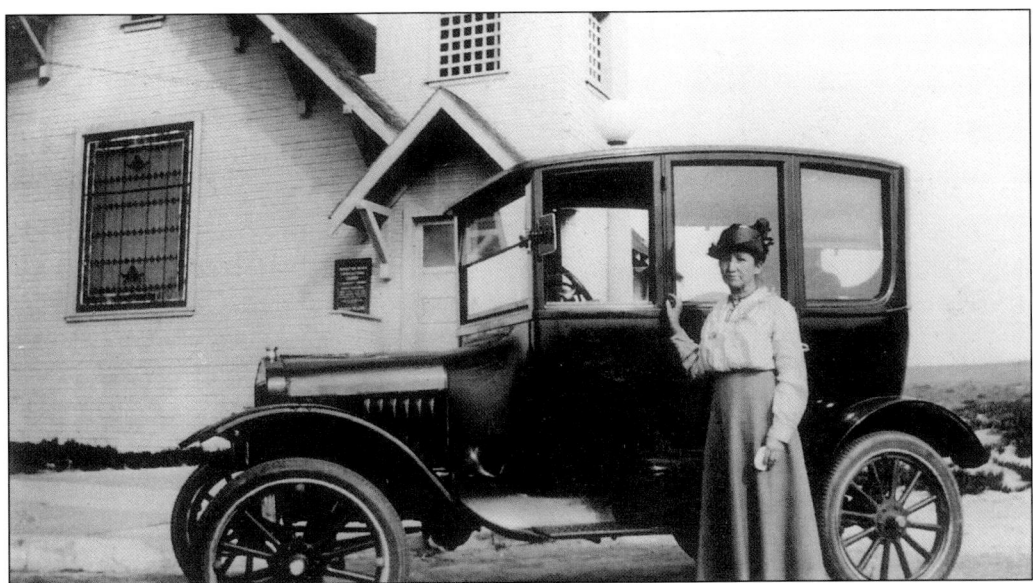

The car created many problems for the city fathers since the streets were still very primitive. Miss Alice Jacobs, Sunday school superintendent, poses with her vehicle in front of the Community Church at Highland and 9th Street, c. 1920

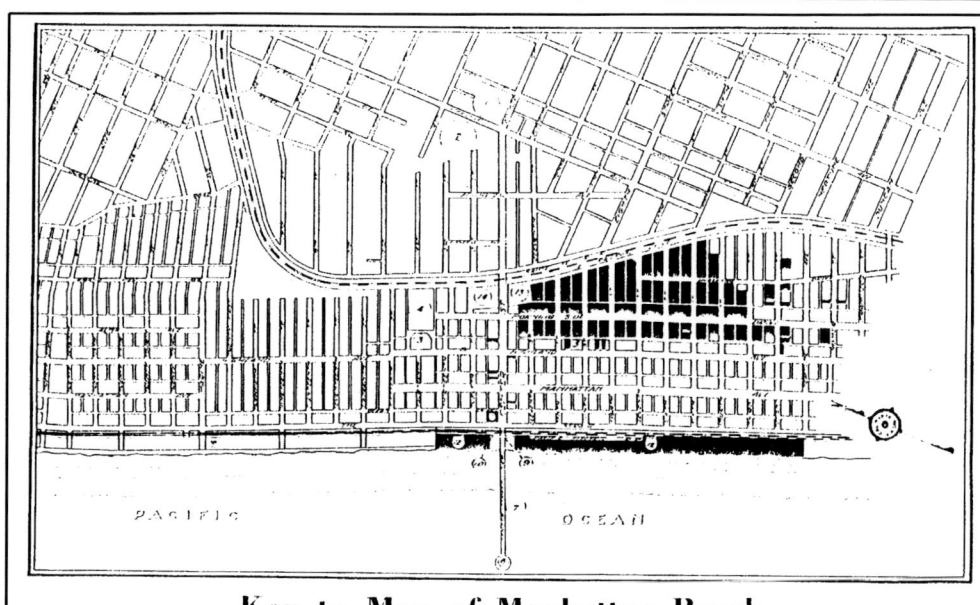

This 1921 advertisement for the Manhattan Beach Development Company promoting opportunities in beach property investment would be but one of many land buying encouragements to come.

Three
SHIFTING SANDS

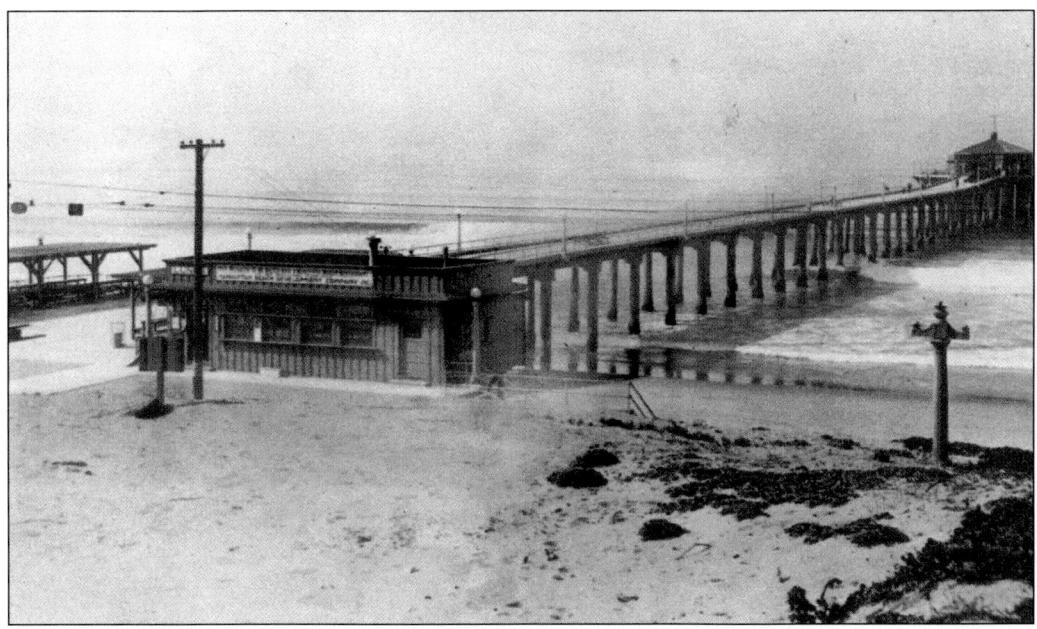

The promise of a building boom in the West following World War I brought many families to Manhattan Beach. The town had its share of moonshiners, inebriated drivers racing through town, and flappers dancing the night away. Still, it was a family town and it cracked down hard on anything that would disturb that image. By the early 1920s, the town had grown to more than 1,400 residents and boasted of having approximately 30 miles of paved roads and sidewalks. Despite these advances, the residents in many areas still made their way over the deserted sand dunes by way of boardwalks laid atop the sand. Dubbed "Queen of the Dunes" and in spite of the problems with drifting sand, the town was well on its way to record building years. The value of building permits issued in the first three-and-one-half months of 1920 was nearly six times larger than in 1919.

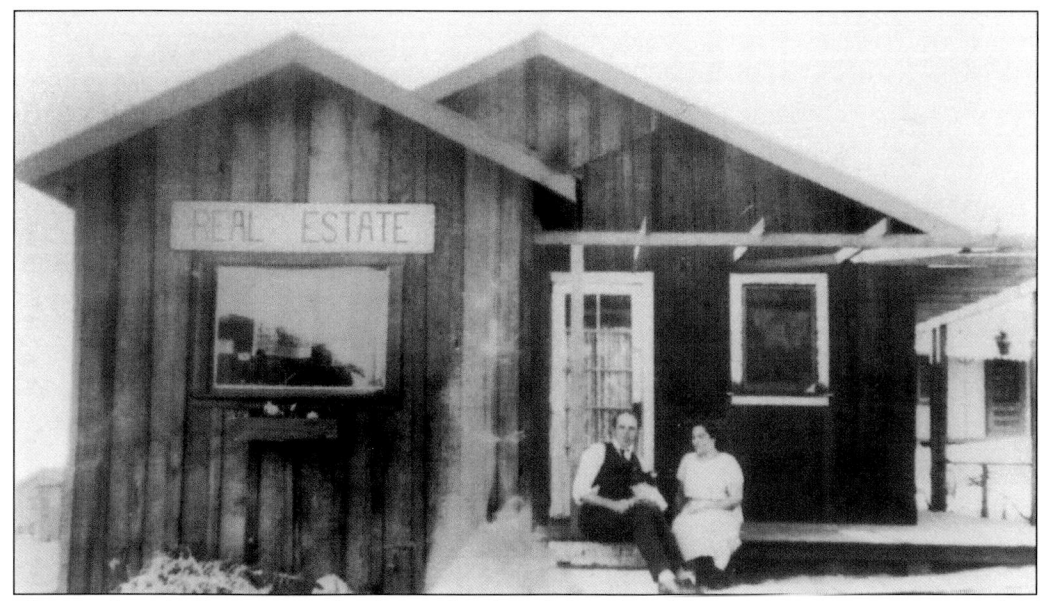

The north end of town was also being developed. Board and batten construction was used in the building of the realty office and home of Mr. and Mrs. G.H. Lindsey.

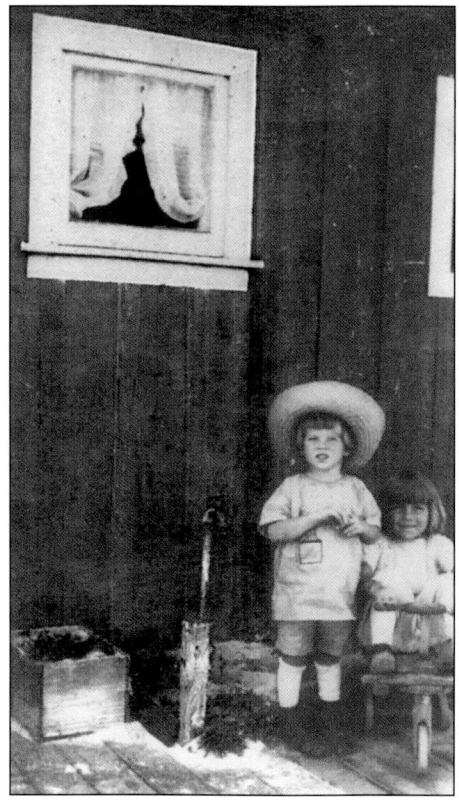

The Lindsay children, Don and Bunny, pose for the camera outside the kitchen window where the water supply for the home was located.

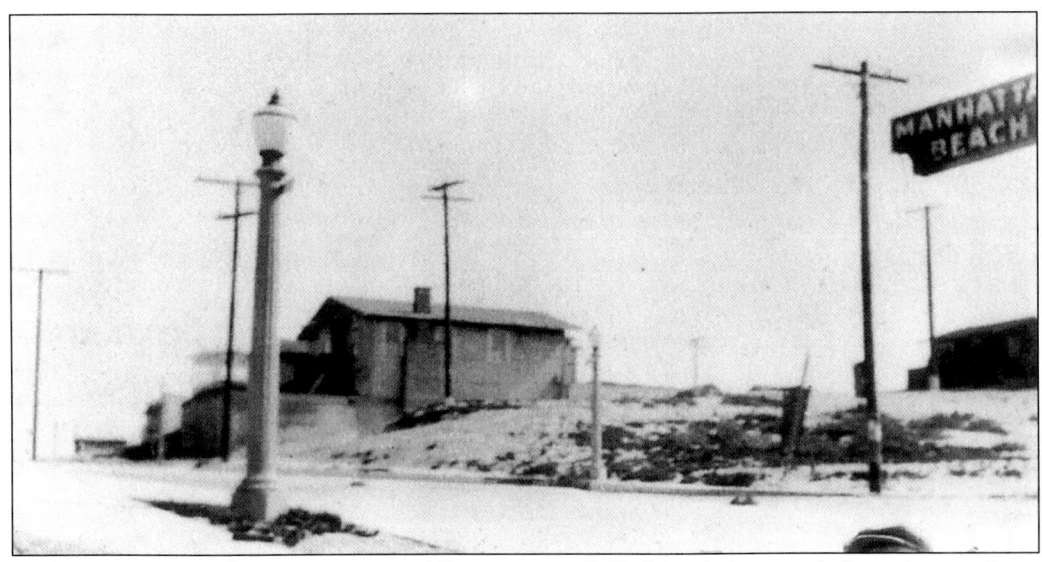
Looking eastward, this intersection of Rosecrans and Highland Avenue defines the northern boundary of the town known as the North-end.

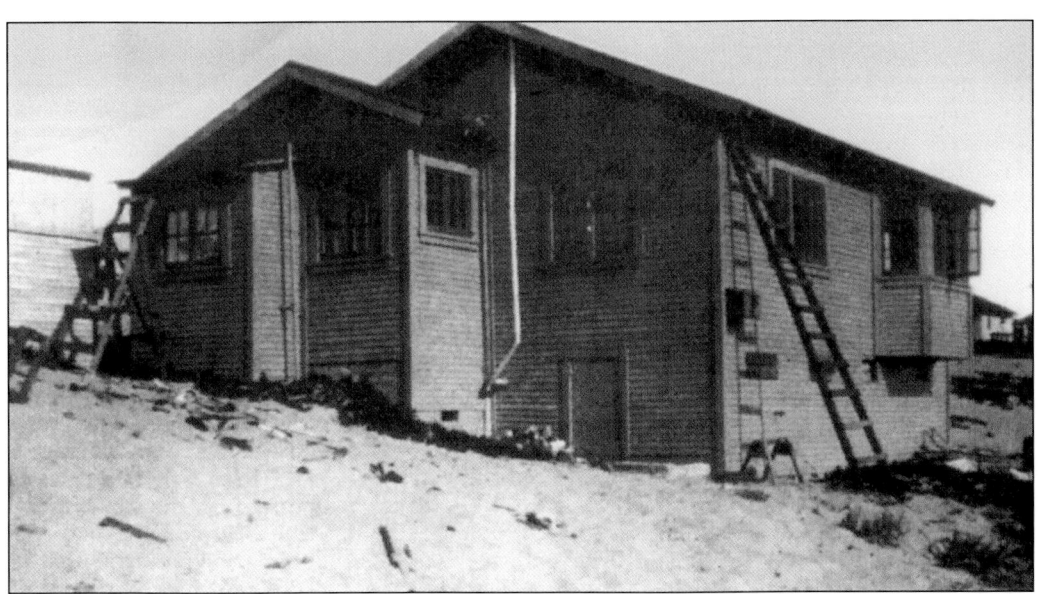
Fred and Lou Dopf's home, located in North-end, was an excellent example of the beach homes that were being built in 1925.

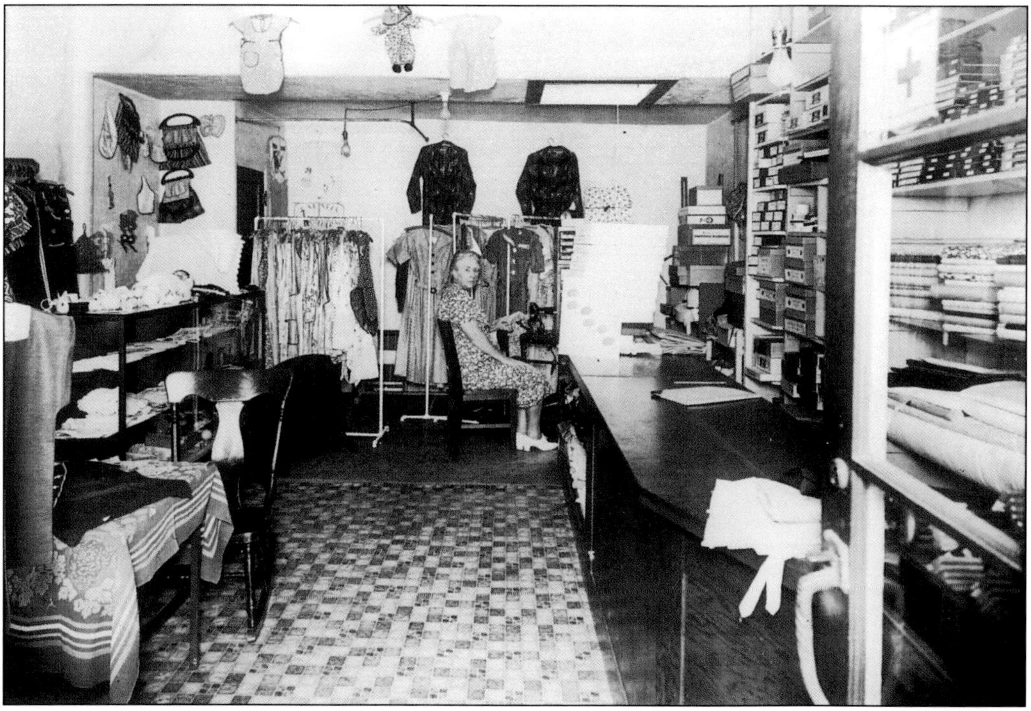

With an influx of permanent residents, more and more retail stores opened. Here are the interior (above) and exterior (below) of Mary Haeberlin's notions store in the business block located on Manhattan Avenue.

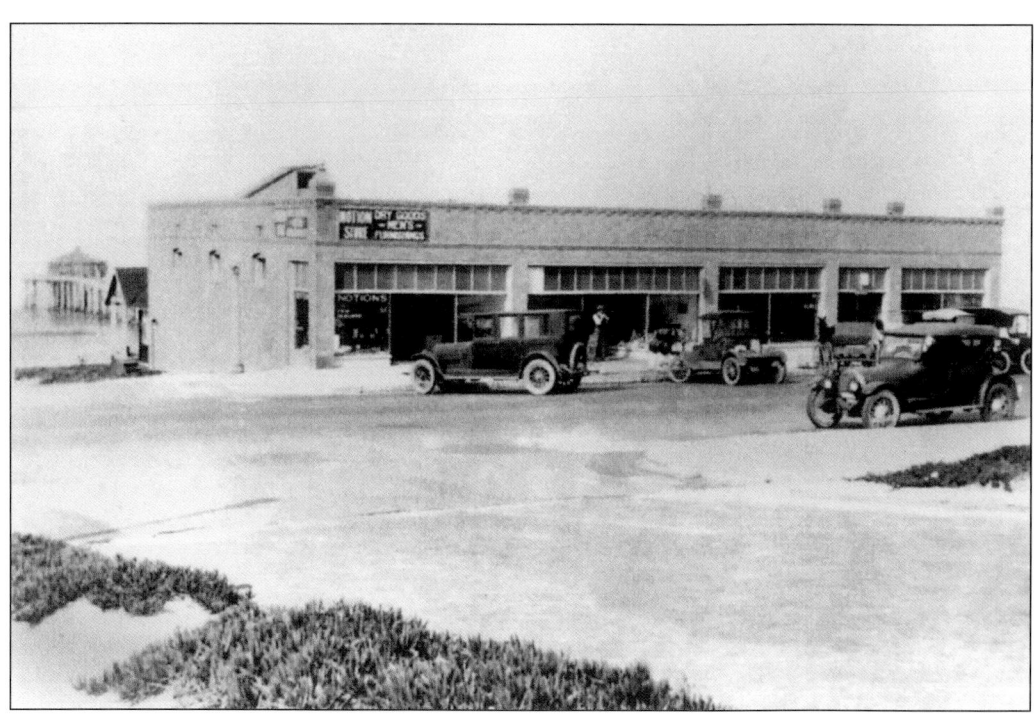

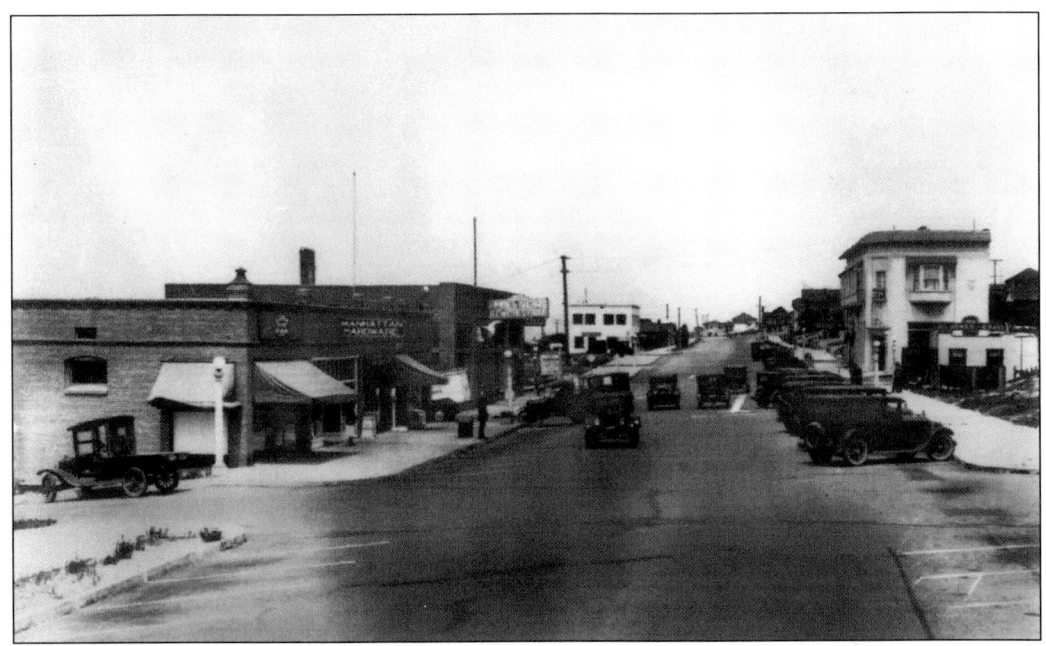

Here, looking north on Manhattan Avenue at the intersection of Center Street (now Manhattan Beach Blvd.) is another business block. It was built with bricks that were made at a site located on what is now Dorsey field, a popular baseball field.

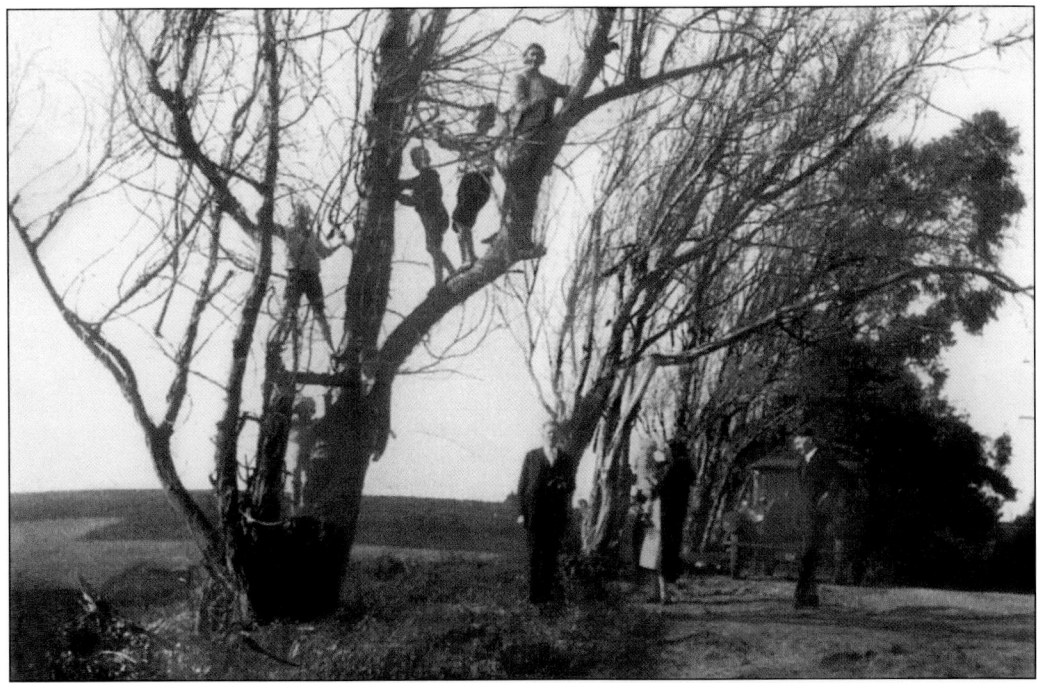

The south end of town was not developing as fast as midtown or the north end. Its rural nature provided the Matthies family with country outings. They are pictured here in 1923, at the corner of Gould Lane in Hermosa Beach and El Camino Real (later to become Sepulveda Blvd.). This corner remains the most southerly boundary of Manhattan Beach.

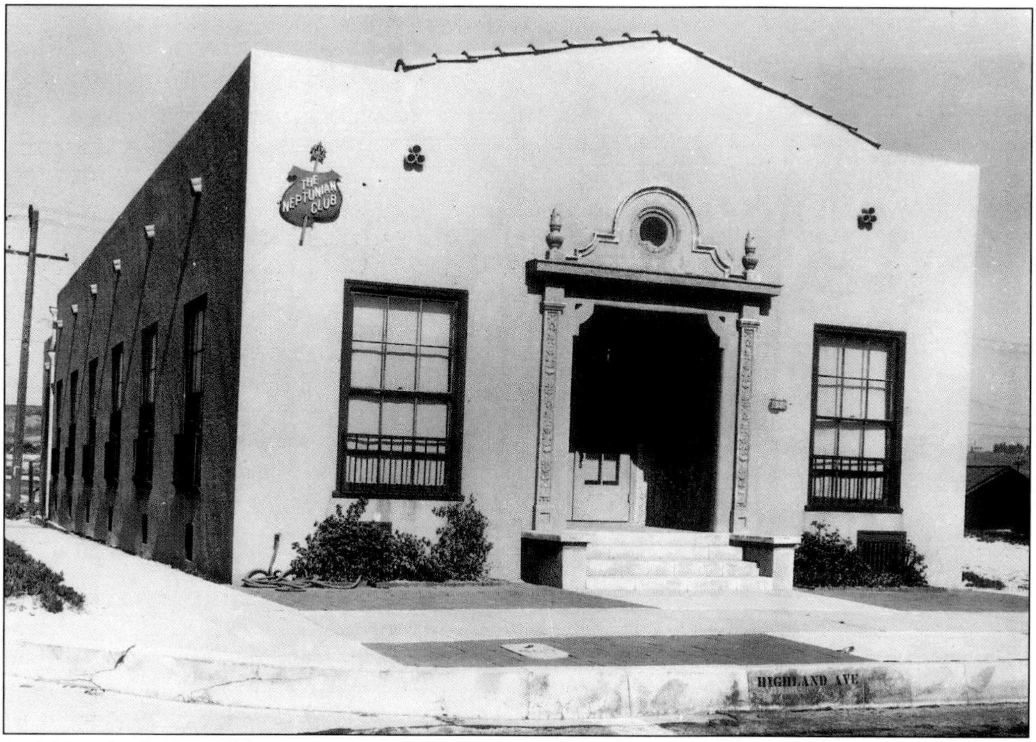

In 1924, the ladies of the Neptunian Club voted to build a clubhouse, which would be located at 920 Highland Avenue. The lot had been purchased several years earlier at a tax sale for $239, plus an additional $300 in order to clear title. The club, through many events, raised $5,500 and work began in early 1925. Fred Young, husband of a charter member, was the contractor who built the 30 by 100 foot structure for a sum of $500.

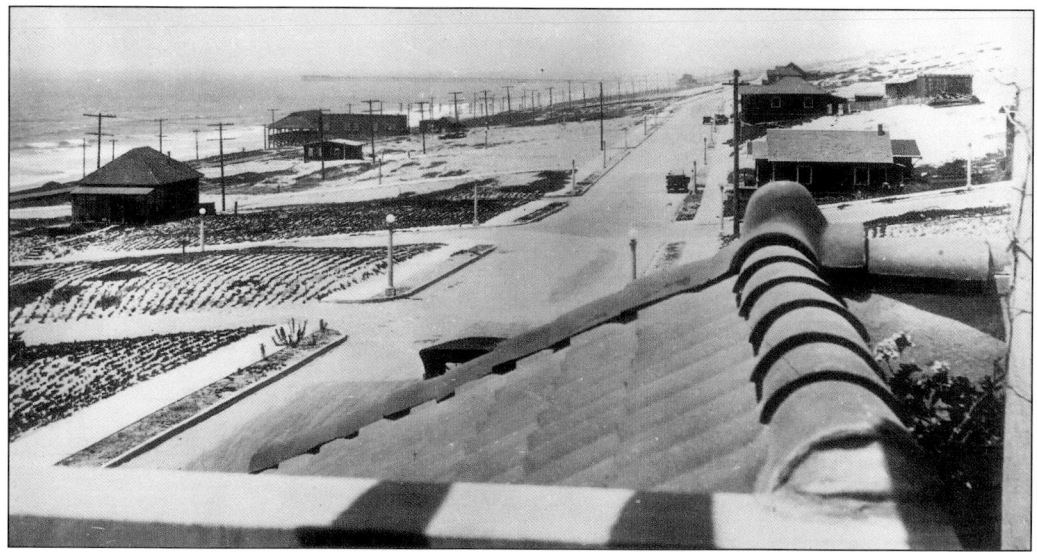

In order to control the shifting dunes, the Neptunian club members and community residents planted row after row of "ice-plant" or "sea moss." In the center of this photo taken c. 1915, Peck's pavilion (razed in 1920) stood between 26th and 27th Street.

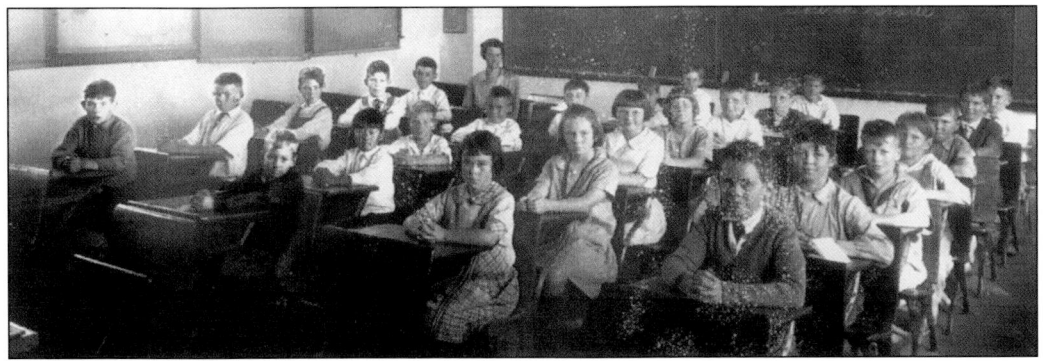

By 1924, there were 207 children and 8 teachers enrolled in the Manhattan Beach school system. Children of the area at this time were from farms, small housing tracts, and the wealthier families along the Strand. It was not uncommon to see children in school barefooted and wearing overalls, or in knickers, high stockings, and white shirts. Appearing in this photograph is the fourth grade class of 1924.

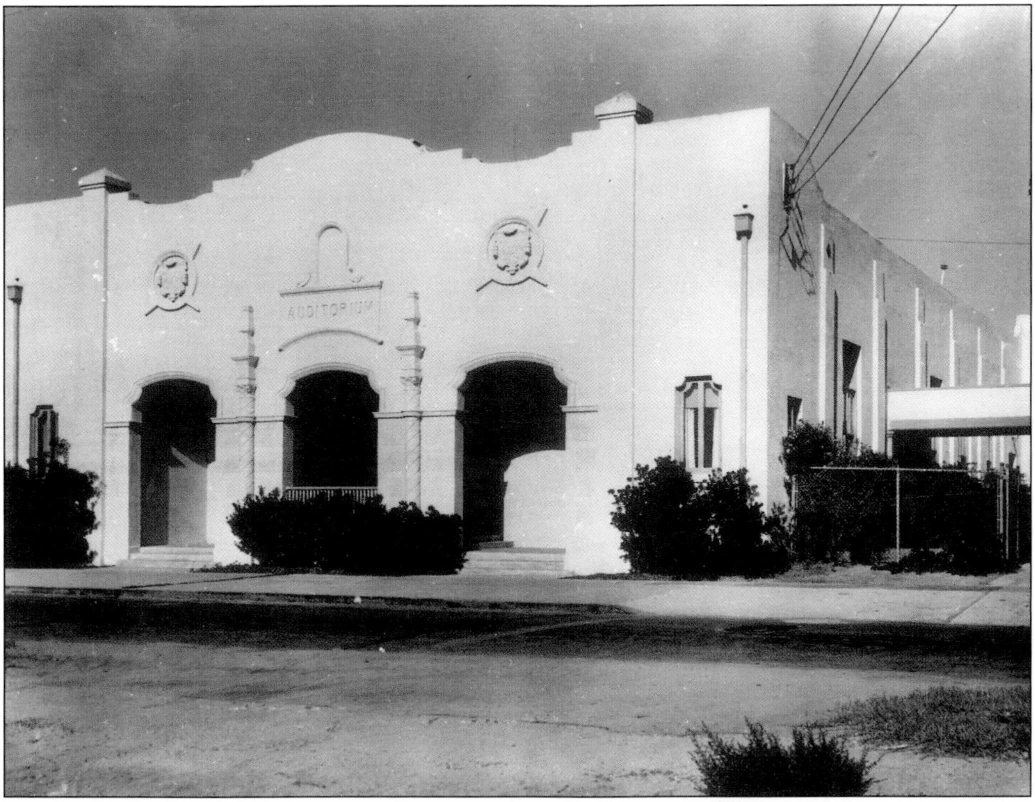

Both the school and the community utilized the Center Street School auditorium. Built in 1925, it was constructed of steel, wood, and hollow tile. Due to the earthquake of 1933, the building was deemed unsafe and was eventually demolished in 1949.

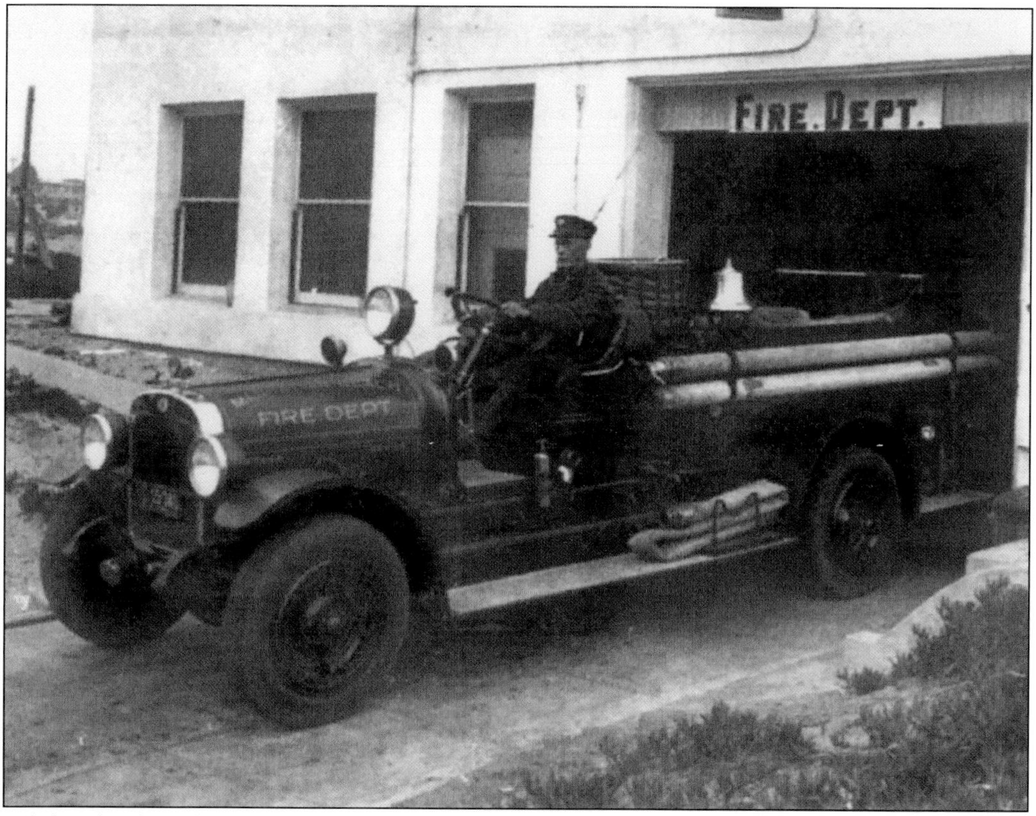

While schools, police, and utilities were supported by the city, fire fighting was last on the list of city improvements. Before 1921, neighboring Hermosa Beach Fire Department fought all fires. After a house fire at 1148 Manhattan Avenue, the town realized it needed its own department. Chief H.L. Hicks, the city's only paid member of the new department, is seen here on a new Seagrave pumper purchased in 1925.

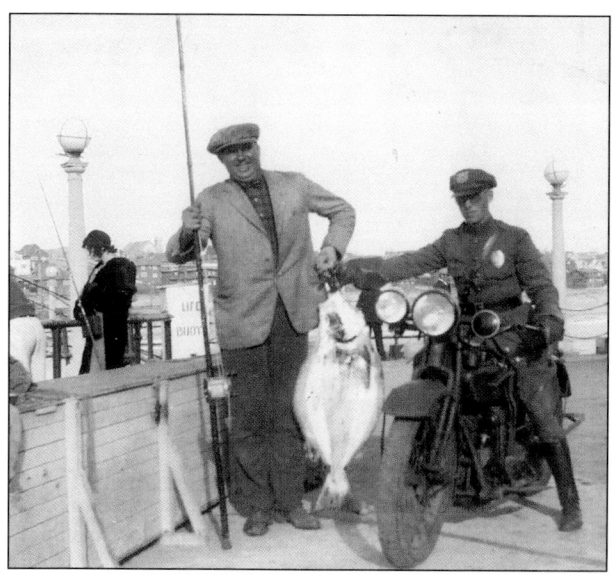

In 1924 Jack F. Garvin, pictured here on the motorcycle, became chief of the Manhattan Beach police department. Chief Garvin worked as the city's only motor officer. The qualifications for becoming a Manhattan Beach policeman were rather simple. One had to own his own car, buy his own uniform and weapon, and be appointed by the city council. The city did buy a motorcycle, red lights, siren for the patrolman's car, and furnished gas for the vehicle. There was only one patrolman, H.S. Boardman, who, with the chief, worked 12-hour shifts, 7 days a week, and was on call 24 hours a day.

In 1924, Howard Zahn, a first generation German American, arrived in Manhattan Beach from Illinois. He first worked for George Peck and later opened his own real estate office on Highland Avenue. His old-world values regarding the importance of land were reflected in the acquisition and development of fine quality homes and commercial buildings. Many of those structures are still standing today.

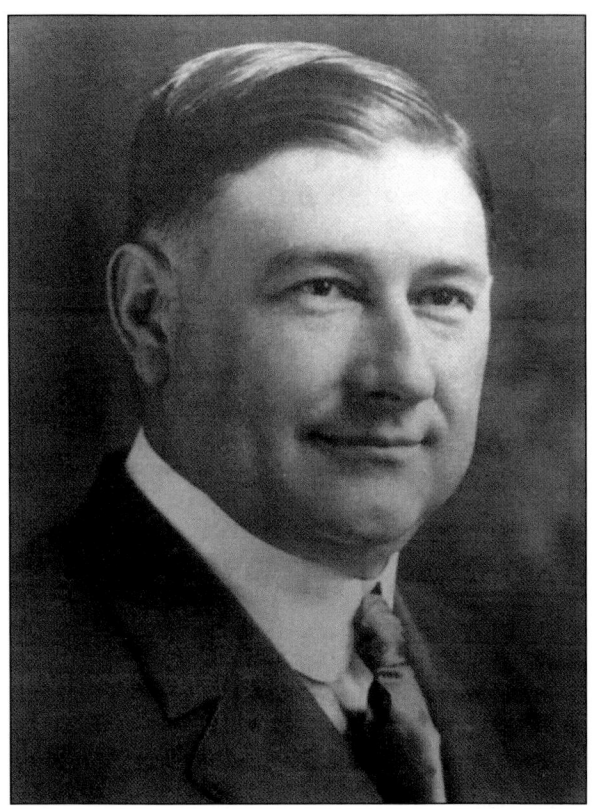

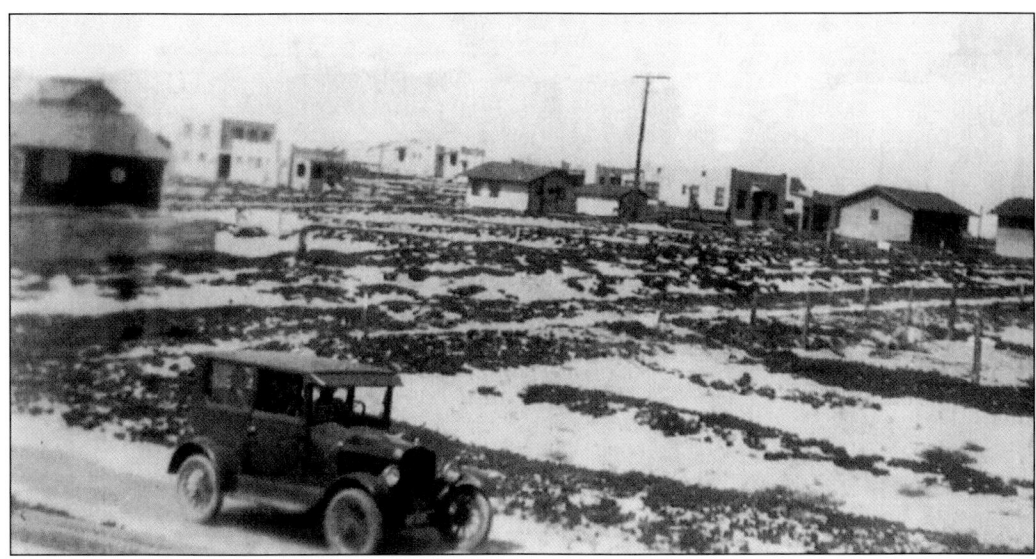

Looking northeast on April 22, 1927, this is one of the many sites that Zahn developed located at 33rd Street in the Northend.

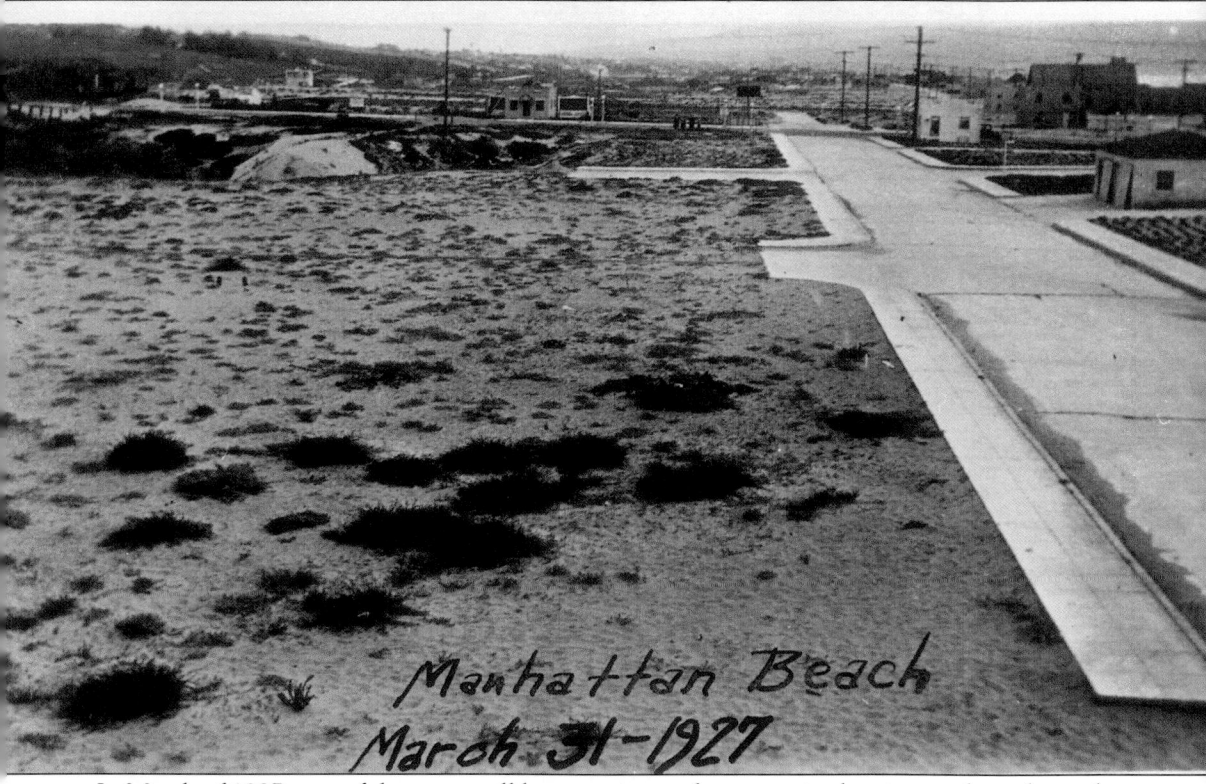

Manhattan Beach March 31 - 1927

In March of 1927, one of the most well known pieces of property in the city was brought to the newsworthy attention of its residents, when T.C. Prouty was searching for a new factory site. This virgin sand acreage was located in the downtown area, bounded by the Santa Fe Railroad on the east, Center Street (Manhattan Beach Blvd.) on the south, Morningside Drive on the west, and the civic center property on the north. The Santa Fe Railway Company had leveled the acreage in 1921–22, intending to build a warehouse and waiting room for their rail line. The construction never took place. The Proutyline Products Company, founded in 1921 by T.C. Prouty, had been operating in Hermosa Beach, manufacturing architectural tiles.

Prouty was an inventor, manufacturer, and visionary. By the time he purchased the land in Manhattan Beach, he had several factories around the country and employed over 6,000 people. In 1929 his sons, Kenneth and Willis Prouty, created the Metlox Corporation, which rapidly became the most successful manufacturer of neon signs across the country.

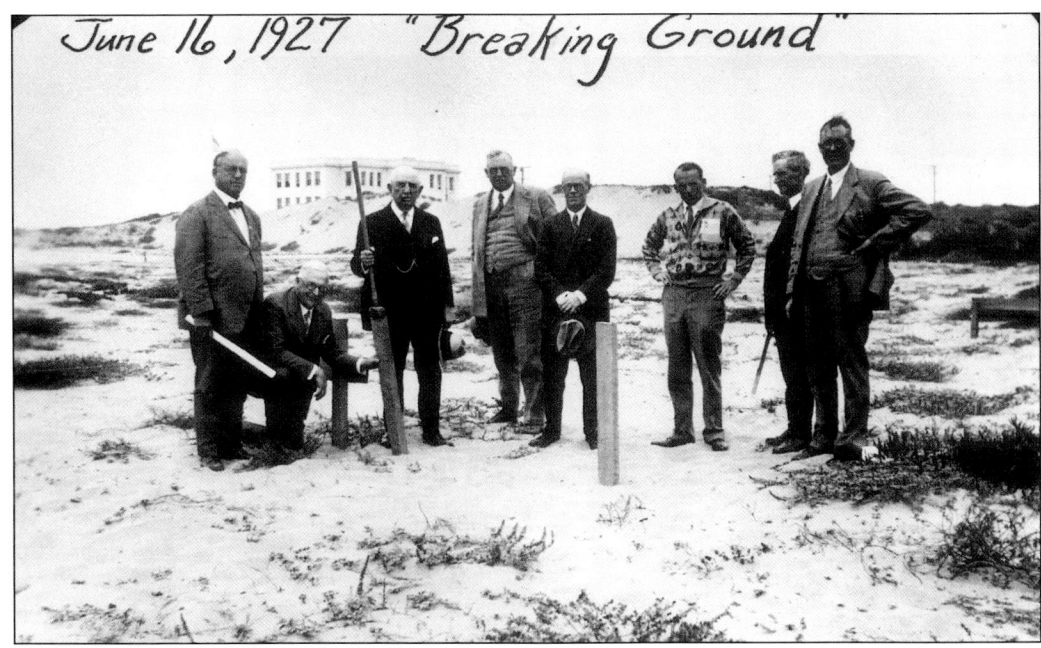

The Proutyline Products Company purchased four acres of Manhattan Beach property from the Tractor Service Company following the sale of their architectural tile plant in Hermosa to the American Encaustic Tile Company. On June 16, 1927, their groundbreaking ceremony (pictured above) launched the development of a new industrial site in the city. Note City Hall in the background.

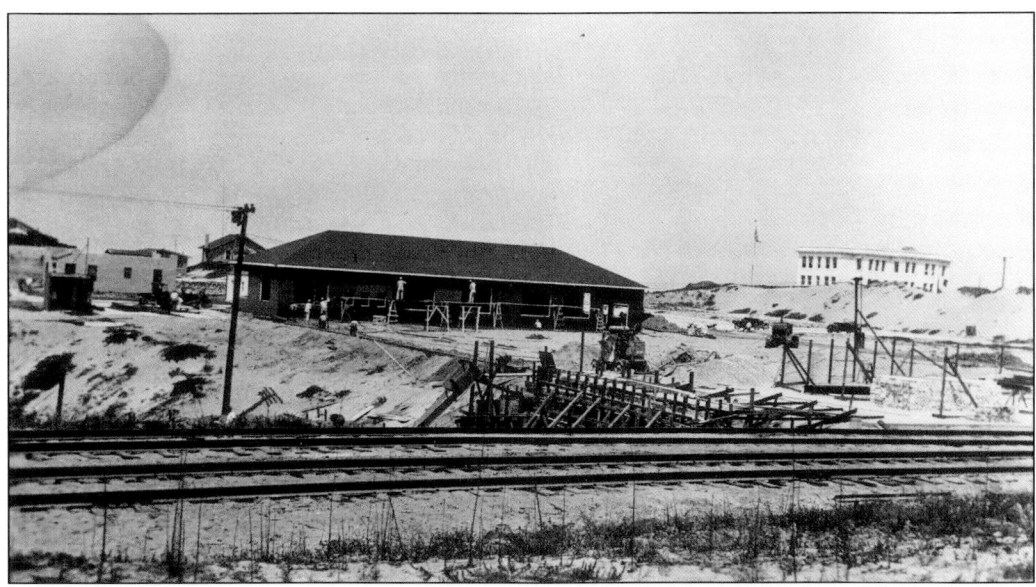

Facing west from the Santa Fe Railroad tracks, the office/experimental laboratory building was the first structure to be constructed. T.C. Prouty had a strong feeling that the South Bay was to become one of the greatest manufacturing districts in the United States and that the Atchison, Topeka, and Santa Fe right-of-way corridor would be developed into an industrial area.

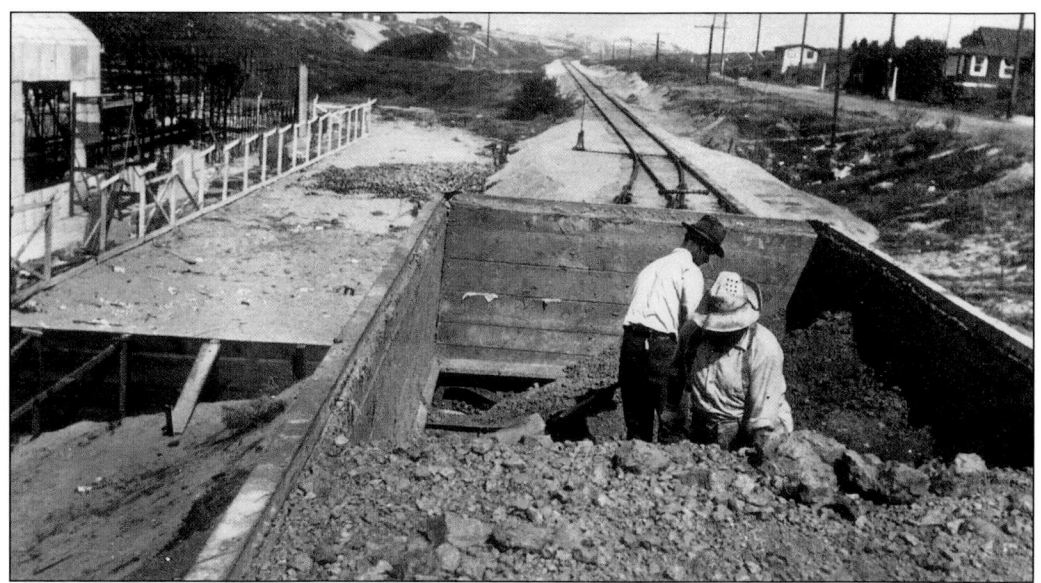

Pictured above, the first carload of clay arrived at the Prouty site on October 6, 1927. Clay was used in manufacturing the Metlox-non-fading tile letters used in the making of Metlox Neon tube signs. Neon gas letters were placed on a tile letter, making it possible to see the sign both day and night. The Metlox Corporation was a subsidiary of the Proutyline Products Company.

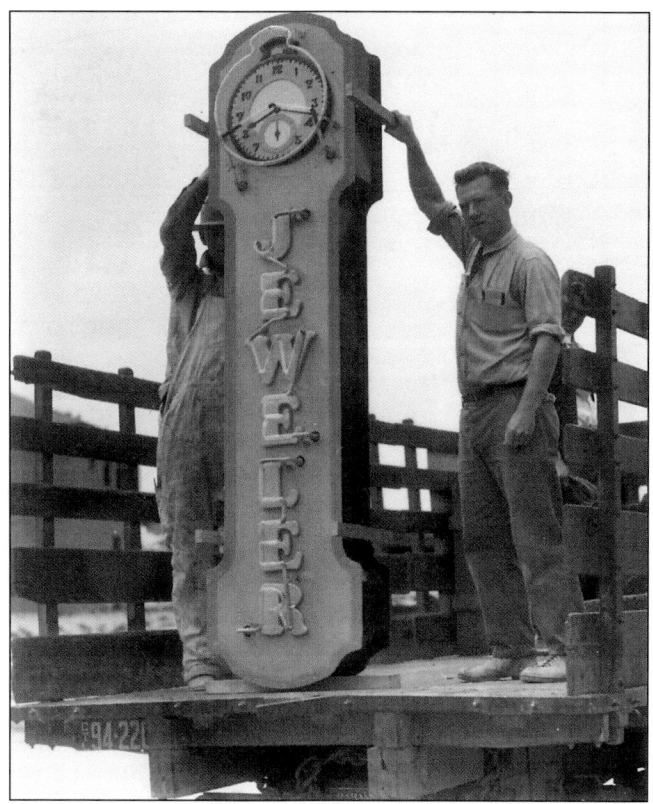

Pictured to the left, C.W. Lockry, superintendent of production, holds a Metlox neon and tile sign for a jewelry store. The new technology of neon light combined with glazed tile work brought an unusual beauty and distinctive appearance.

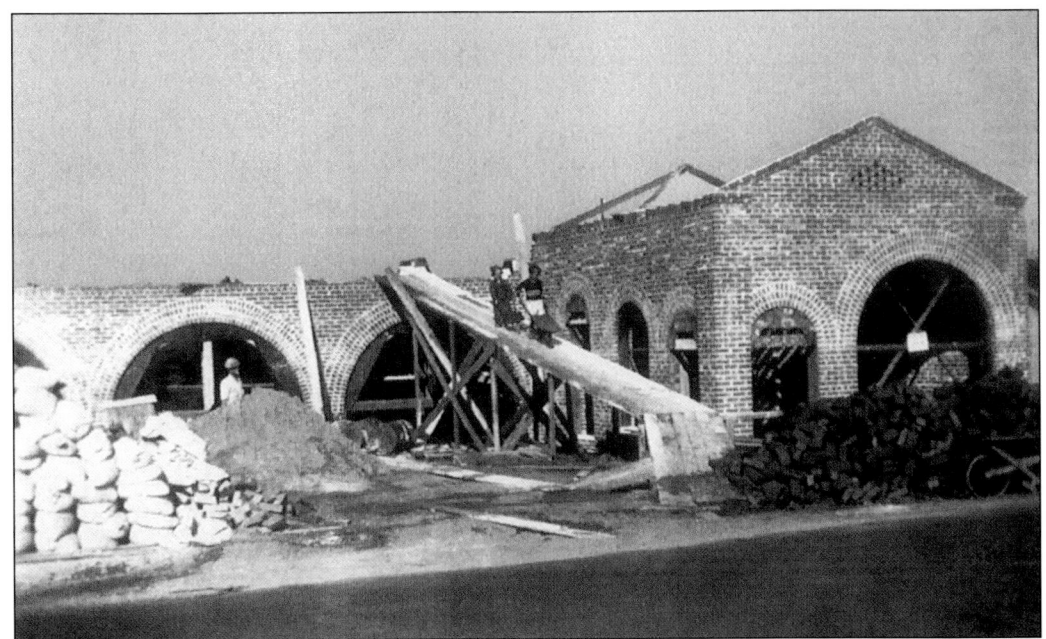

In 1929, realizing the influence car transportation would have on the area, Howard Zahn saw the need for quick and easy access to commercial buildings for shoppers. He envisioned "drive-in" storefronts, the forerunner of the strip mall. Zahn, truly ahead of his time, designed, built, and owned the first building of this type in Manhattan Beach.

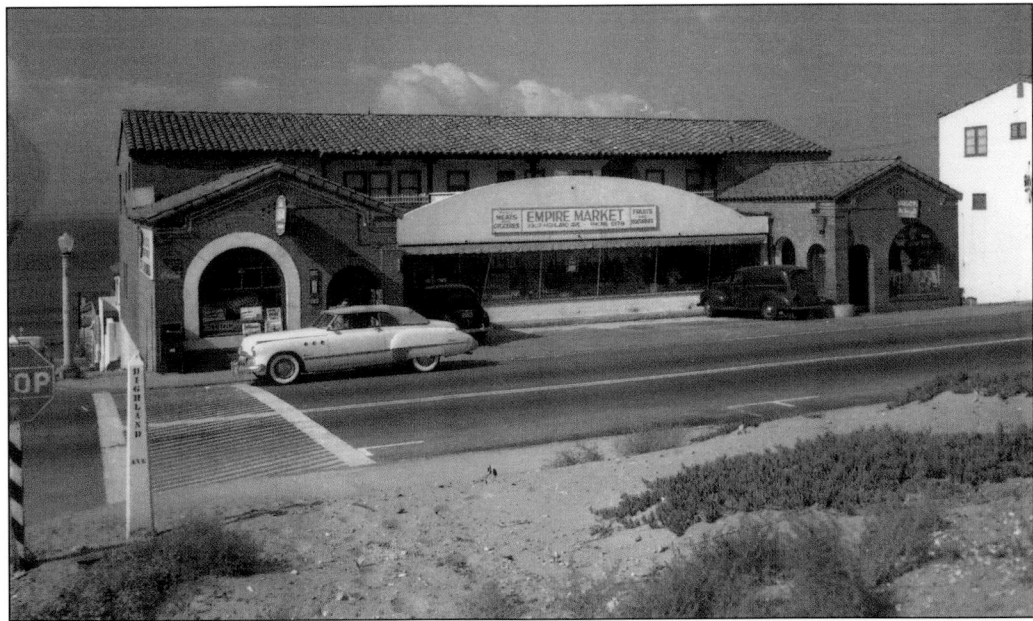

The finished product featured a tile roof, concrete foundation, and 13-inch thick brick walls, which were later covered with stucco. Located on the corner of 33rd Street and Highland Avenue, the market opened in early 1930. Originally known as the "Camp and Clark Drive-in Market," it contained a grocery store, barbershop, and radio store. The building can still be seen today. (Photo c.1940s)

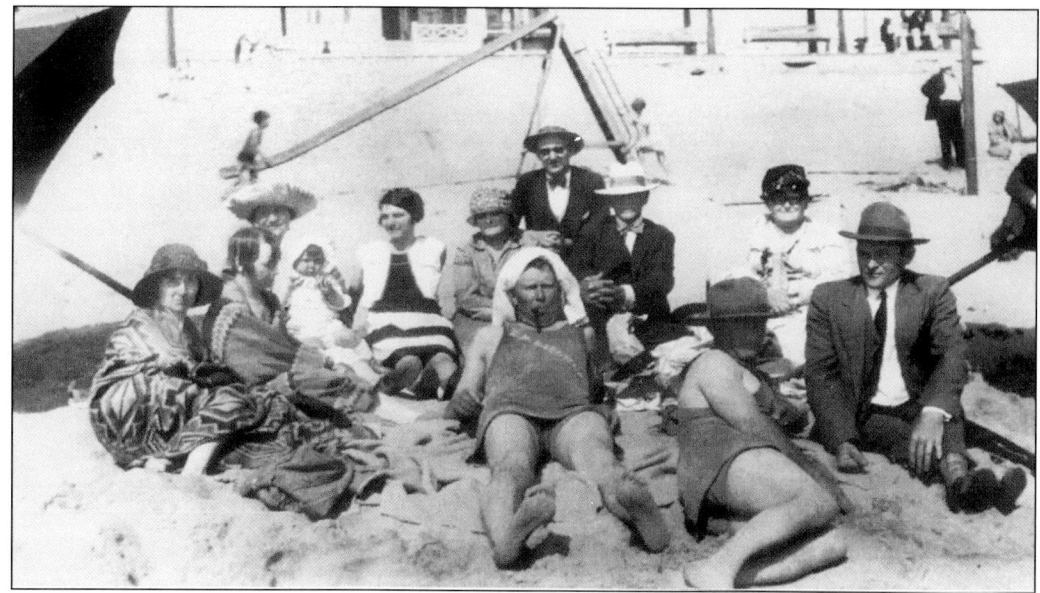

During the summer, the population doubled as the people poured onto the beach. At the beginning of the decade, Manhattan was a resort town, but by the end of the Jazz Age, many summer visitors had become permanent residents. Here a family, some in their Sunday best, enjoys the beach at the foot of Marine Avenue.

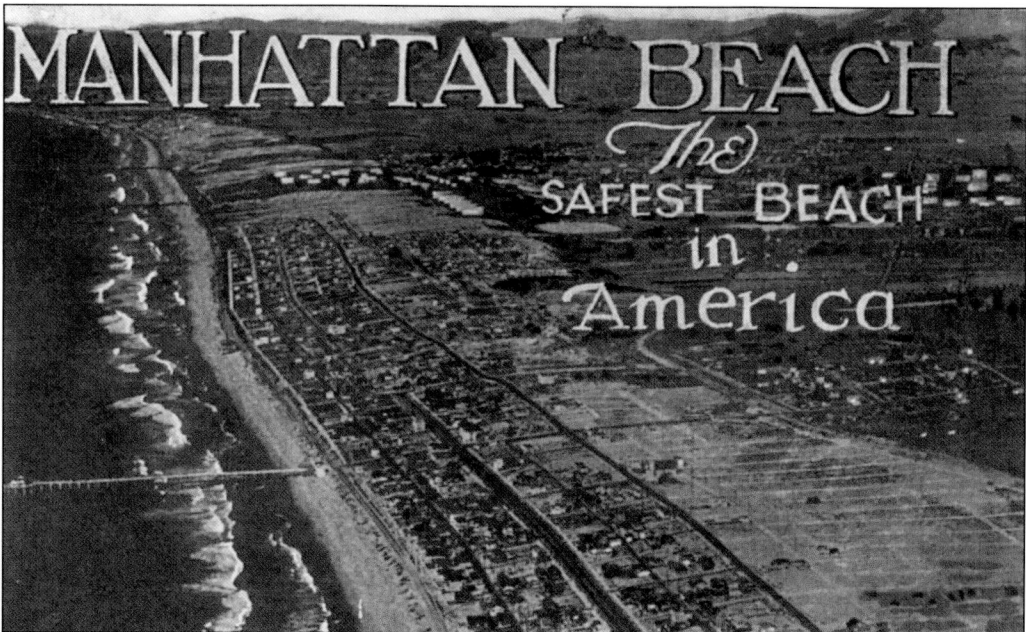

The beach continued to be the center of attention. In order to promote the town, a Chamber of Commerce was formed in 1920; however, the community did not embrace it. By 1926, an alternative group to the chamber had been formed, determined to put Manhattan Beach on the map as one of the outstanding cities in the Santa Monica Bay. More then 50 residents were members of the organization called the Manhattan Beach Booster. In 1927, the group put out a promotional pamphlet entitled "Manhattan Beach the Safest Beach in America."

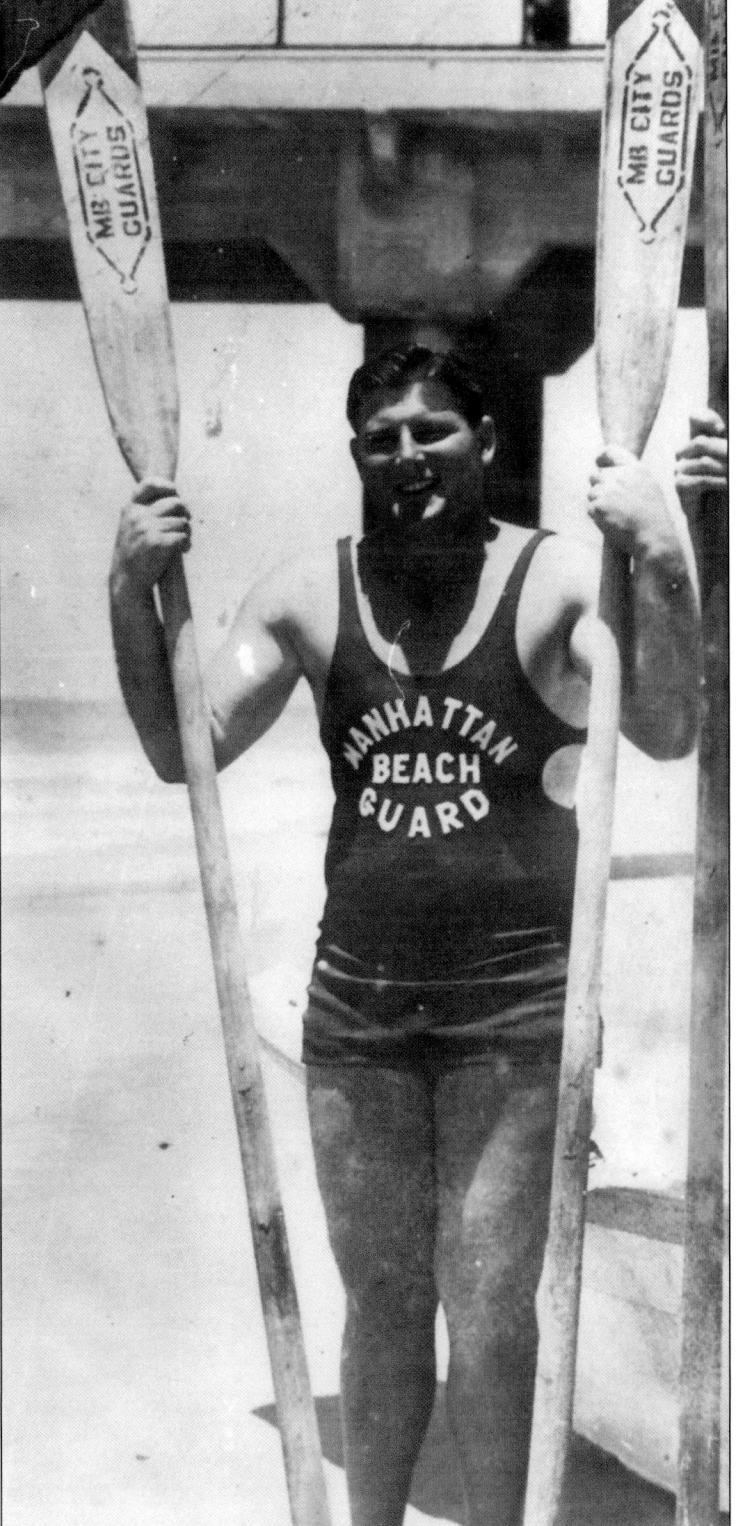

In 1927, being billed as the safest beach in America was a bit overstated. Coastal riptides could be dangerous and even deadly. Because of this, the city started a lifeguard program in the late 1920s. In the beginning, lifeguards were limited as to the amount of service they could render for they had to borrow equipment from Redondo Beach to the south. However, by 1935 the city had purchased a dory for rescues and a resuscitator. Here, lifeguard Jack Thompson displays two dory paddles.

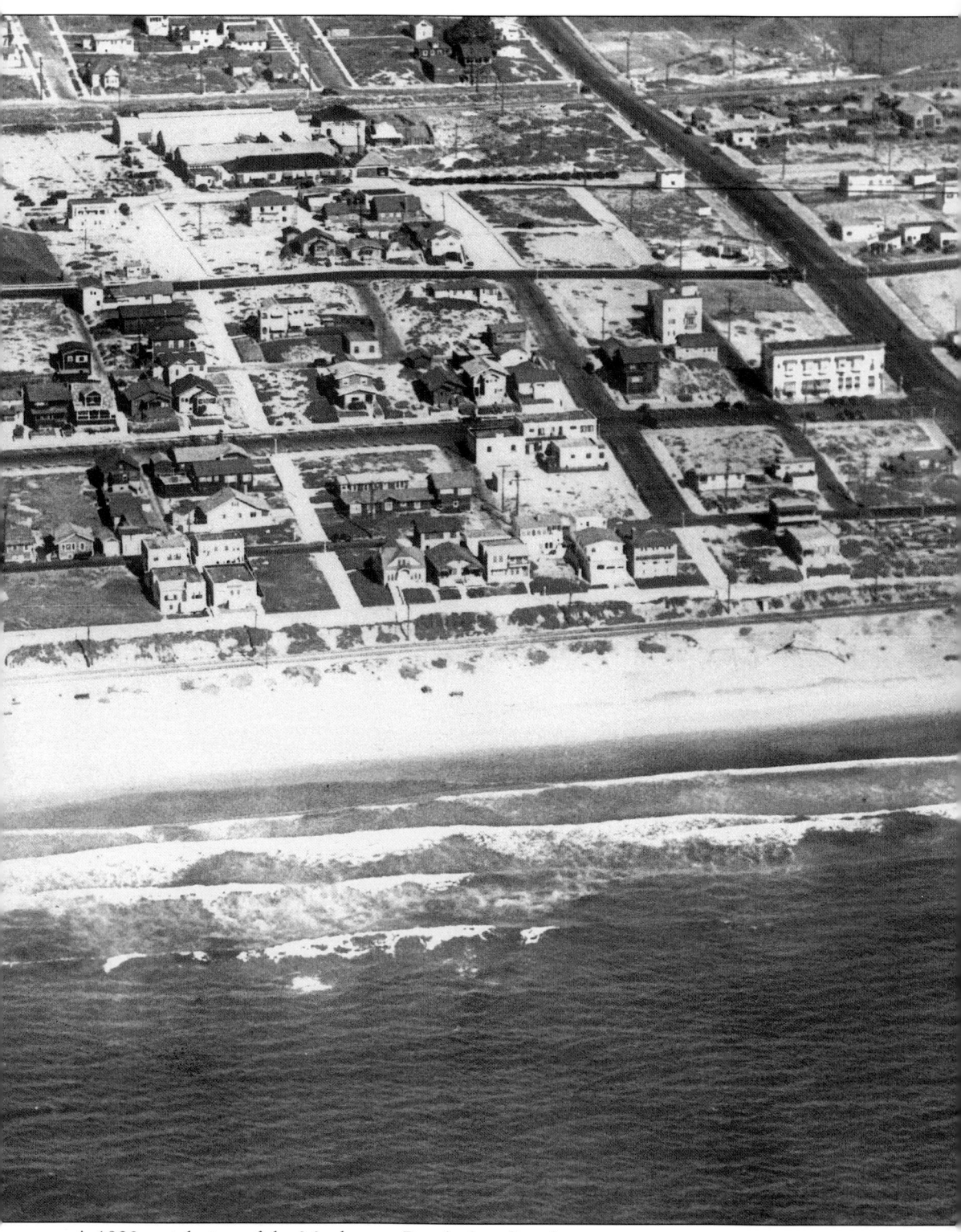
A 1929 aerial view of the Manhattan Beach shoreline featuring its signature sports pier.

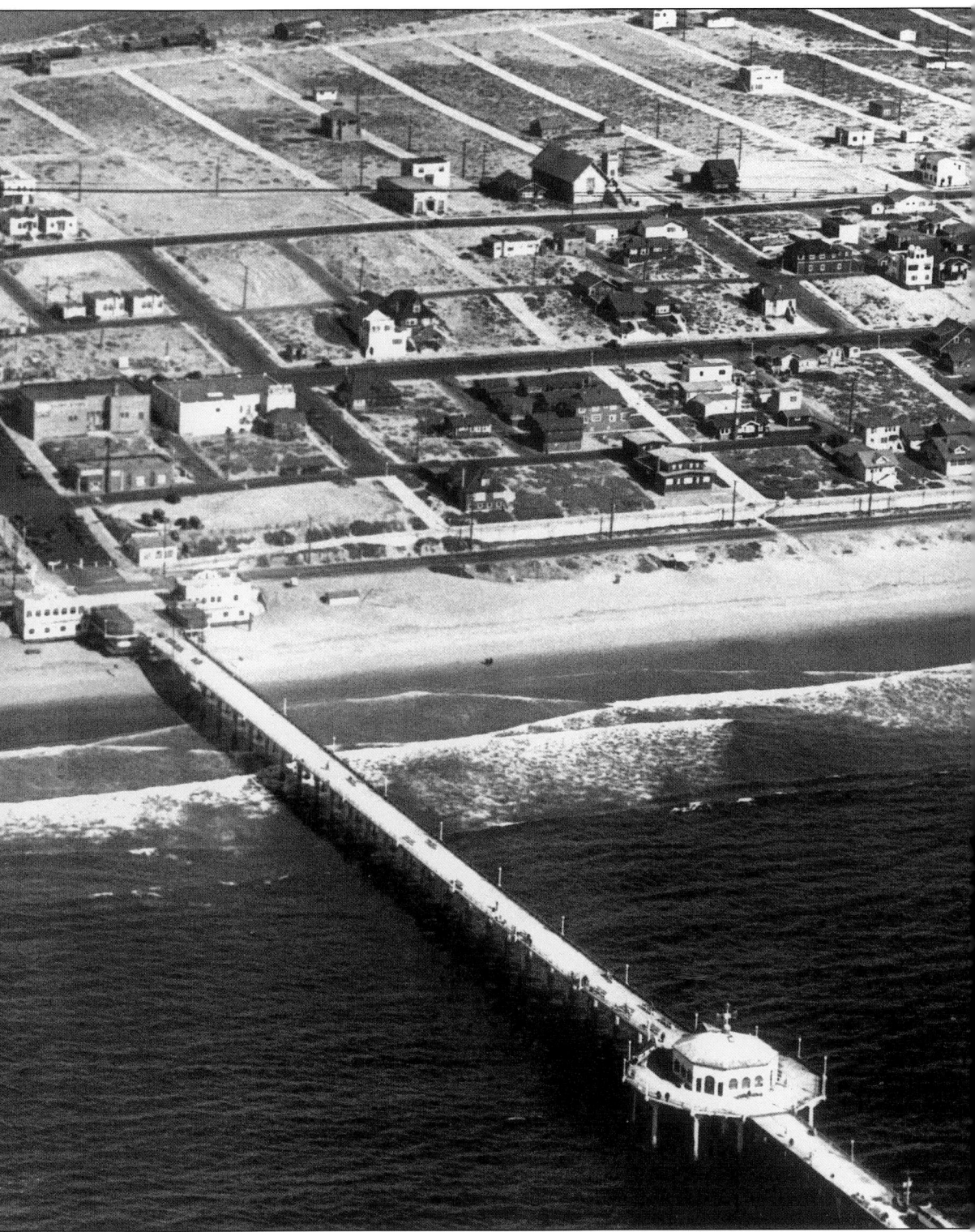

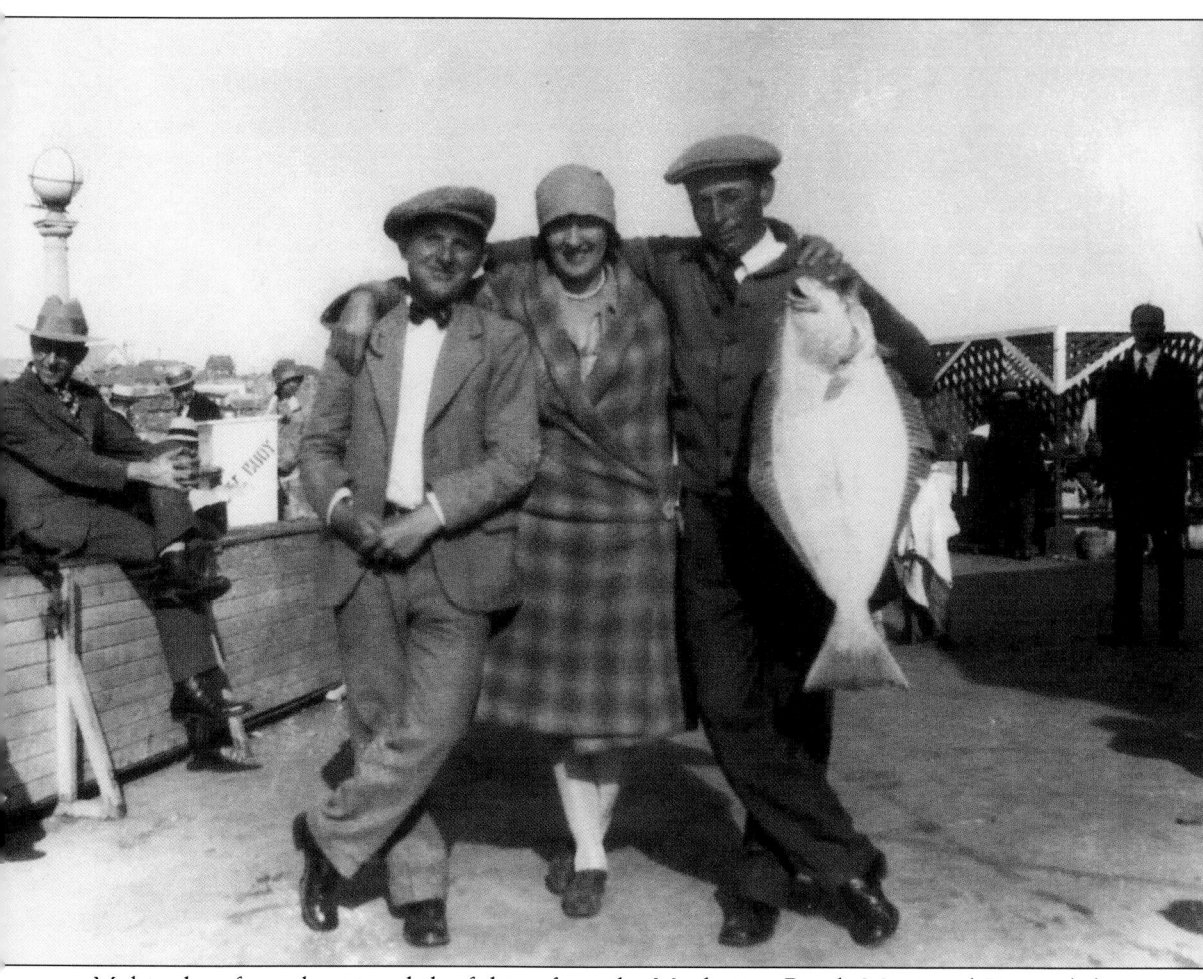
Multitudes of people enjoyed the fishing from the Manhattan Beach Municipal Pier and the bounty from the Pacific shoreline continued to lure them throughout the 1930s.

Four
RAPID GROWTH

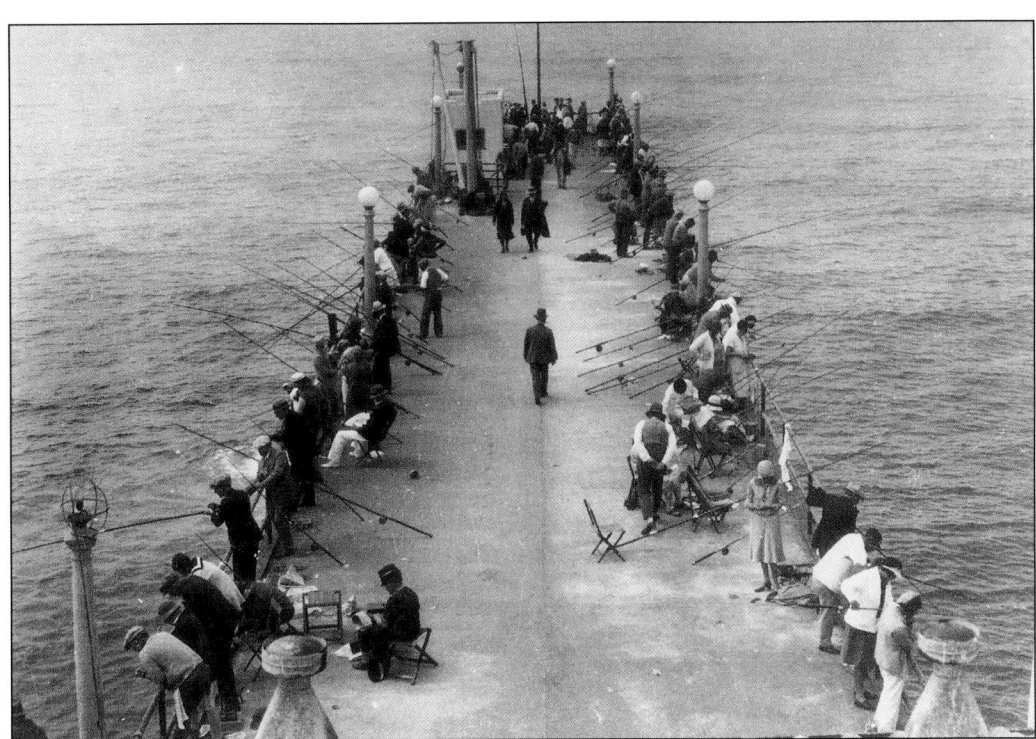

In the 1930s, sun, sand, and sky were the things that drew celebrities and ordinary folks alike to Manhattan Beach. During the depression decade, beach lovers could claim—in the words of a popular song—that the best things in life are free. Fishing and swimming were obvious favorites. To make fishing even better, the pier was extended in 1928 at virtually no cost to the city. Captain Larsen of Redondo Beach oversaw the construction of the extension and ran a shore boat between the pier and his fishing barge, the "Georgina," which was anchored off shore. Hundreds of visitors used the municipal pier extension, fishing year round. Several people in town feared the pier would change the family nature of the city by bringing in too many outsiders.

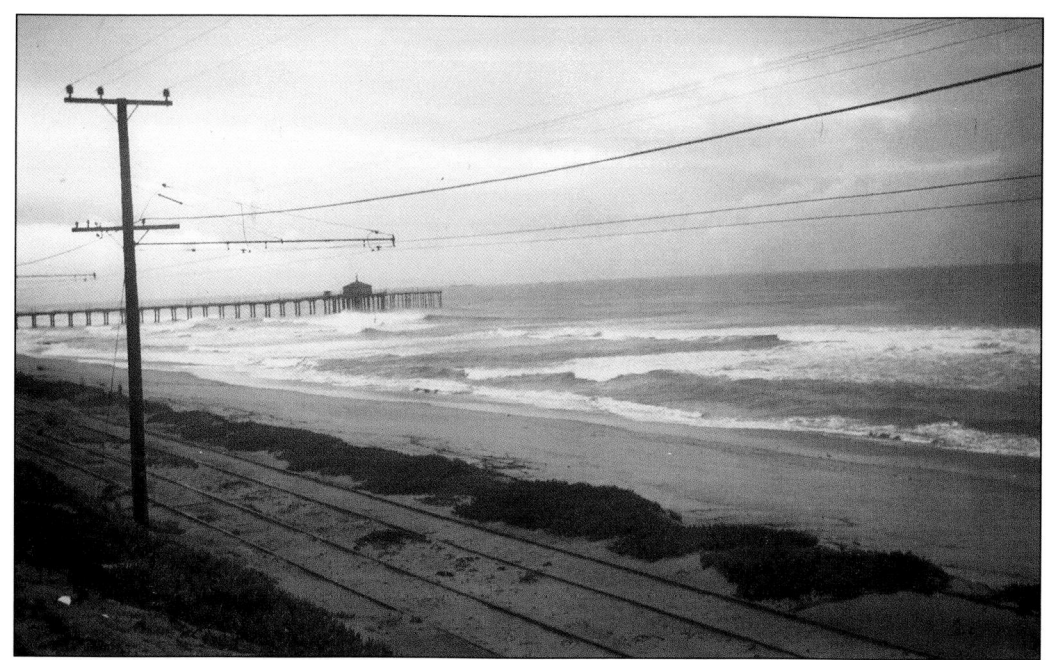

Looking from the Strand, one can observe the Red Car trolley tracks, the shallow beach, the pier, and extension. The extension was destroyed in a wild winter storm in 1940/41.

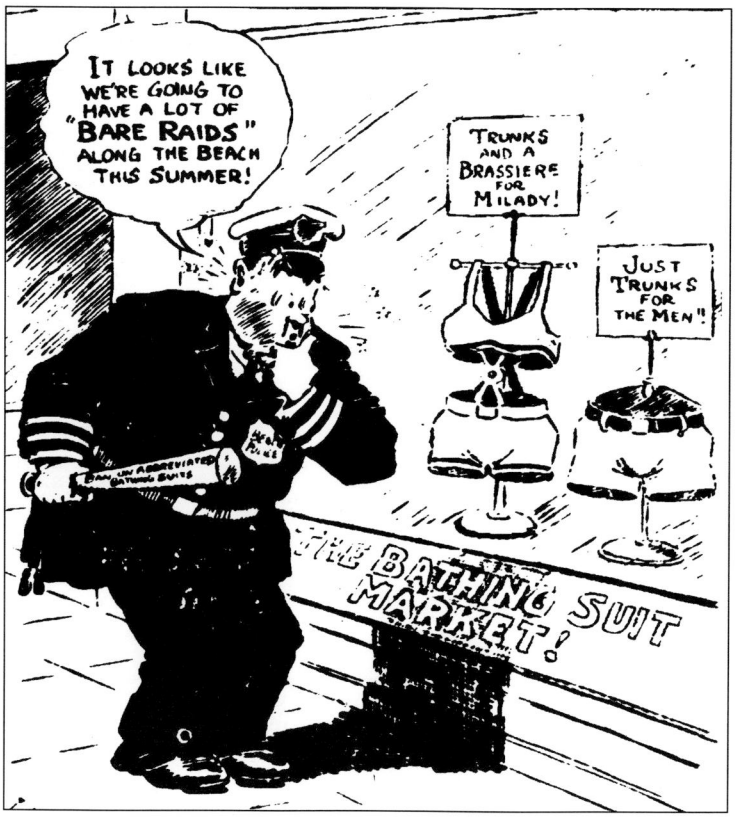

In the middle of March 1930, 25,000 people came to celebrate the beginning of beach season in droves. The same flapper era that had brought in short skirts also brought a trend to more comfortable sports clothes and briefer bathing suits. In 1933, Manhattan Beach officials modified the dress ordinance. Men were now allowed to sport bathing trunks on the beach and women could wear two-piece bathing suits, but everyone had to cover up if they wanted to walk on the pier or the Strand.

The Ward children enjoying a sunny day at the beach in front of their grandmother's home at 12th and the Strand. Left to right: William, Shirley, and John Ward.

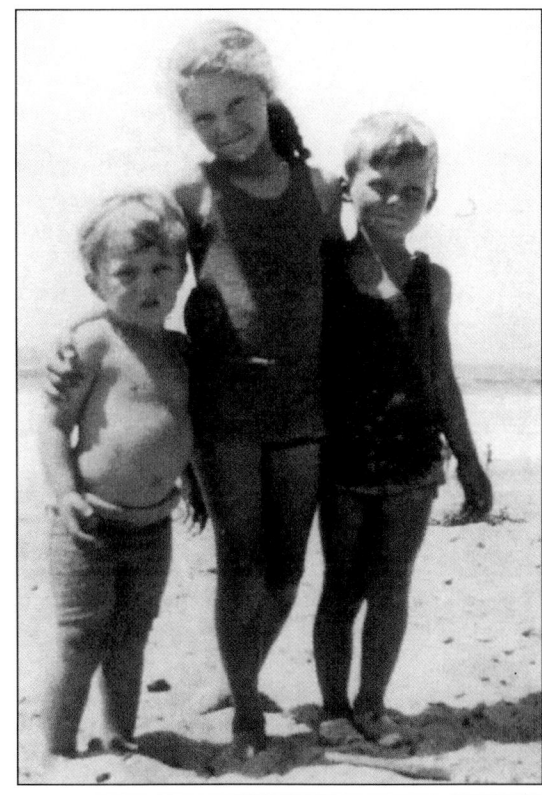

"Fisherman" came in all ages! Here a young lady proudly displays her catch of the day from the Manhattan Beach Municipal pier.

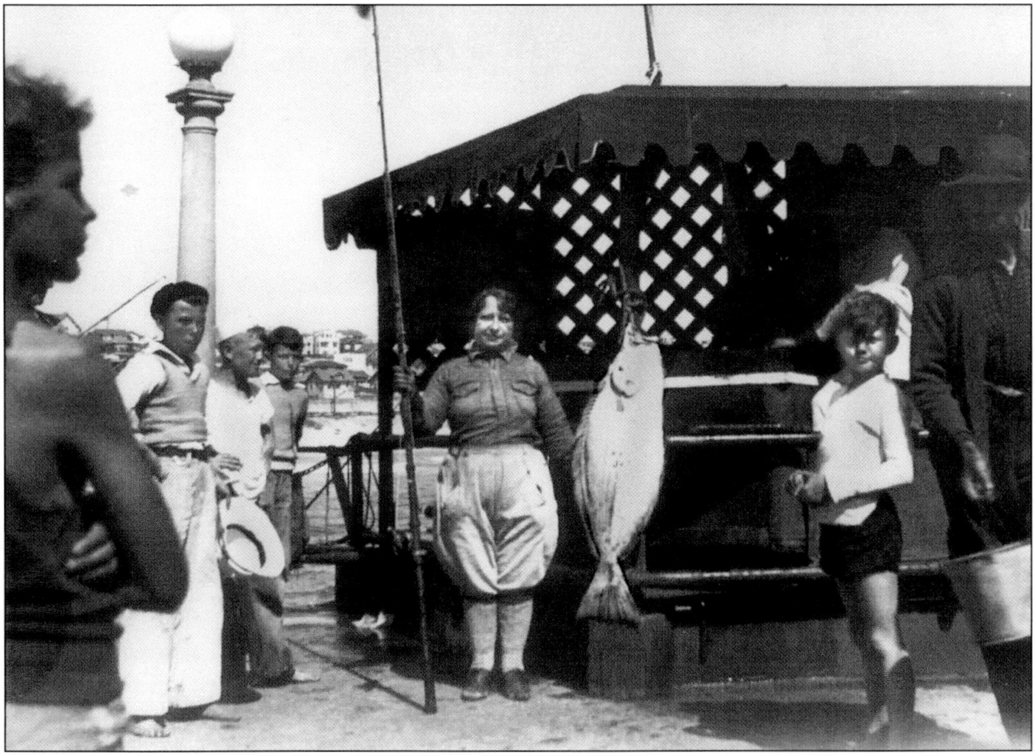

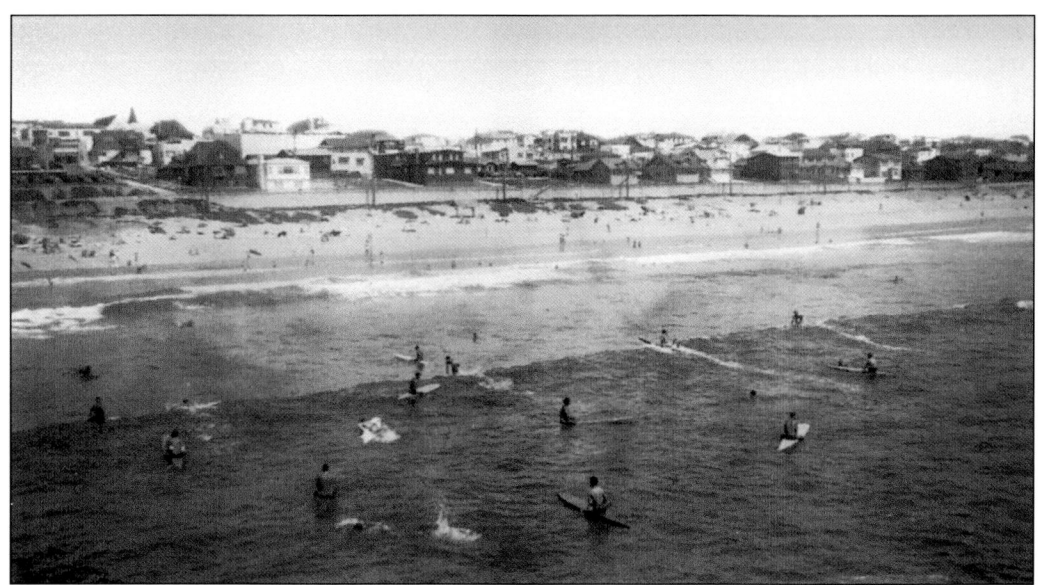

Surfing was also a big sport for the water-loving public. A surfing club had been formed with its meetings held at the pier.

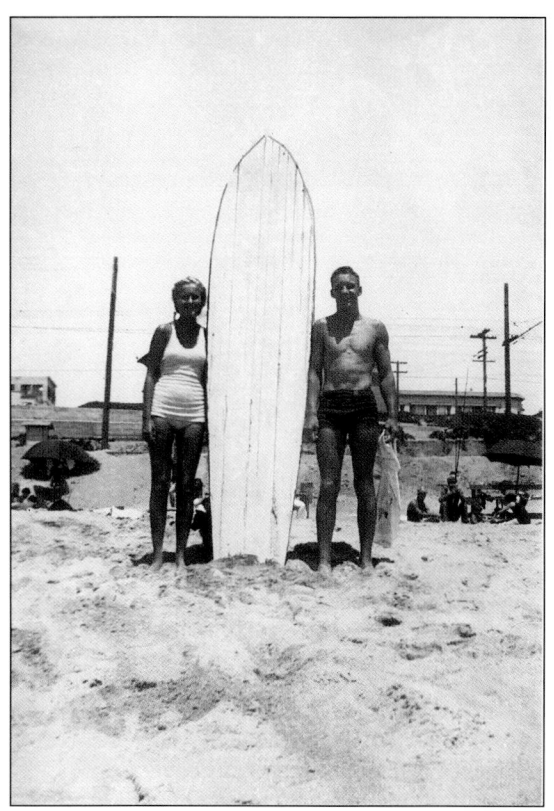

John Dale with his friend, Lynn Carver, who later became known as Virginia Sapson, movie starlet. In 1930, Dale built one of the first surfboards out of 2 by 4 inch laminated soft pine. Often the pine lumber was acquired by cutting down the city's pine posted stop signs. Dale was also a member of the "Water Rats," a group of young men whose turf was the beach.

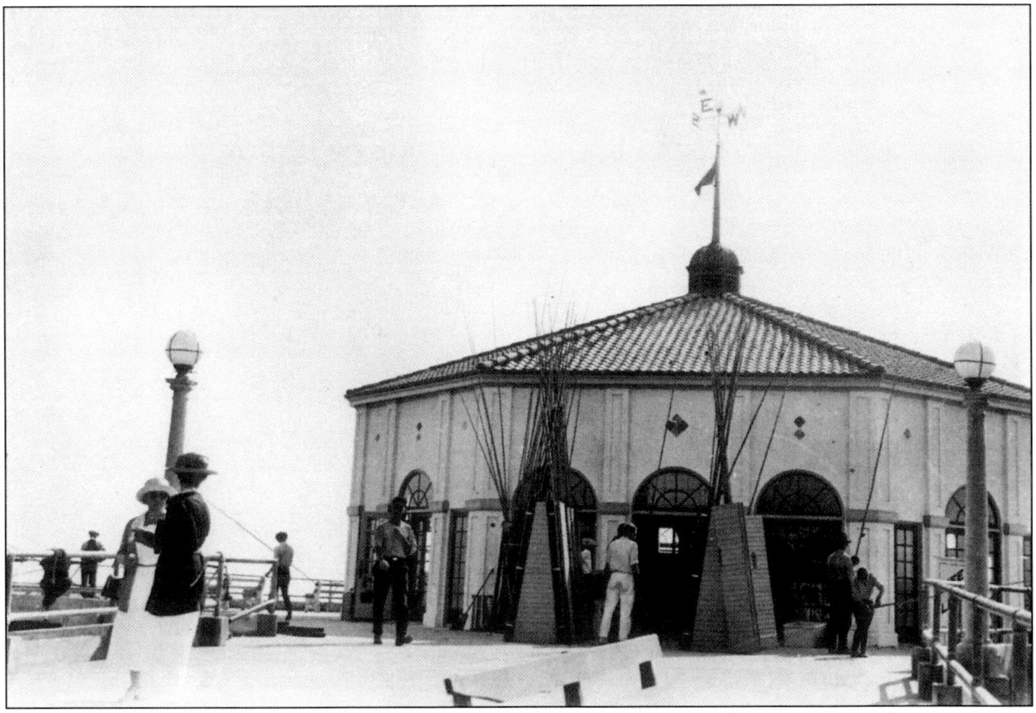

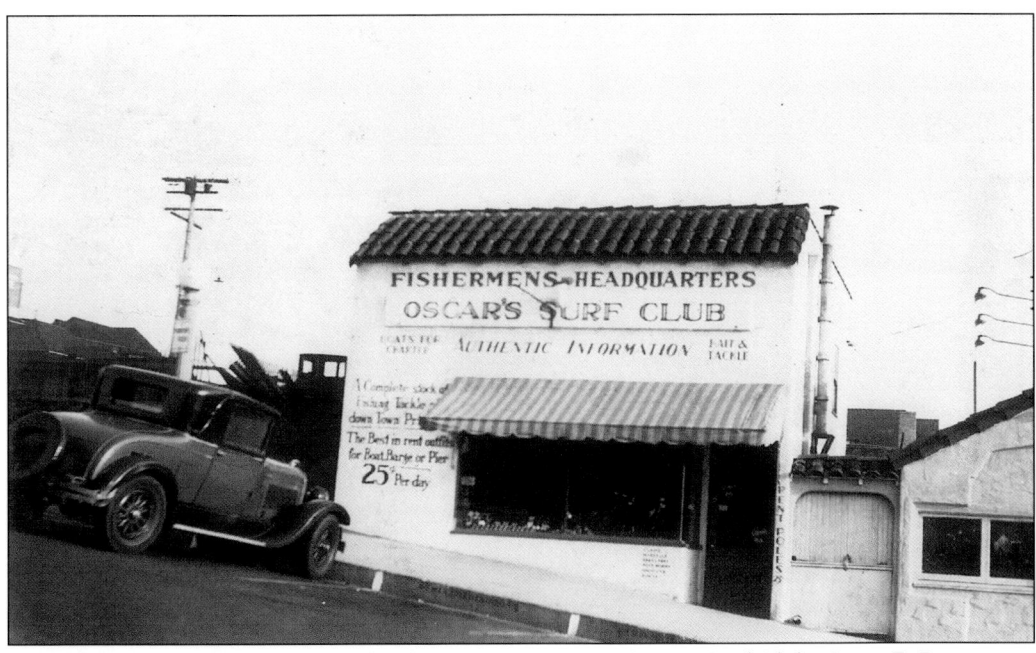

The "roundhouse," or pavilion, at the end of the pier was a busy place year round.

One of the very active stores in the downtown area was Oscar's Surf Club. Oscar E. Bessonette opened this business on Center Street after he lost his lease for operating the tackle and bait concession at the end of the pier.

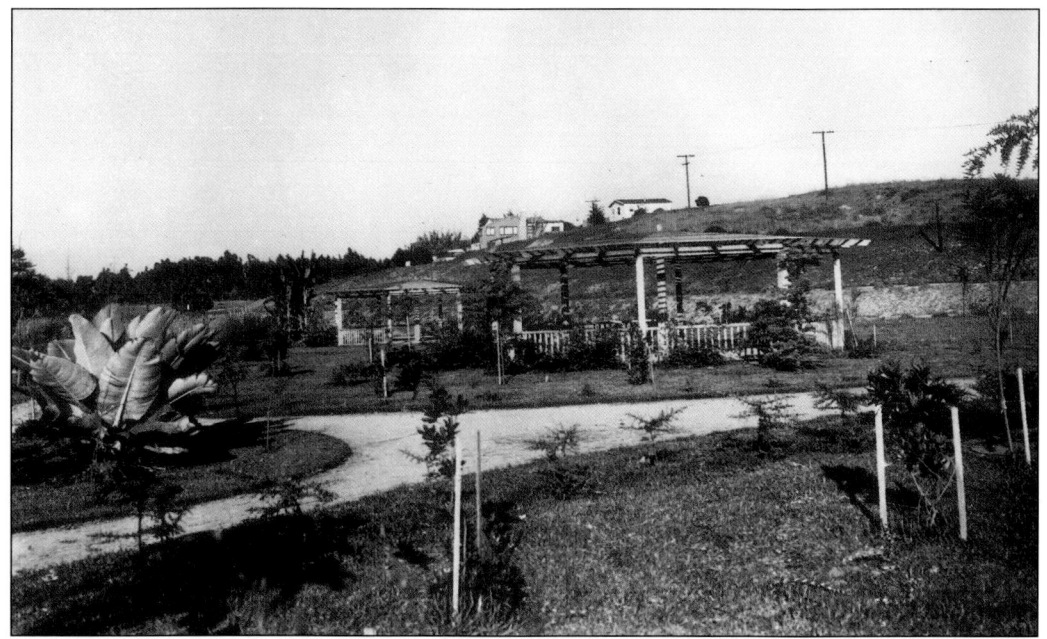

Not only was the pier and beach a popular place, but city parks were being developed. The county built Live Oak Park, once the site of a trash disposal dump, with federal relief funds on 5 acres of land donated to the city by George Peck. In the summer of 1932, more than 1,200 cubic feet of dirt were moved by 26 unemployed men making hundreds of trips back and forth along plank runways to fill in the ravine. The park was named after the 50 live oak trees that were planted on December 9, 1932.

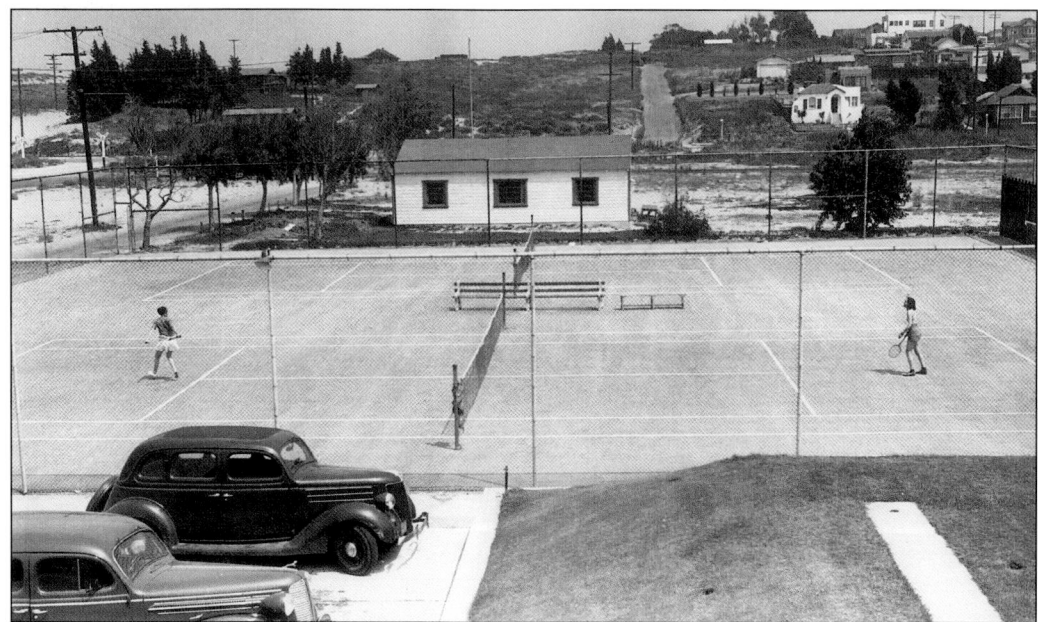

Tennis courts were also built by the Works Project Administration (WPA) in 1933 at the rear of the City Hall. The original tennis courts were erected after the Lions Club had leveled the sand in 1927.

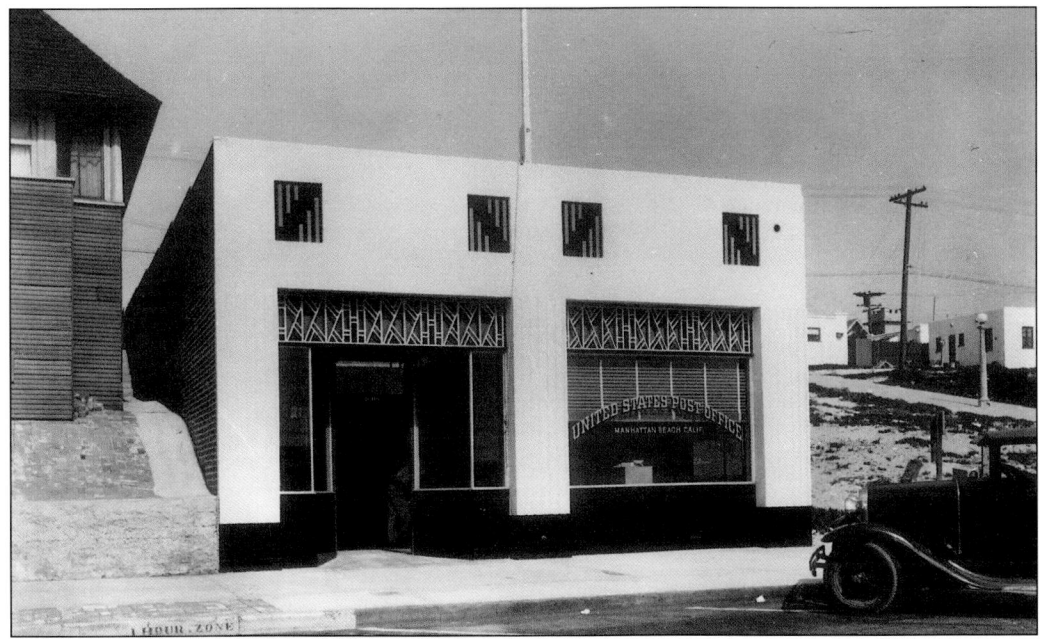

In 1933, the town showed its growth when the first freestanding U.S. Post Office was built. With an art deco design, the building was engineered and built by E.L. Nollan of Los Angeles. The 26 by 57-foot structure located at 116 Manhattan Avenue was leased for 10 years to the U.S. Government.

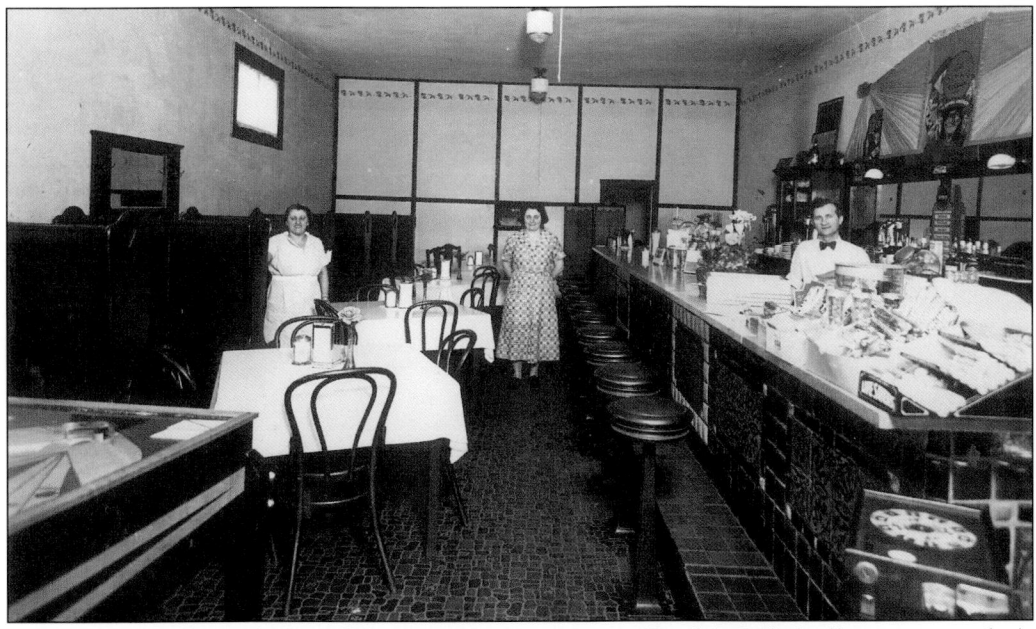

One of the popular and successful restaurants in town was Ercole's Cafe (still operating today), located at 1101 Manhattan Avenue. Joe Ercole was a native of Asti Piedmont, Italy, coming to this country as a young man. He came to Manhattan Beach in 1916 where he opened a small grocery store, which he soon expanded into two stores. In 1922 he took over a small soda fountain at the present location, turning it into a full restaurant and cocktail lounge.

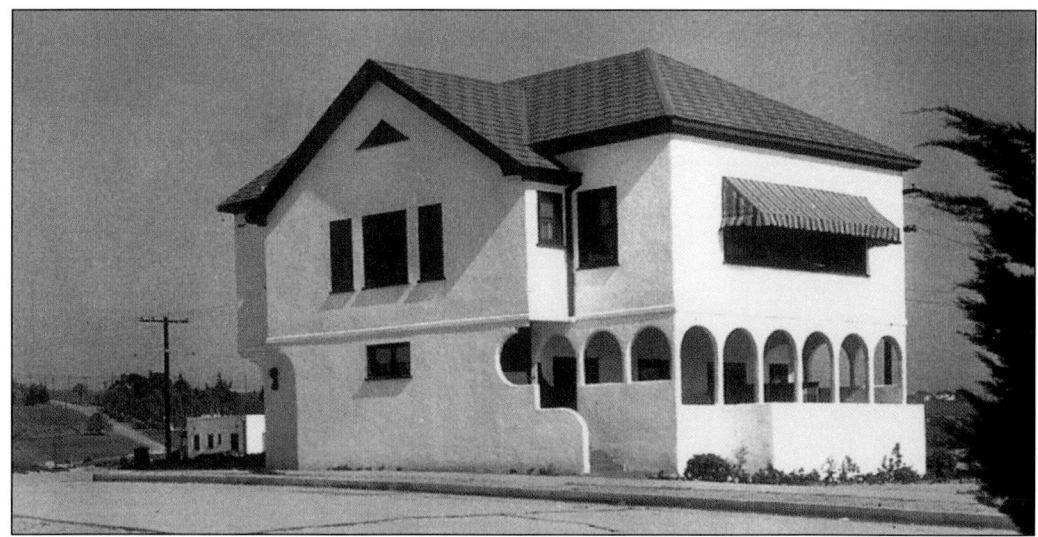

The landscape was rapidly changing with the construction of new and bigger homes. An example of the trend was this home built for Irma C. Joslyn in 1933, designed by architect T.P. Mitchell and built by Frank Koontz. In 1944, Irving Sckol altered and enlarged the floor space by enclosing all the arched openings with windows

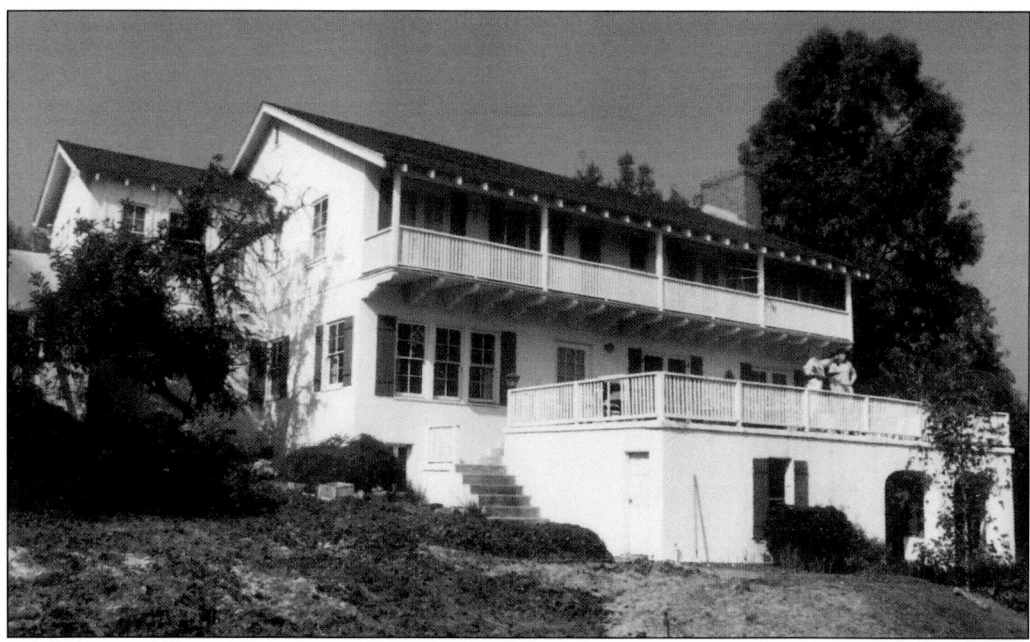

The community's low profile and family orientation did not escape celebrity notoriety. Mr. and Mrs. Gouverneur Morris owned this Monterey revival style home built east of Sepulveda Blvd. and south of Second Street. As a young boy, James Kirkwood Jr. lived here with his mother Lila Lee, a well-known movie actress of the era, as houseguests. A tragic event took place during this period, when the body of a Reid Russell was found in a swing on the estate. In later years, James Kirkwood would write a book entitled *There Must Be A Pony* portraying the events which led up to the alleged murder and developments of the case. Opinions as to the cause of death varied and the case was never solved.

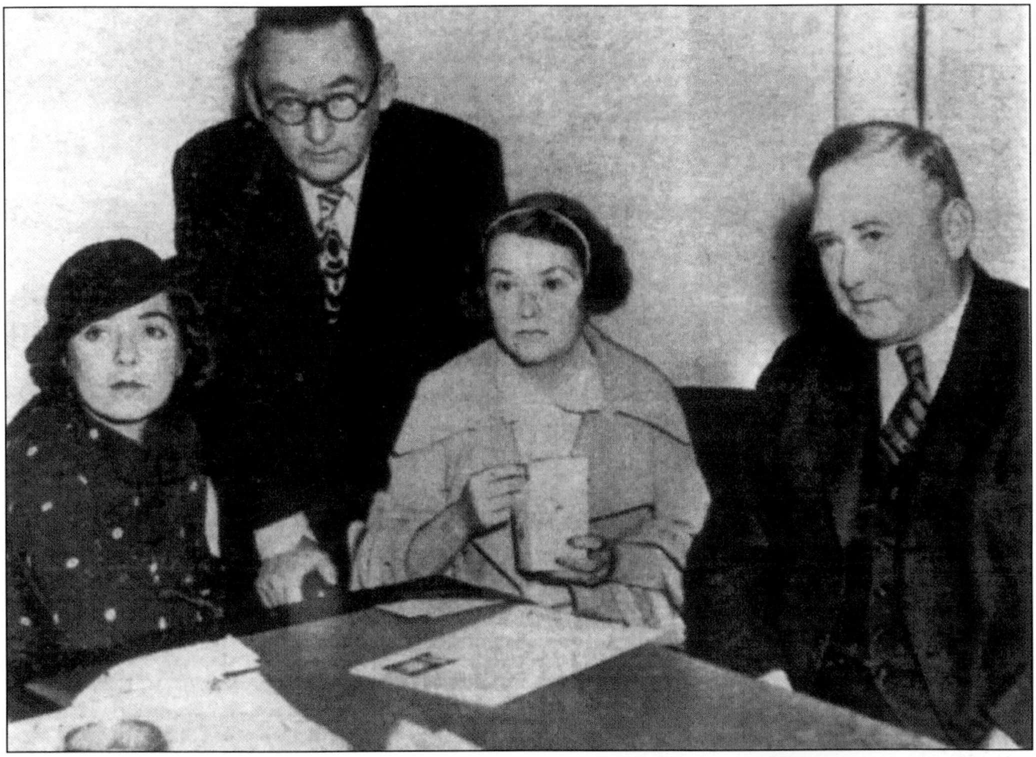

In 1936, details leading up to Reid Russell's mysterious death were told to the chief investigator, Captain Clyde Plummer. It was Plummer's belief the death was a love slaying. However, others felt that Russell met his death because he knew too much about an international smuggling ring. Left to right: Lila Lee, Mr. and Mrs. Gouverneur Morris, and Captain Plummer.

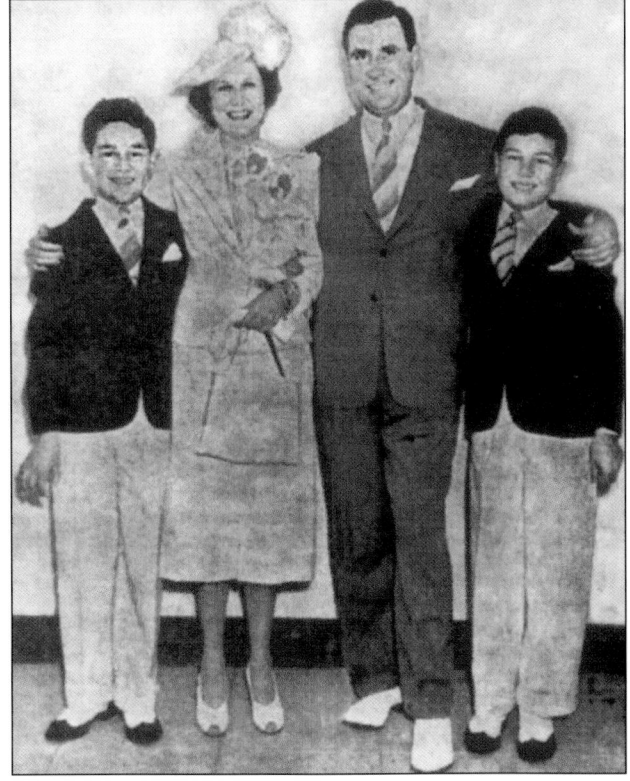

In 1938, another celebrity made the local newspaper. Lita Gray Chaplin, former wife of Charlie Chaplin, married Arthur F. Day Jr. at American Martyrs Catholic Church in Manhattan Beach, in the presence of her two sons, Charles and Sidney Chaplin. The couple had married prior to this date; however, it was found that Lita had not yet received her civil divorce papers. This required the couple to perform the religious ceremony again.

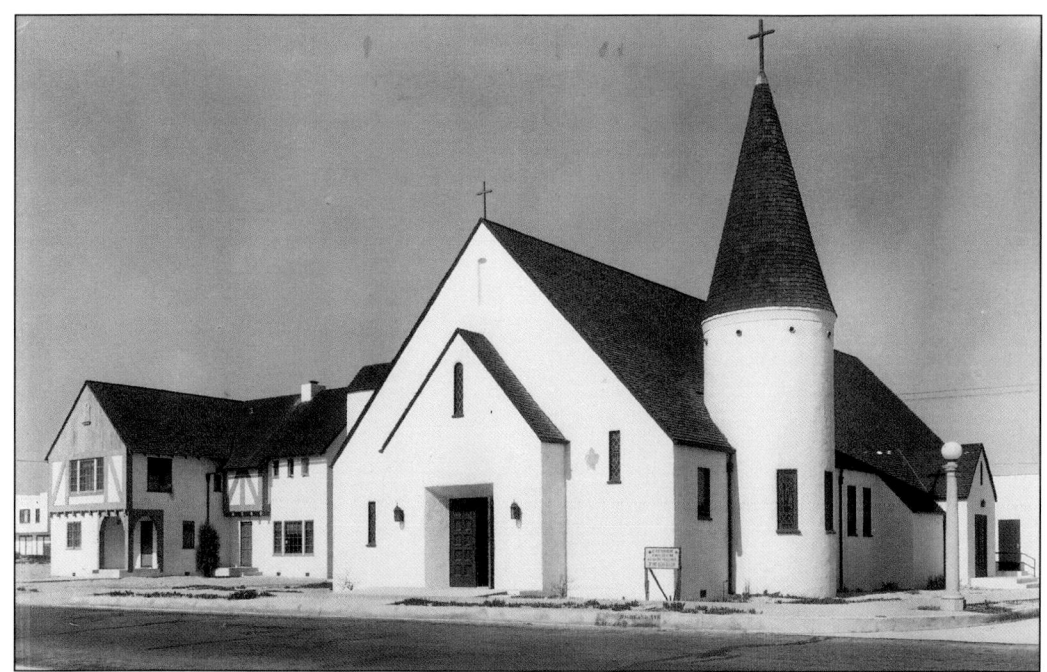

The first American Martyrs parish was constructed in 1930 and dedicated on August 30, 1931. It was modeled closely after an old French church in Normandy at a cost of $18,000. Always drafty and sandy, this structure, located on Fourth Street, was finally razed in 1957 following the erection of a new parish in a different and more prominent location.

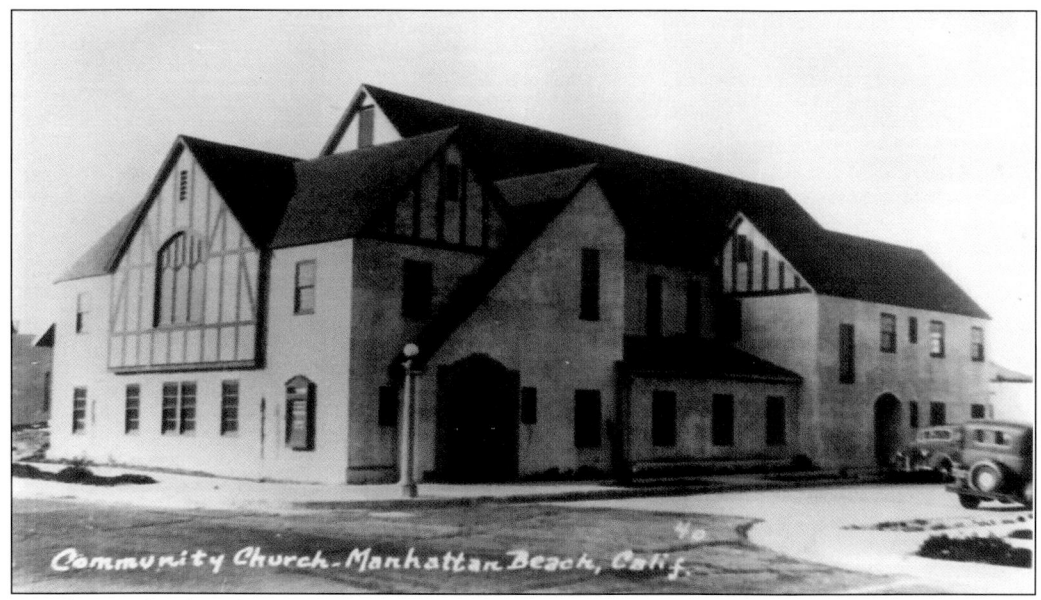

Another early church structure was a small community church. Following the earthquake of 1933, it was condemned in 1935 by the city building inspector as an unsafe structure. The cornerstone was laid for the new edifice (seen above) early in 1937 and dedicated in 1938. The impressive new church served well for many years. While still standing today at the corner of 9th and Highland Avenue, it is now a private residence and apartment complex.

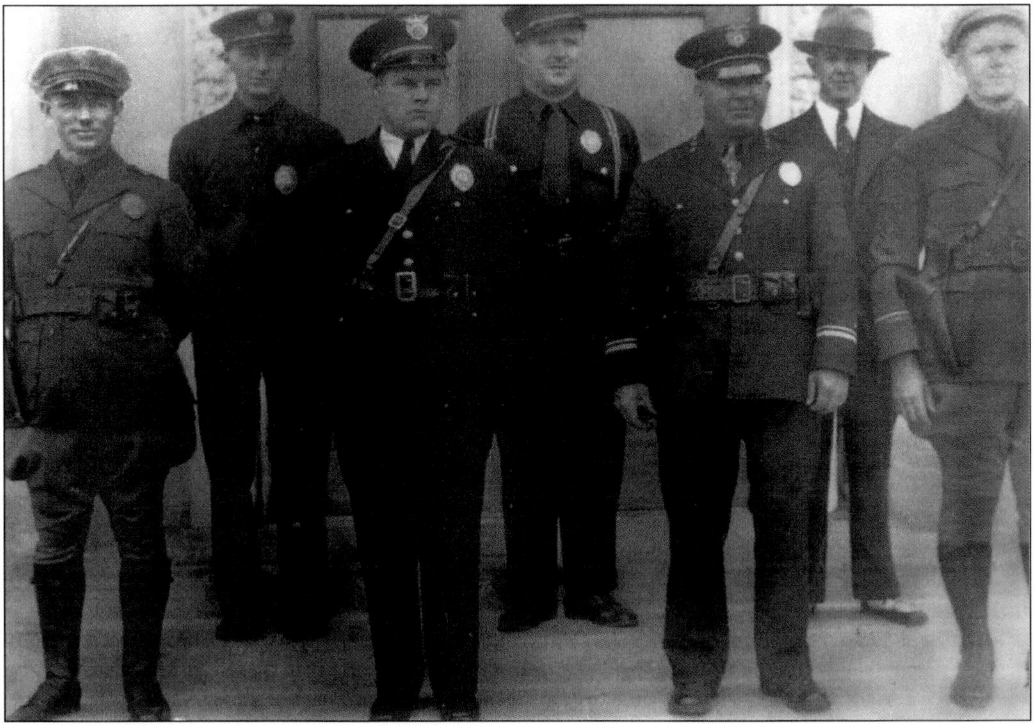

The fire and police department continued to grow with Alex Haddock as president of the Fire and Police Association. The department included, from right to left: C. Whitehead, R.H. Swian, H.G. Sights, F. Root, A. Haddock, W. Plotner, and C. Koon.

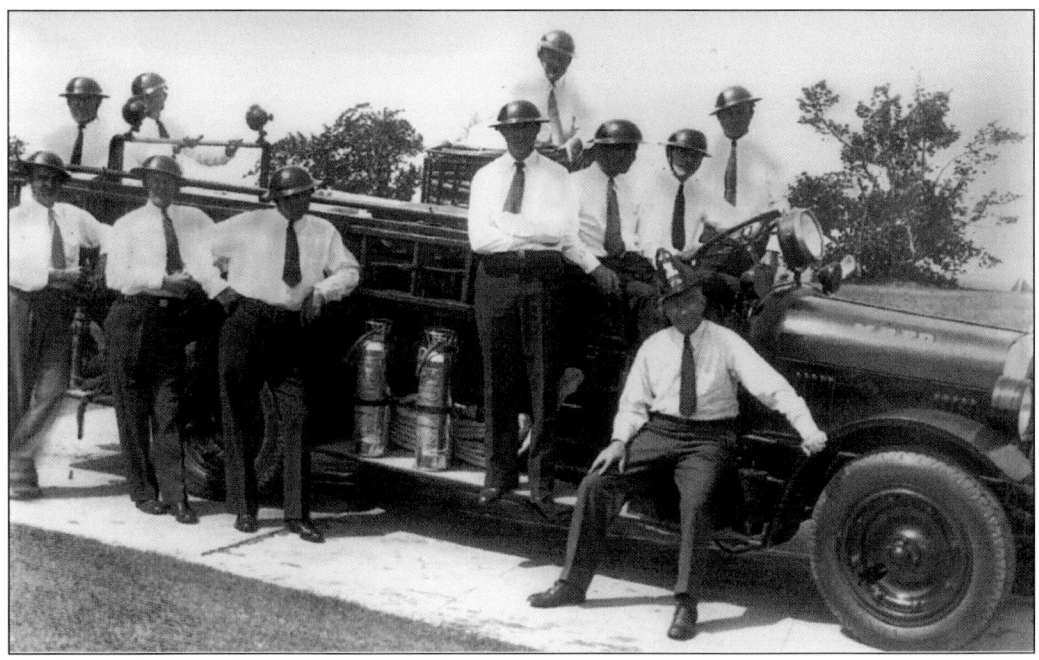

In 1936, the fire department was still a volunteer organization. This group photo was taken during a routine fire drill.

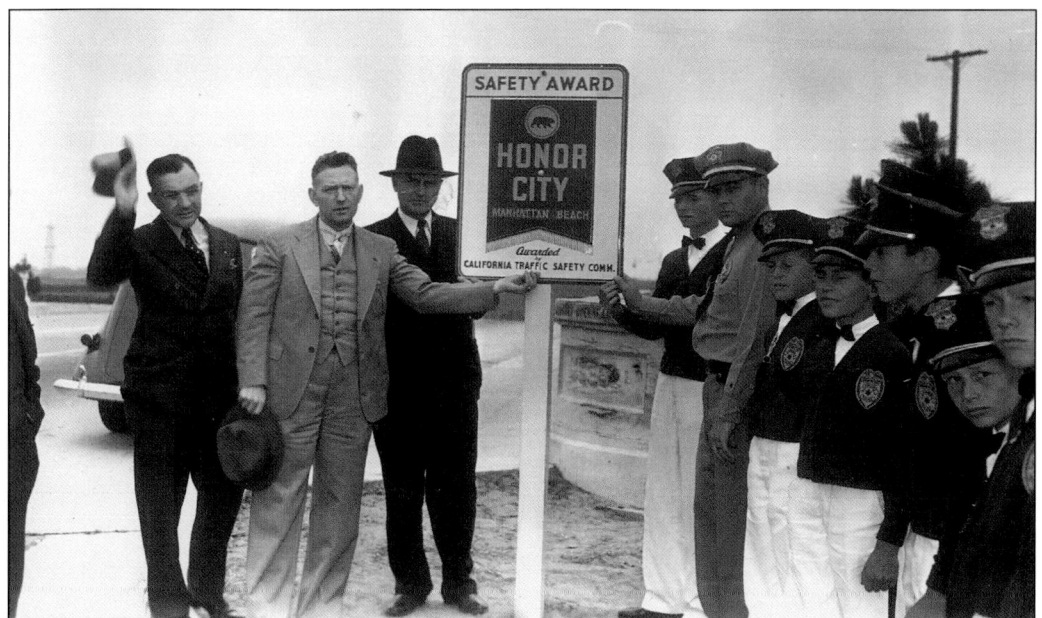

The town boasted of having only one accident in the whole year, even going so far as to accept a state safety award to prove the claim. However, a report in the "Manhattan Beach News" disputed the statistic by citing many car accidents, drunk driving, and disturbances of the peace during that same time period.

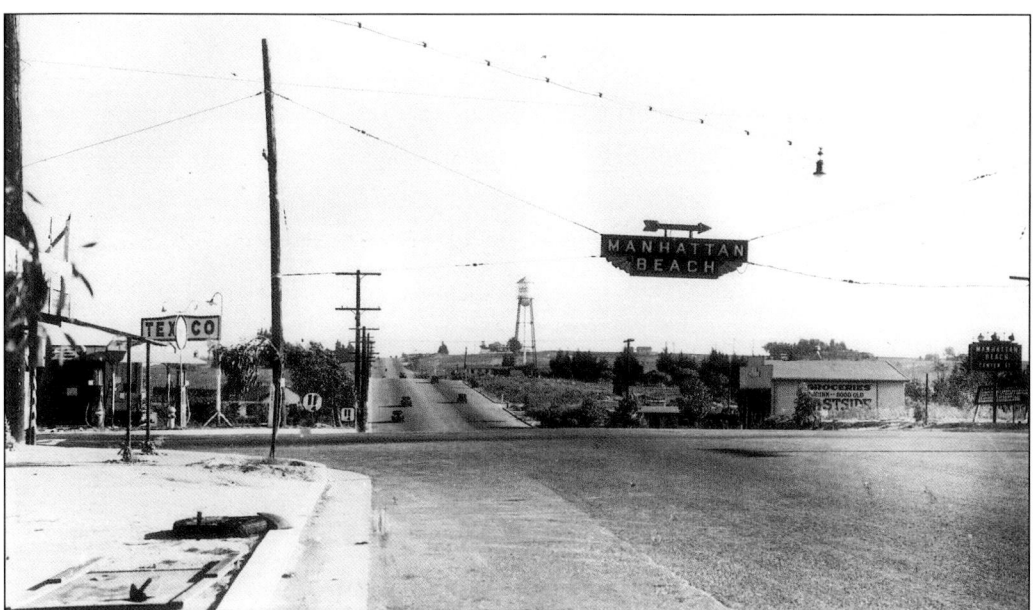

Road construction was probably least affected by the depression. The biggest project during this period was the paving of Sepulveda Boulevard, a rough, eucalyptus-lined road formerly called Camino Real. The stretch of this road from Rosecrans Avenue at the north end to our southerly boundary was officially named Sepulveda Boulevard by Ordinance 389 on October 20, 1932. At the intersection of Manhattan Beach and Sepulveda Boulevard hung an identification sign made by the community's major pottery industry, Metlox.

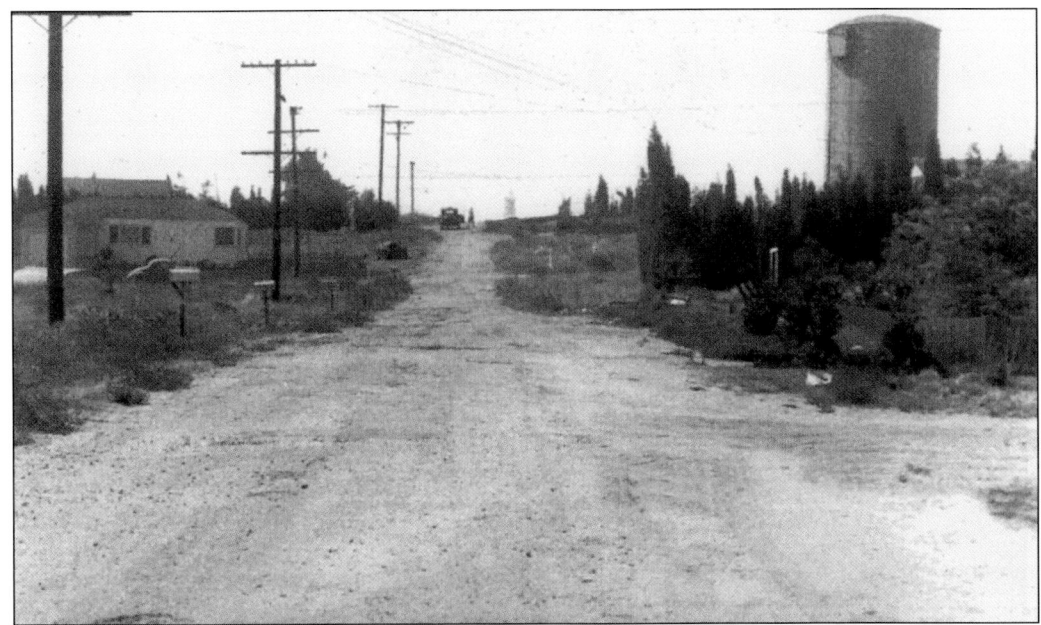

Both county highways and local streets were improved. Larsson and 5th Street had the old paving removed by hand and the street was widened. The municipal water department tower, built by the WPA, was located at Larsson and 2nd Street. The 36-foot diameter and 63-foot high tower containing 450,000 gallons of water supplied the increased city population.

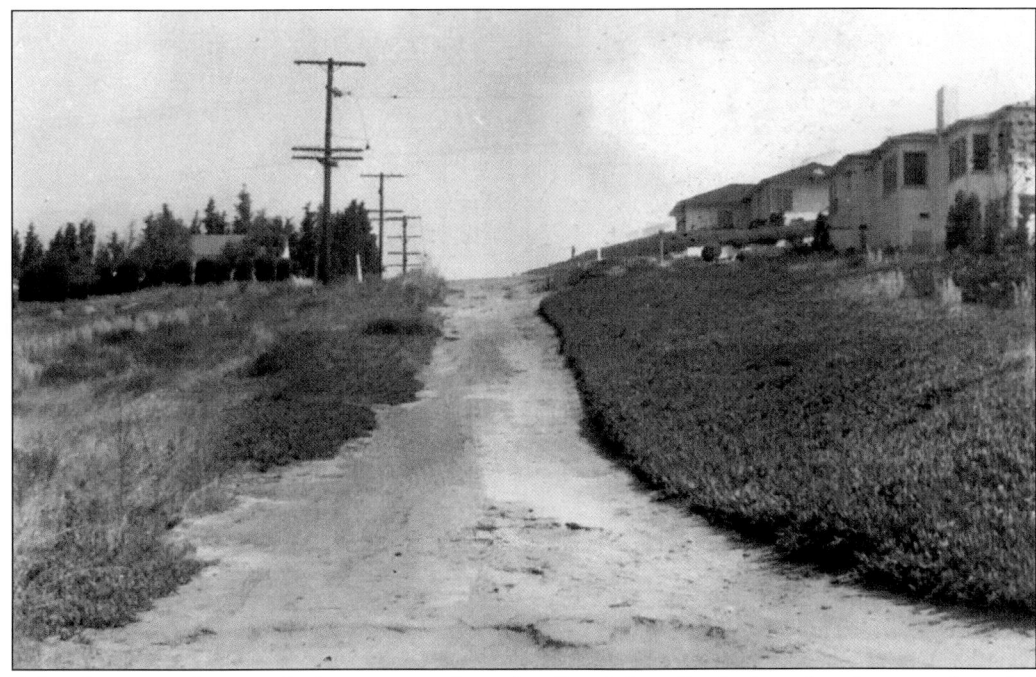

After the manual removal of sea moss or "ice plant" and the oil caked road surface was shoveled into trucks, Pacific and 8th Street were widened and paved.

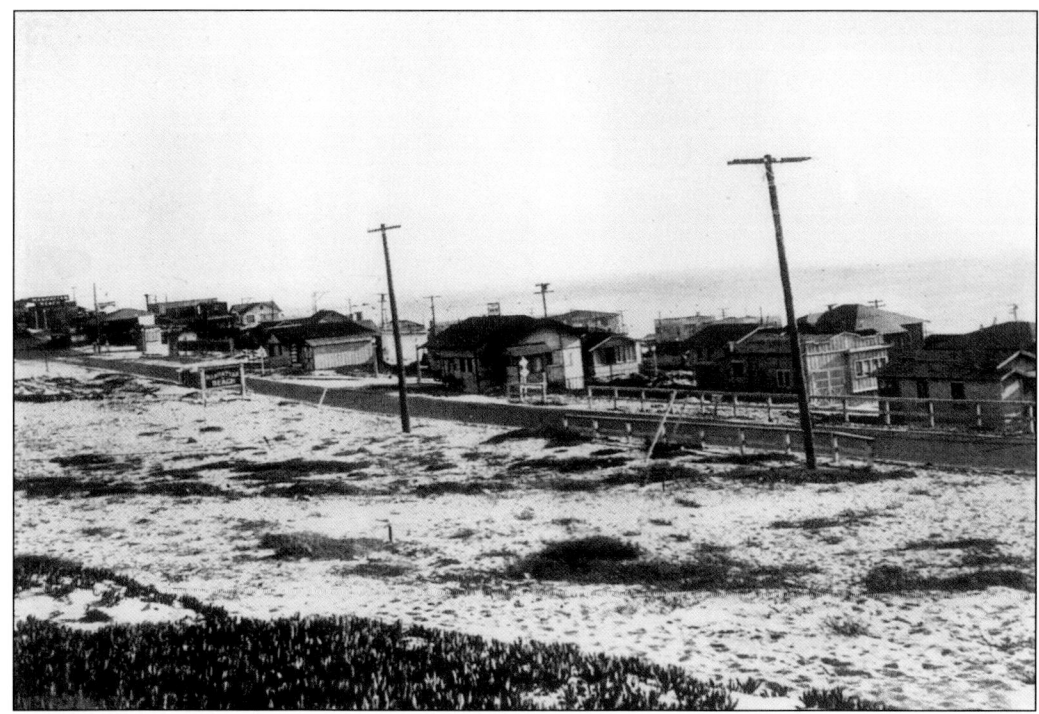

The Northend entry into Manhattan Beach, referred to as the El Porto area, saw slower development. However, the road was completely paved and continued up the coastline as a viable artery.

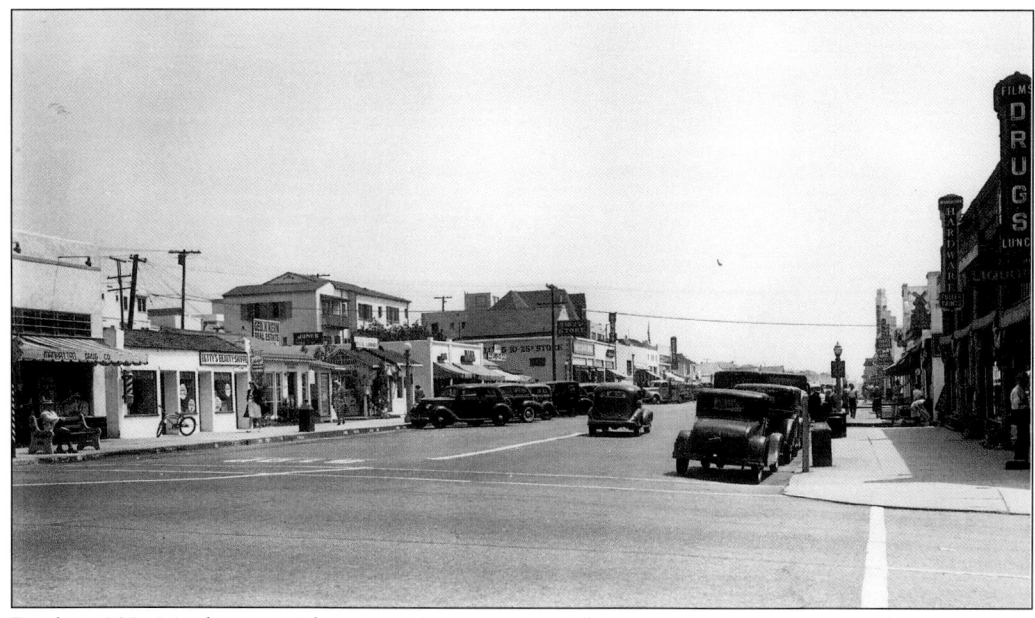

By the 1930s Manhattan's "downtown" area saw Manhattan Avenue completely built out with parking on both sides of the street and busy shops lining the avenue.

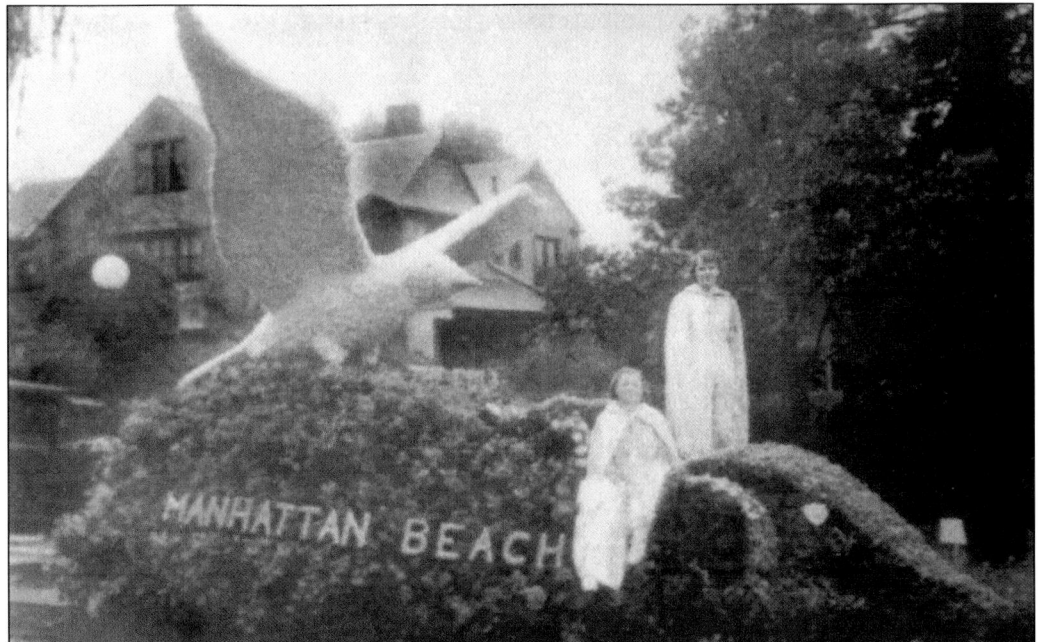

As progress continued throughout the city, the civic prestige of entering a float in the Pasadena Tournament or Rose Parade drew serious attention from the community. An attempt to compete in 1915 failed when, after a devastating winter storm, finding a shelter big enough for the float became impossible. Finally, in 1934, the city entered its first float which depicted a graceful white sea gull with huge outstretched wings alighting on the edge of the Pacific.

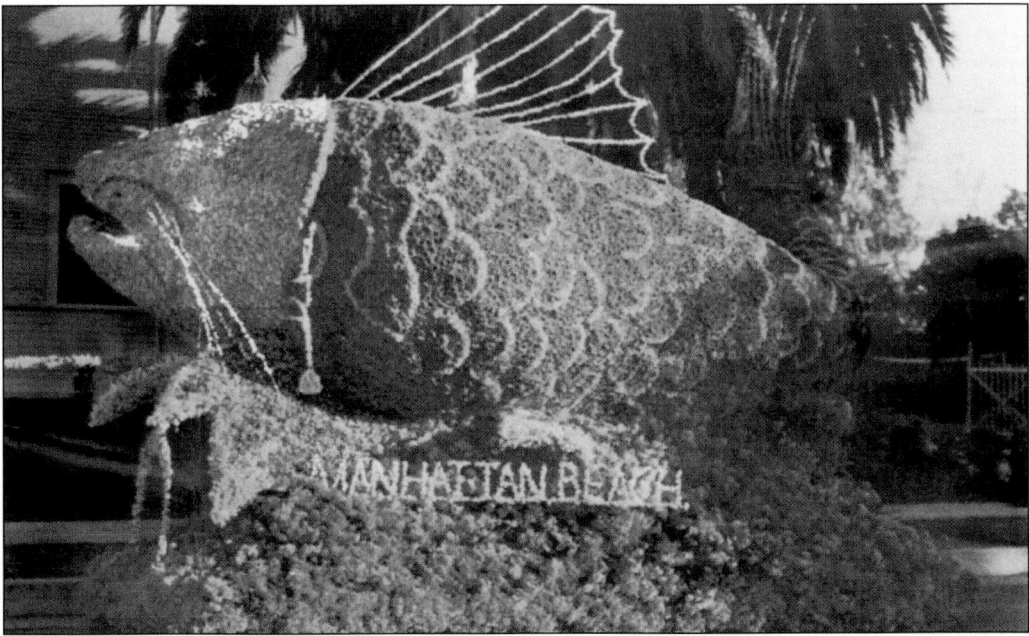

In 1937, the city had an award-winning float, "Fisherman's Romance." The 32-foot gold fish was made of orange, marigold, and yellow pompoms. The eyes were made of shaded delphinium, stevia, and maidenhair fern with foam of white narcissus.

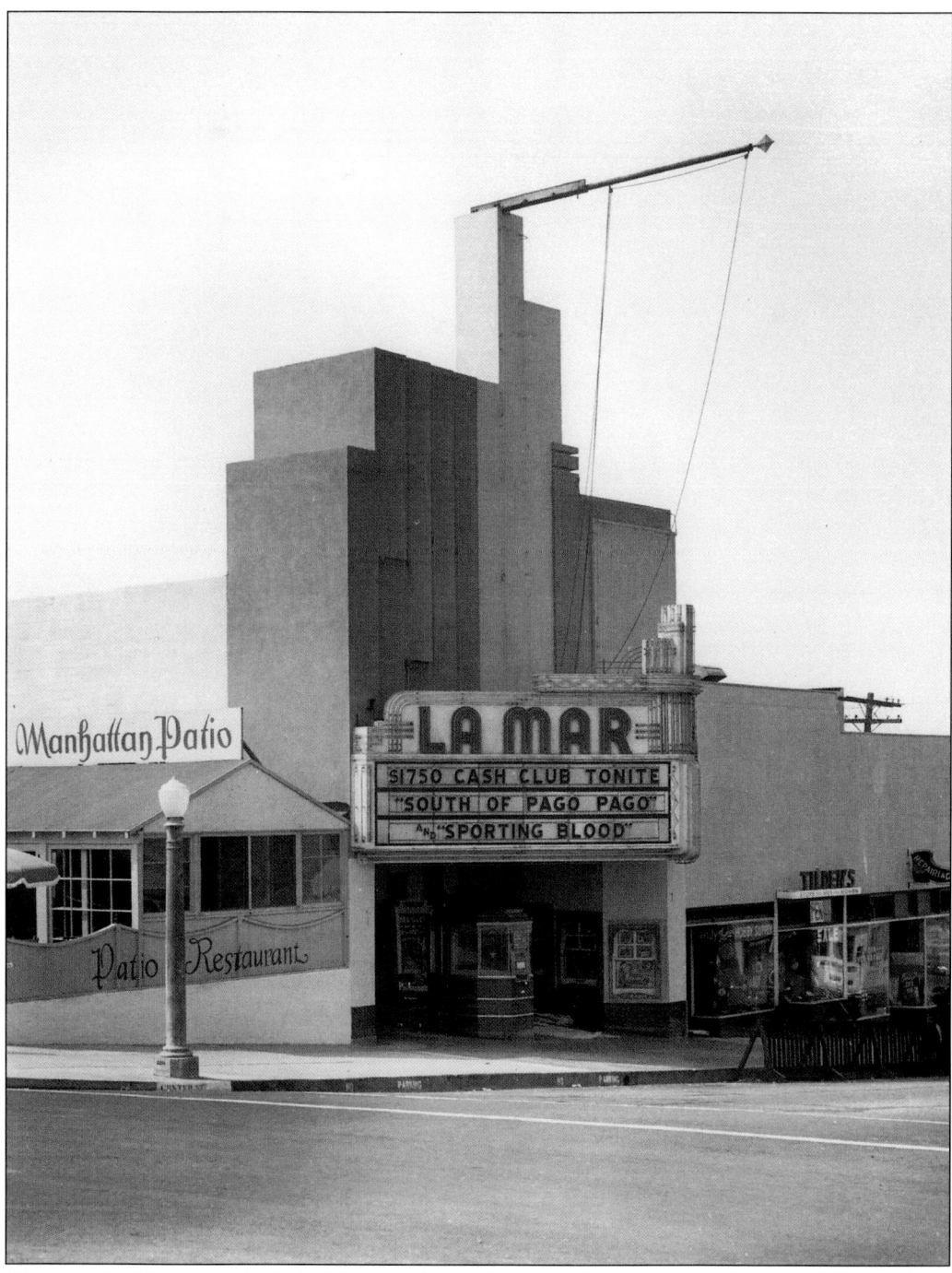

The La Mar Theater, which had its grand opening in 1938, was located in the 200 block on the south side of Manhattan Beach Blvd. The structure represented one of the outstanding art deco structures in the state of California. At a cost of $65,000, the theater's interior exhibited new modernistic sea motifs, blue ceilings, and mirrored walls. After being a landmark for many years the structure met its demise in 1978.

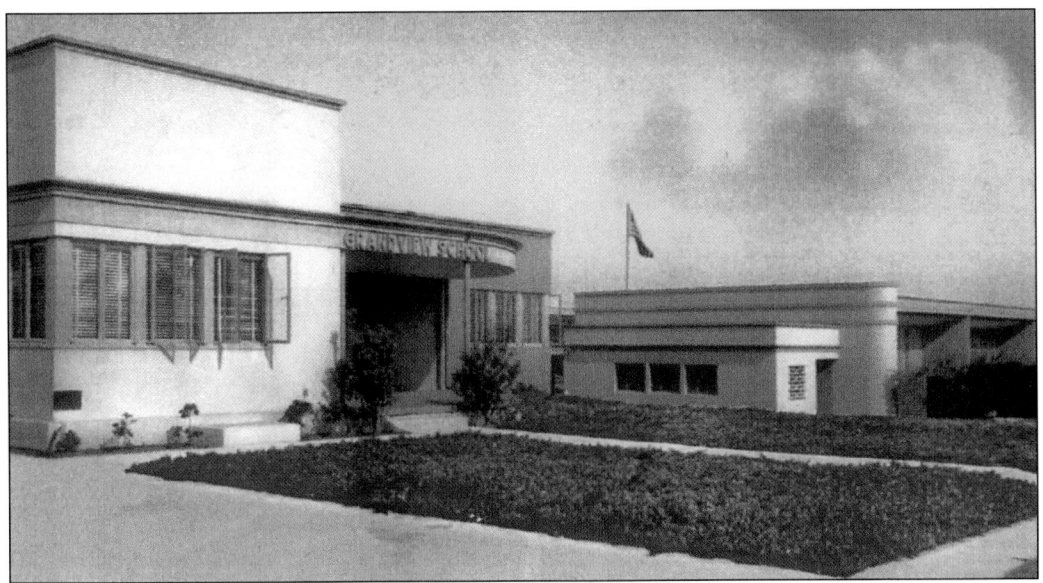

With an increase in the student population, a new second school was needed. The school district had acquired land and the WPA was ready to construct the building using local craftsmen. The city paved the remaining 141 feet left of unpaved Grandview Avenue in order to reach the new site. The facility, with a streamline style of architecture, created an open, functional space with eight individual classrooms opening onto private patios.

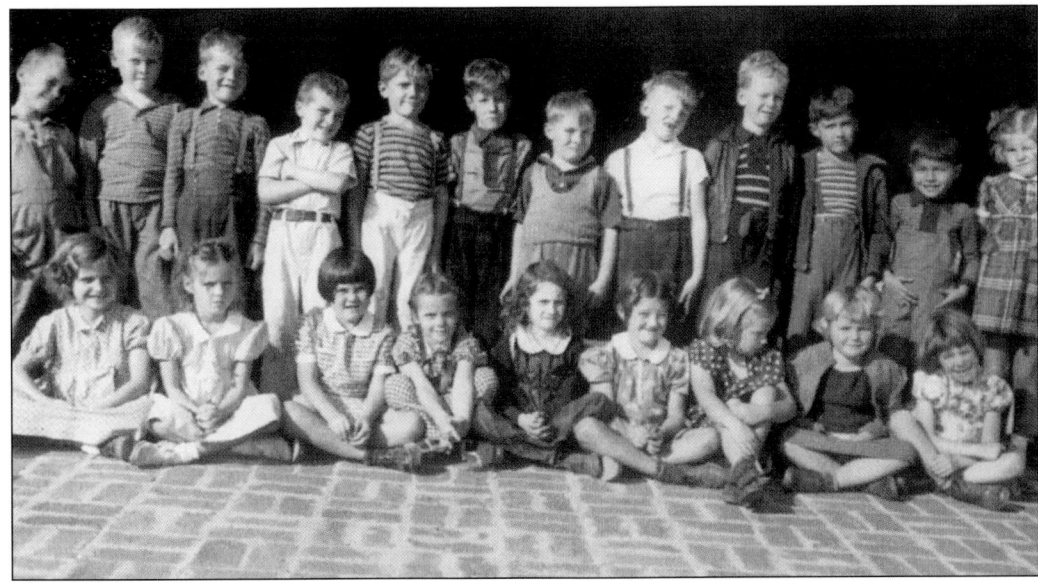

This 1939 photo records the first class of first graders at the new Grandview Elementary School.

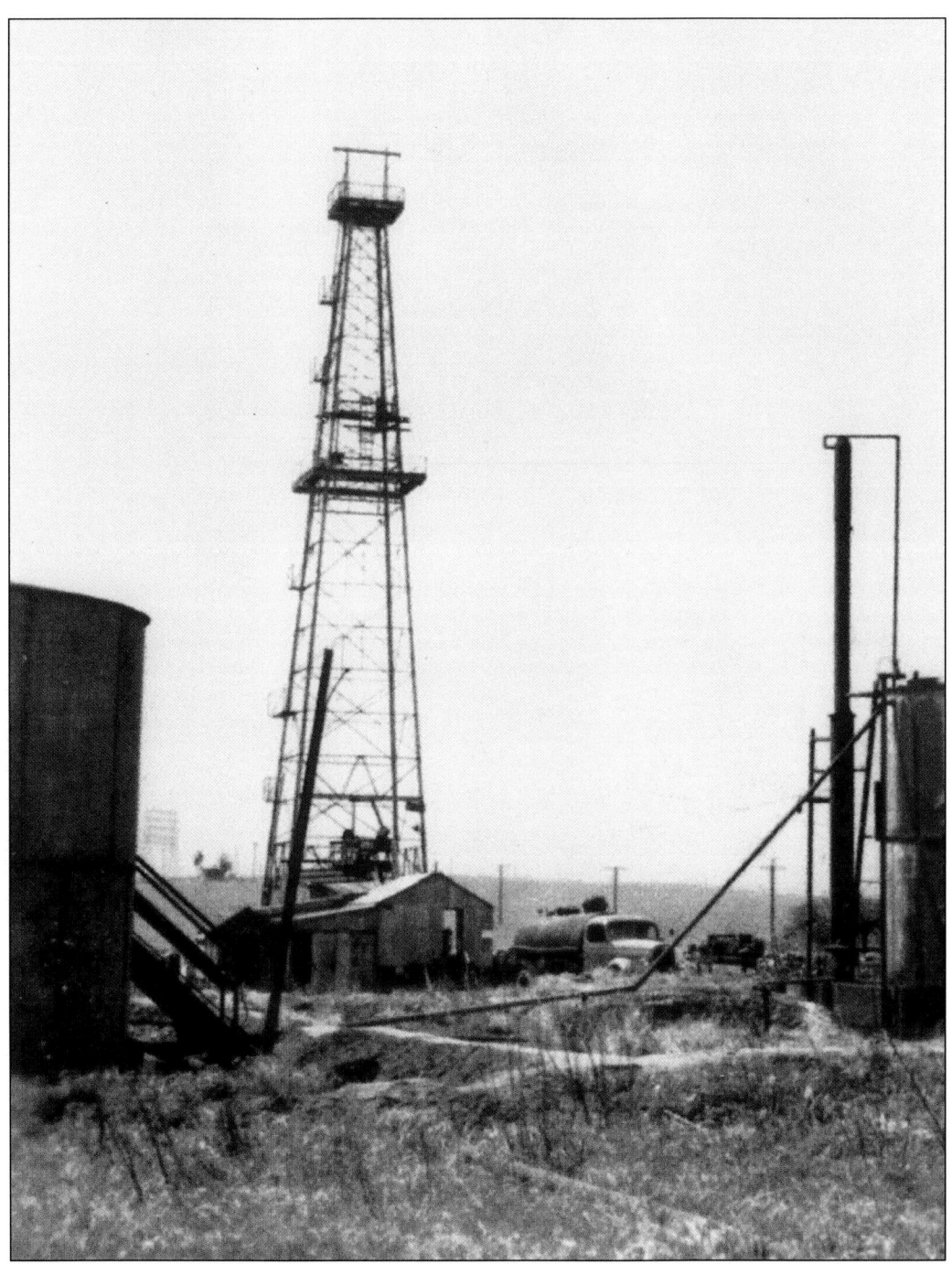
With all the new development in town and much of the good land held in oil leases, the city passed an ordinance in 1939 forbidding any drilling west of Sepulveda Blvd. There were also restrictions and regulations placed on drilling east of Sepulveda Blvd. A $500 permit fee as well as a yearly $500 license charge was put into place. If the new rules were not followed there was a possibility of a $300 fine or three months in jail or both. That effectively ended oil drilling in Manhattan Beach.

Five

END OF AN ERA

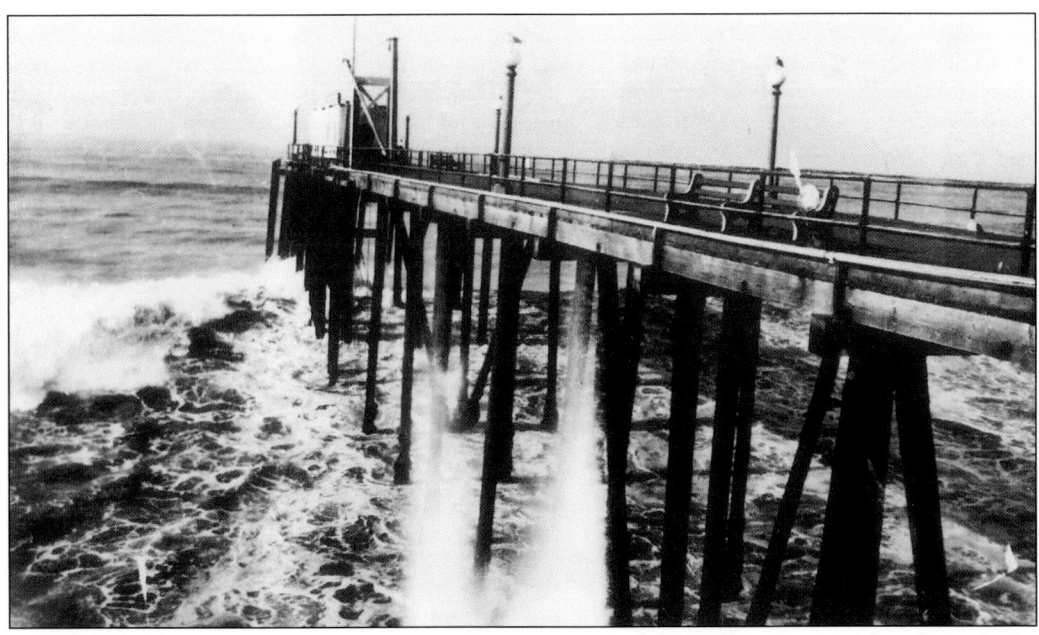

In the early hours of January 9, 1940, Manhattan Beach awakened to the new decade with the arrival of a violent storm. The pounding surf and fierce winds signaled the inevitable collapse of the wooden pier extension. Forty feet of this popular fishing segment built in 1928 was carried out to sea. Along with it went the city winch, a gasoline station formerly owned by Standard Oil, and a lifeguard dory. The next morning several of the pilings still left had come loose at the base and swung suspended from the deck as battering rams ultimately demolishing half of the remaining structure. It was never rebuilt.

In 1940 and 1942 other dramatic changes came to Manhattan Beach. A population boom and a growing town saw all parts of the community developing. Manhattan Beach was one of the fastest growing cities in the state of California with a gain of nearly 300 percent over 1920. By 1940 approximately 3,200 homes existed in Manhattan Beach; most were located west of Sepulveda Blvd. This increase in population allowed the city to build many new facilities.

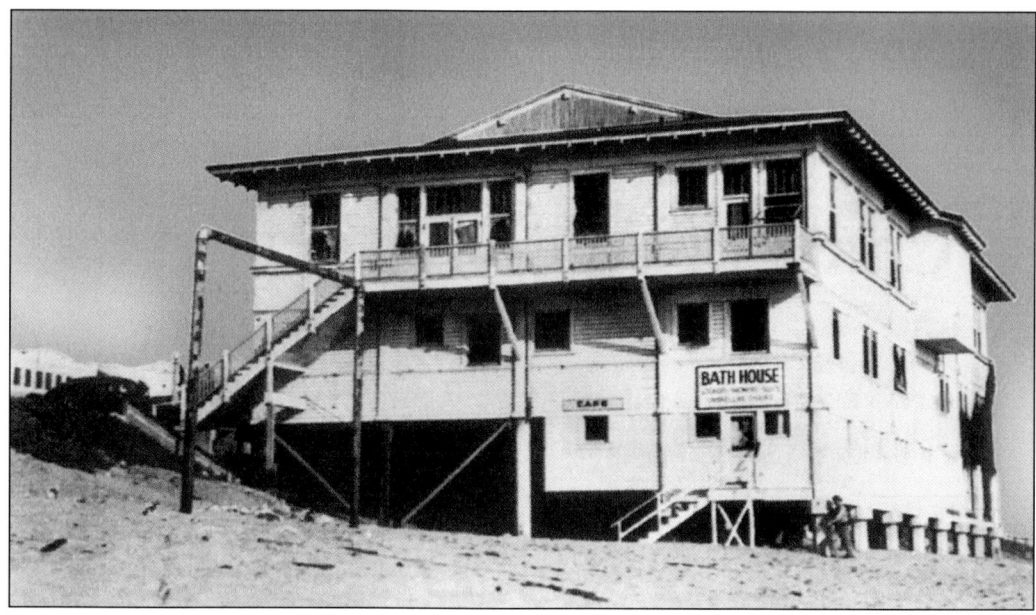

After many years of service the Marine Pavilion, built in 1917, gradually fell into disrepair. For several years the council had struggled with its disposition. Not until it was damaged by fire under suspicious circumstances was it demolished in 1941. The lumber was salvaged and used in the construction of a new street department warehouse at 8th and Larsson Street.

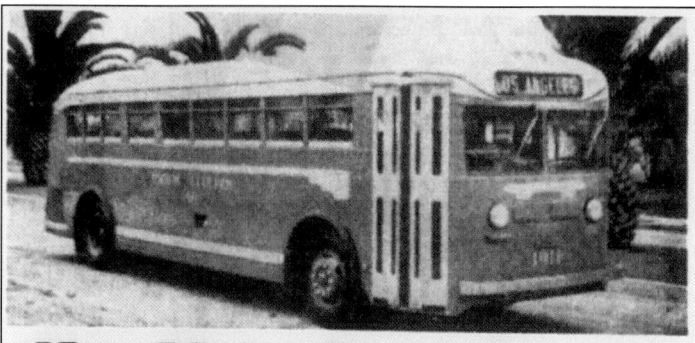

Advertisement proposing new motor coach service between Los Angeles and the beach communities.

In many ways, the '40s marked the end of an era and the beginning of a new one. Nowhere was it more evident than the gradual phase-out of Pacific Electric cars. The P.E. had lost $30 million dollars on the Red Cars since 1925, so in the spring of 1940 the company claimed the bus service offered a better and cheaper transportation.

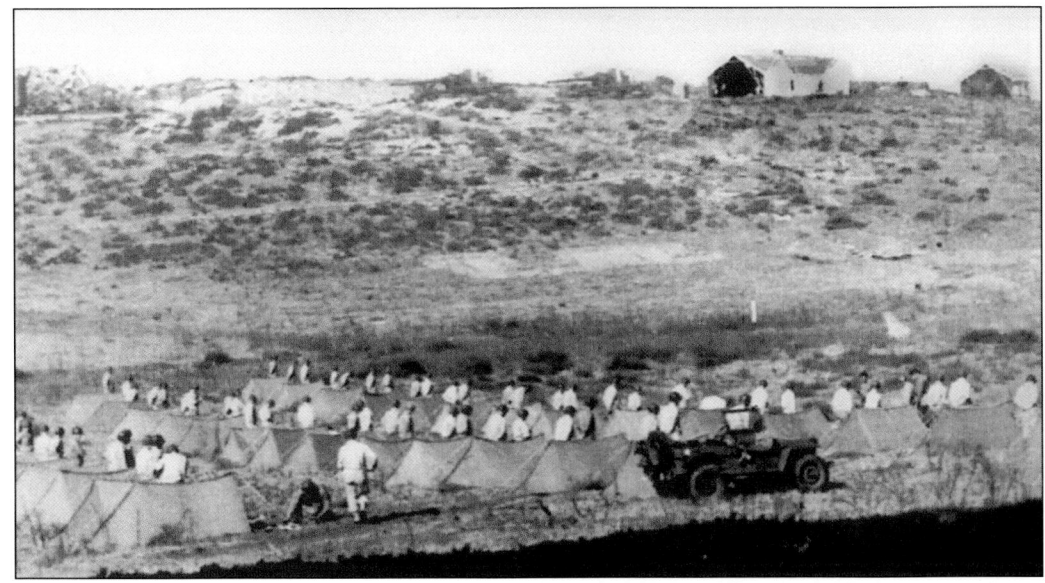

In 1941, with the advent of World War II, rearmament reduced the ranks of the unemployed and the WPA soon passed into history. After Pearl Harbor was bombed, Battery E. Coastal Artillery arrived in town from New Jersey on Christmas Eve. Approximately 100 soldiers camped out in Live Oak Park the first night and were later stationed between 18th and 19th Street on Flournoy Road. They were there to protect the coastline and brought with them two 8-inch railroad battery guns. On the horizon, two rollaway houses can be seen; they were used to conceal the guns from air surveillance.

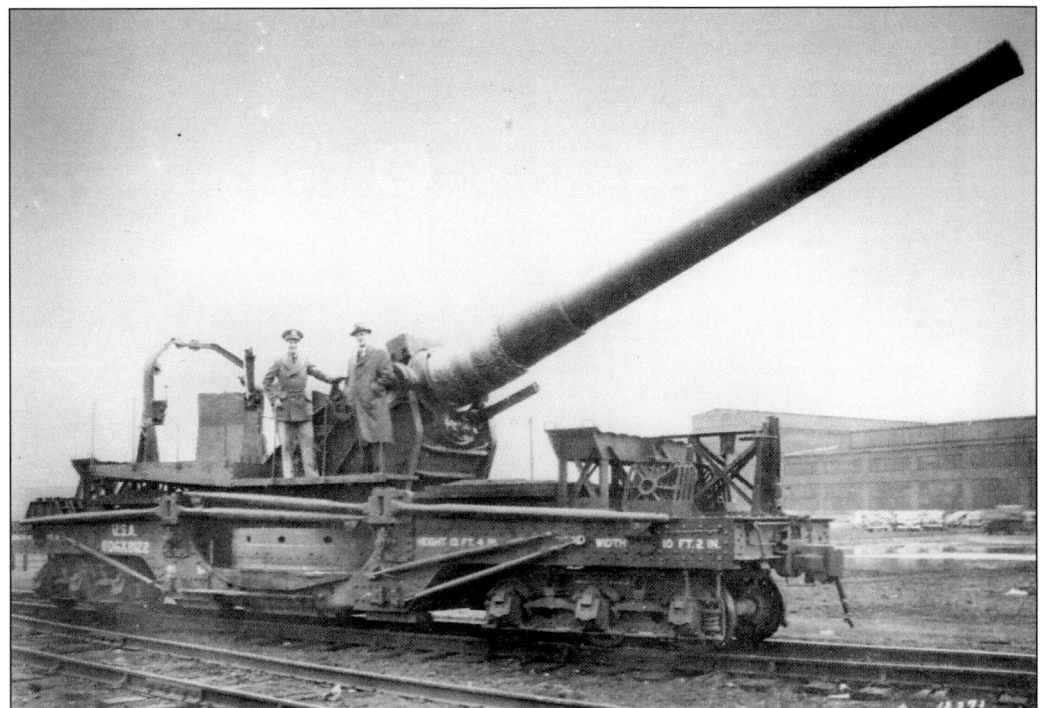

One of the 8-inch railway battery guns used in coastal defense.

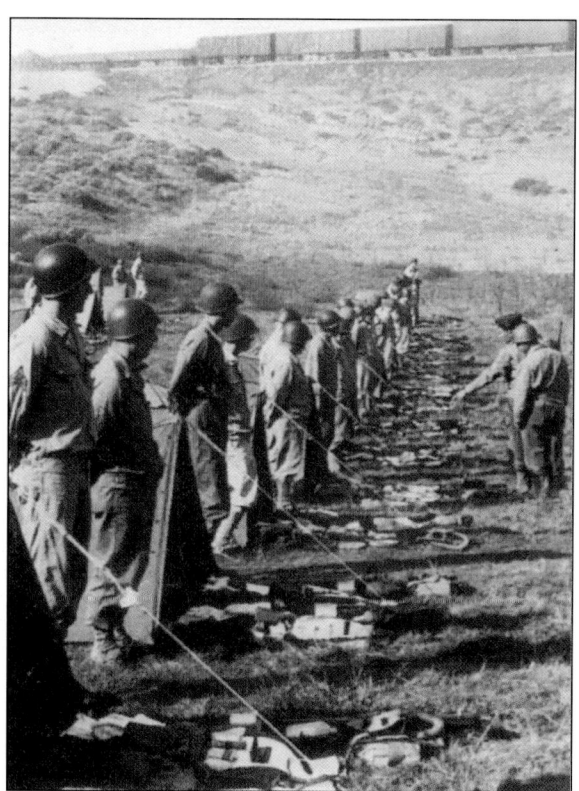

These men are undergoing an inspection in the field. Hundreds of lots in the area of 18th and 19th Street were designated for the government's use. This area was occupied by the railroad spur and bunkers, which served the coastal defenses.

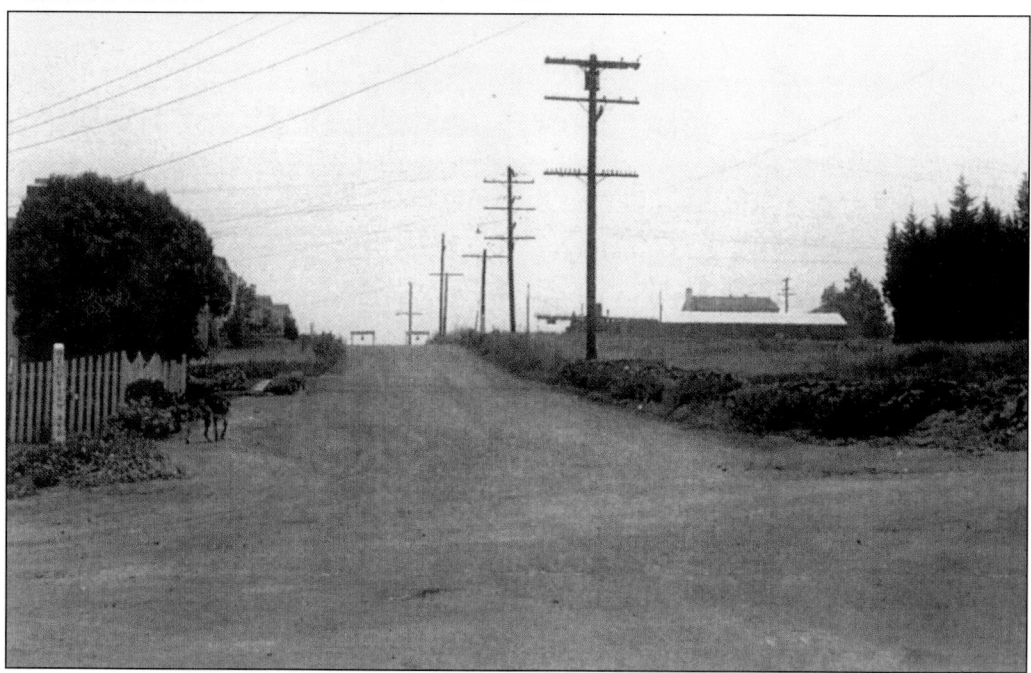

There were other places in town where there were military installations. Along the ridge of the hill at John and 9th Street, structures can be seen housing the Search Light Battalion in readiness for the possible defense of Los Angeles.

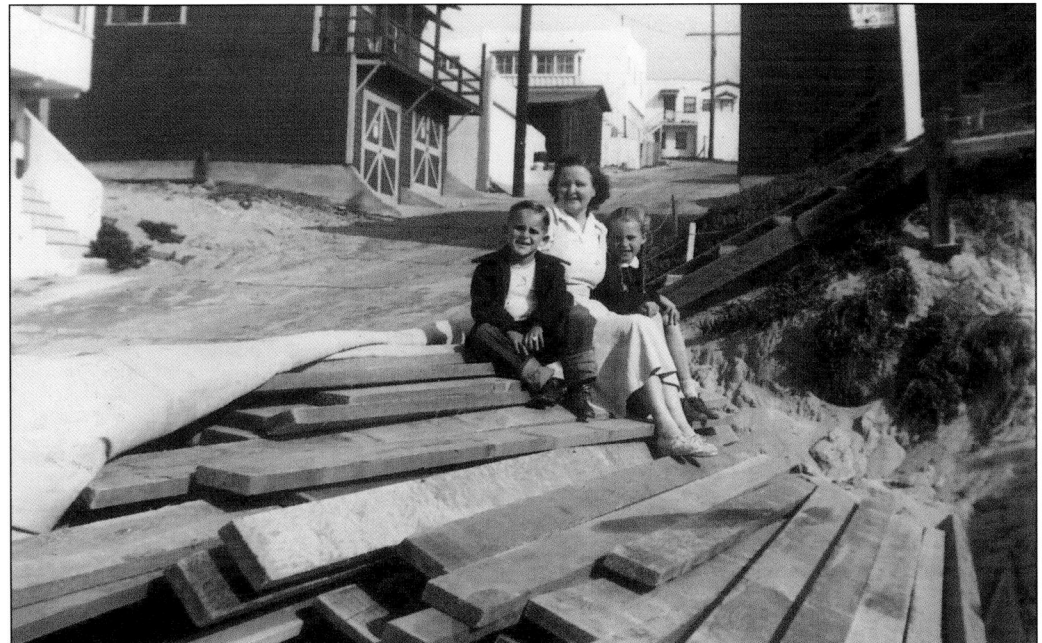

Eloise Loomis, along with children Ken and Ellen, who lived on 19th Place, are seen here perched on a stack of lumber that had washed up onto the Manhattan Beach shore. Japan's submarines in the Santa Barbara and Catalina channels were torpedoing ships. The day before Christmas in 1941, the lumber schooner "Absaroka" was sunk off Point Fermin in the Catalina channel.

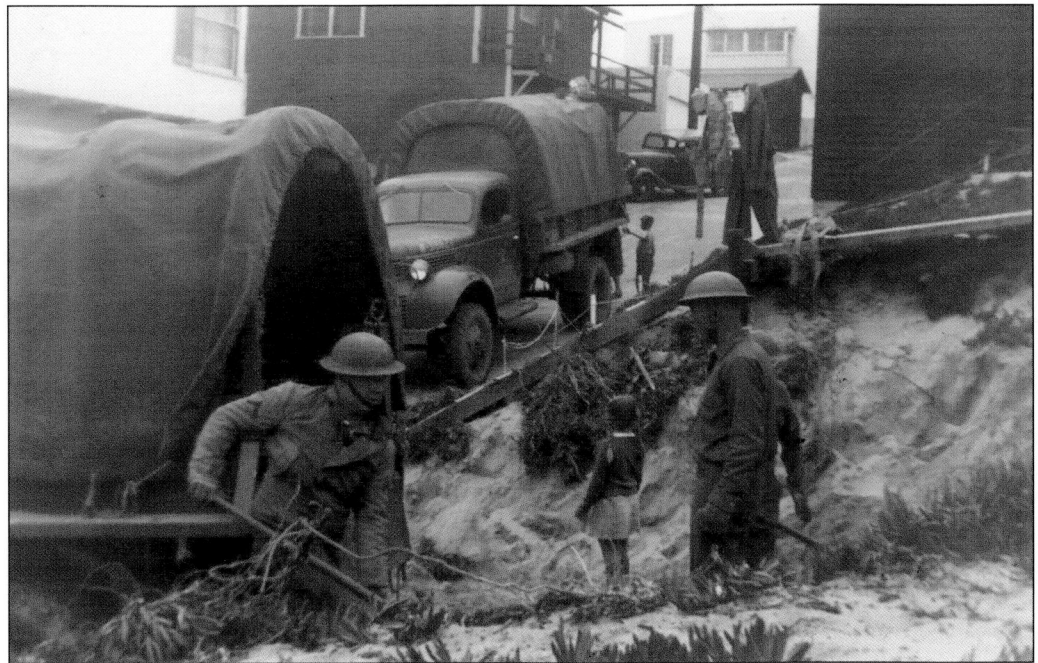

In 1941, soldiers filled bags with Manhattan Beach sand to be used to protect the airplanes hangared at Mines Field, which is now the Los Angeles International Airport.

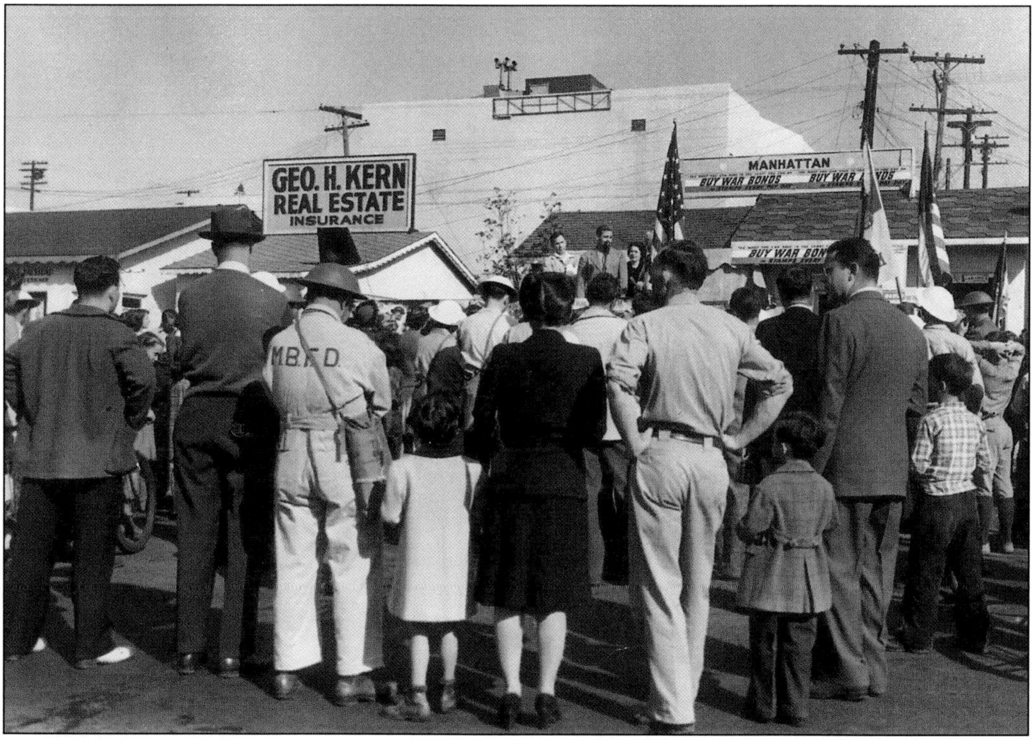

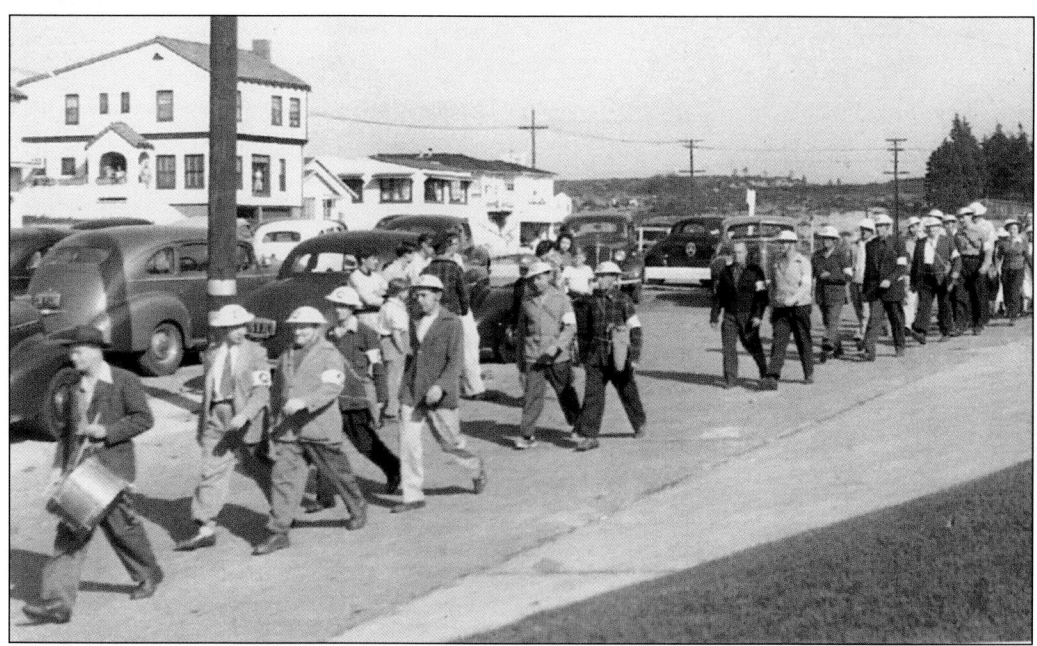

Bond drives were frequent events held at the victory house on Manhattan Avenue. Other victory houses were setup as places where soldiers could go to write letters, listen to music, or just relax.

Here at home, the men who were not called into military service often served in civil defense units. They played a very important role in training the citizens in emergency preparation.

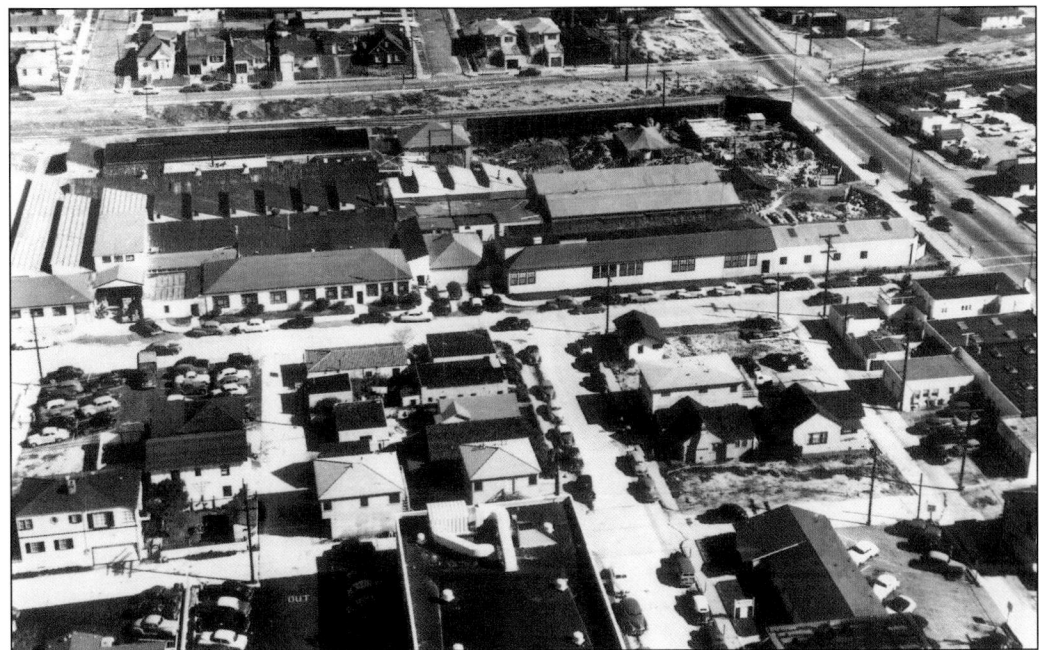

During the war, the Proutyline Products Company produced military shell casings, nuts and bolts, and machine parts for military use. With the end of the war in 1945, one of the biggest financial transactions was the sale of the Prouty/Metlox Pottery Company. The plant now covered the entire site located on Morningside Drive and Manhattan Beach Blvd.

The new Metlox owner Evan Shaw and customers examine one of the many designs of dinnerware in the Metlox showroom. After the purchase by Shaw, the company pulled out of its financial slump to become a world leader in ceramic ware.

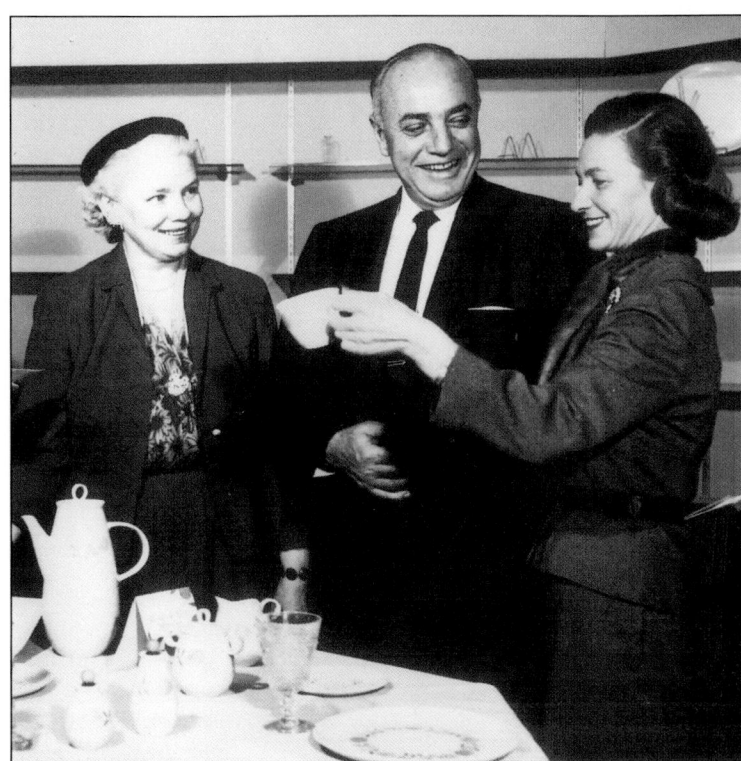

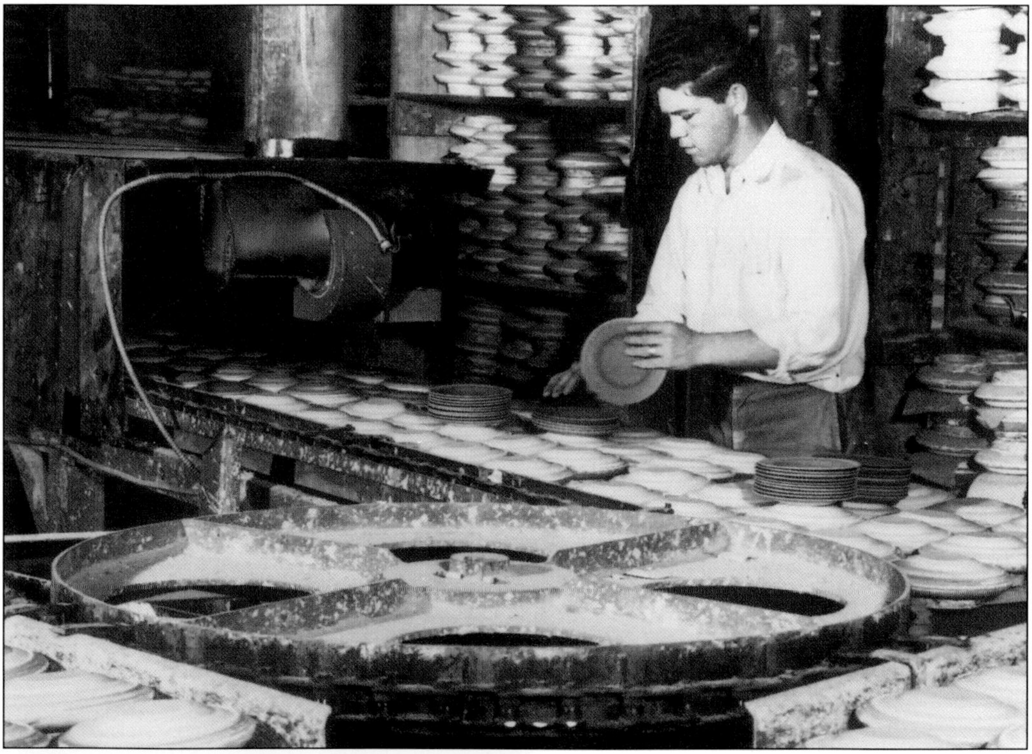

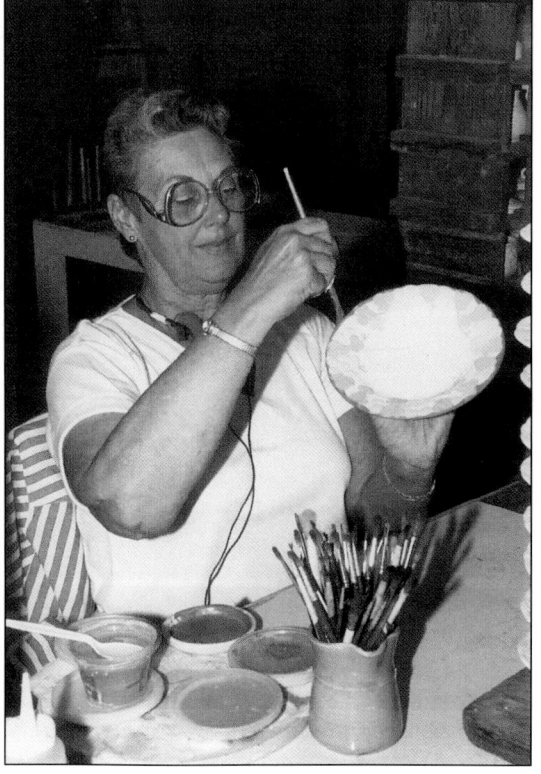

One of the many processes a clay piece went through before it could be painted: the piece, while still on the mold, was run though a gas flame dryer. This hardens the clay sufficiently for safe removal in less time.

It took talent and a steady hand to paint the many designs produced by Metlox. Many local residents, particularly women, found employment in this well-known pottery factory.

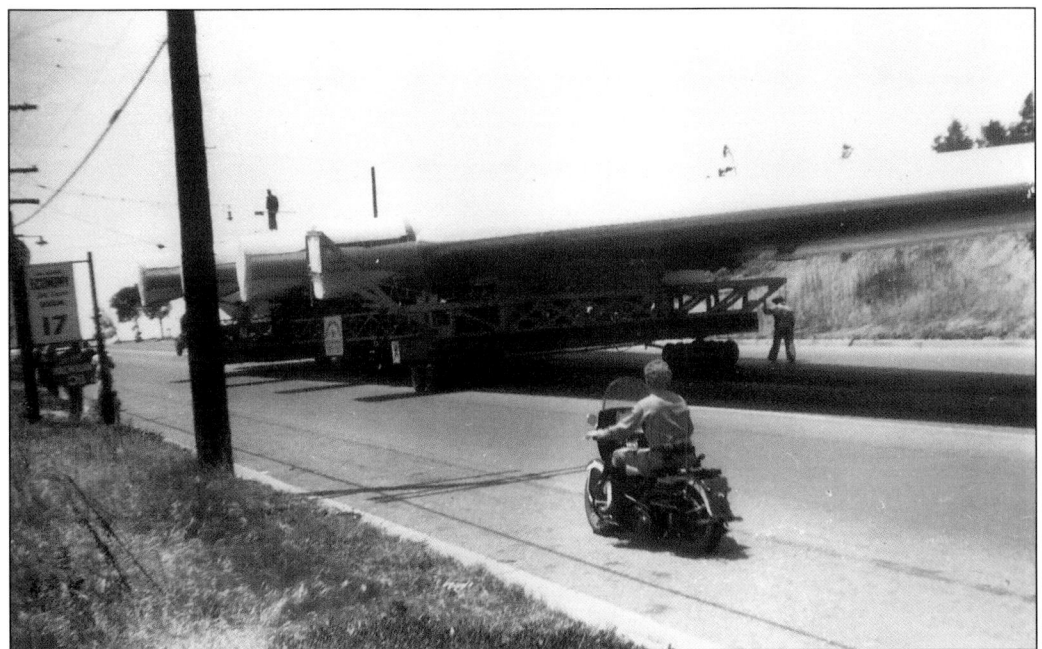

In June of 1946, an enterprising young man, Howard Hughes, oversaw the transport of the "world's largest flying boat" through the South Bay on its way to Long Beach. The plane, nicknamed the Spruce Goose, had been built in Culver City in a time span of 17 months. A section of the left wing of the plane was moved up the hill at Sepulveda Boulevard and 2nd Street.

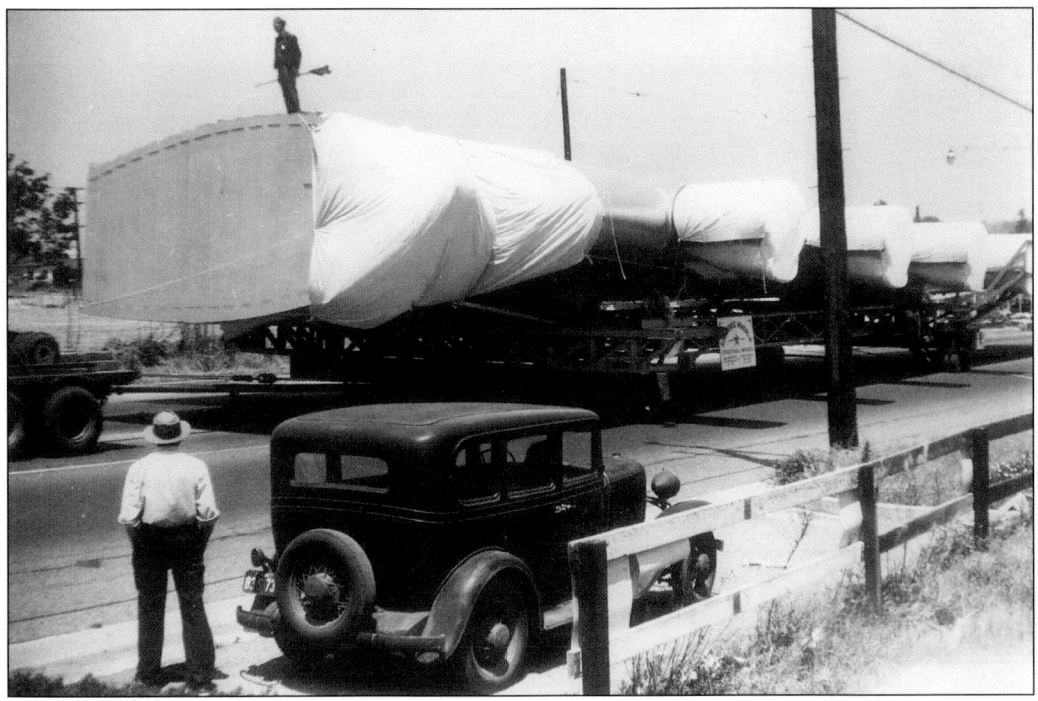

Manhattan Beach resident Frank Bauer watched the activity as a man stood on top of the wing with a broom. The broom was used to push up wires suspended over the road.

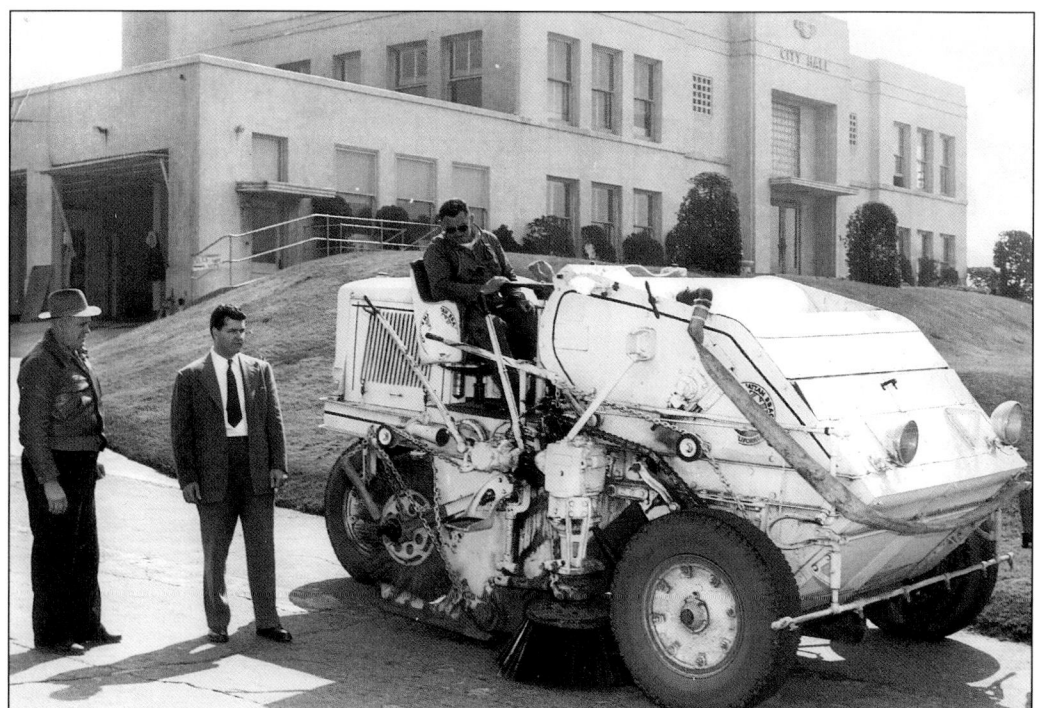

On August 1, 1948, Clifford G. Petrie, second from the left, took office as the first city manager. Petrie wasted no time in getting to work. One of his major projects was a street cleanup campaign. Standing with the city manager is Mr. Kuhn. Mr. Smith is seated on the street sweeper.

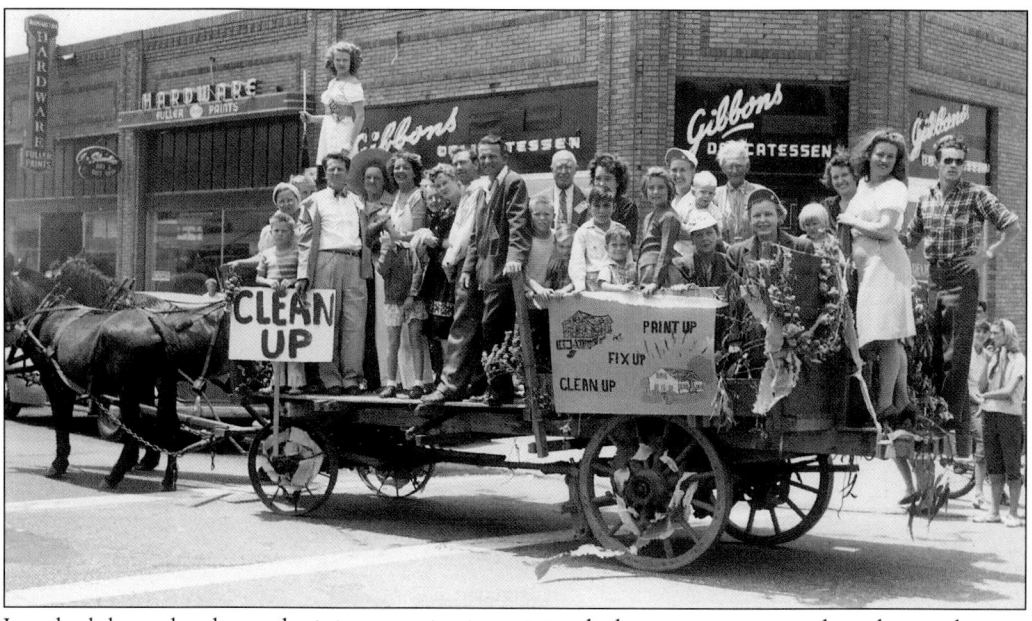

Local clubs, schools, and civic organizations joined the movement with a huge cleanup campaign aimed at beautifying the city, the beach, and homeowner's property. Aiding the volunteers were special city trucks picking up rubbish free of charge.

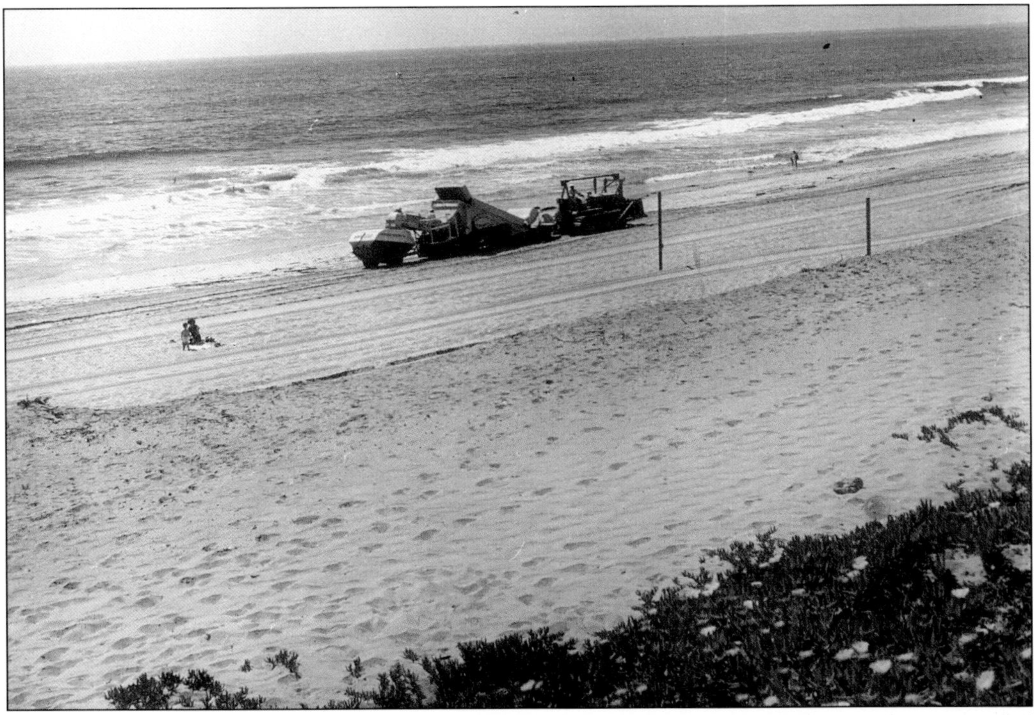

The clean up of the county beach was an urgent priority. A tractor-drawn machine traveled over the sand, raking to a depth of 6 inches. The machine was capable of cleaning the beach at a minimum rate of 1,500 square yards per hour.

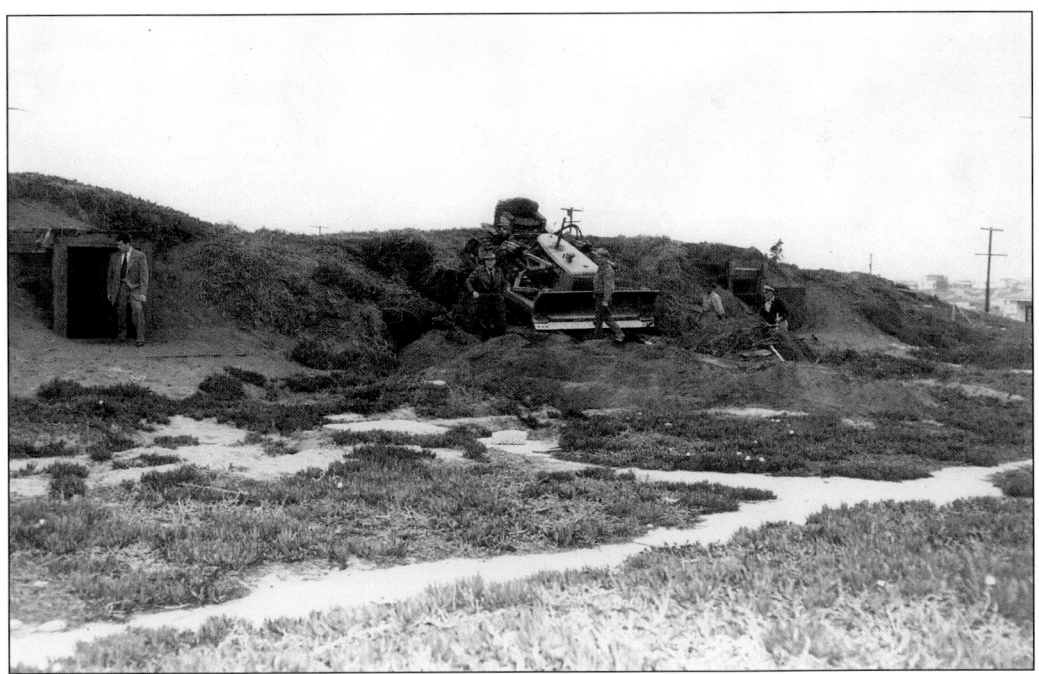

The powder and projectile storage bunkers used by the army during World War II were dismantled, filled in, and made ready for home building lots.

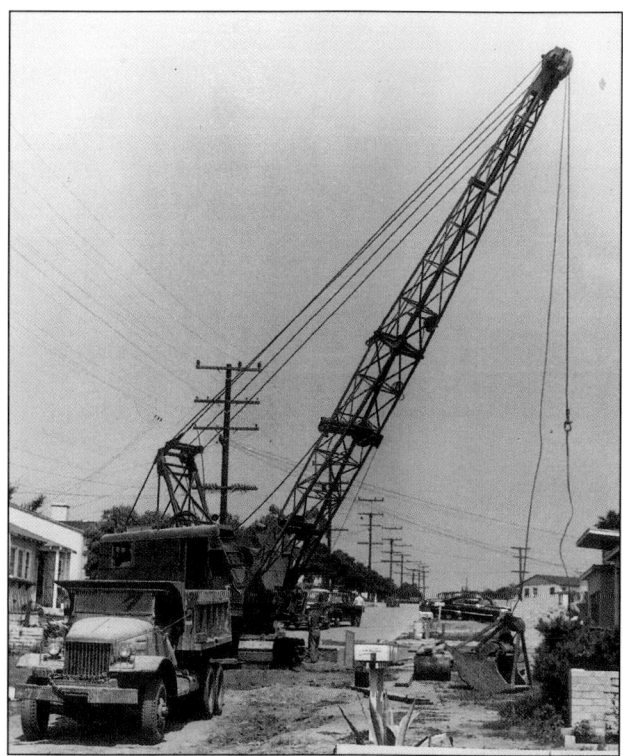

The late '40s were years of rapid transition from the depression and World War II economy into an era of peace and prosperity. One of the major expenditures was a new sewer system. Shown here is the work being done on one of the sewer tunnel's intersections. In August of 1949, a new sewer pumping station located under the Strand walk at 27th Street went into effect. Lifting waste material 65 feet from the oceanfront to the city's eastern boundary, it joined the county's Sanitation District No. 5 system.

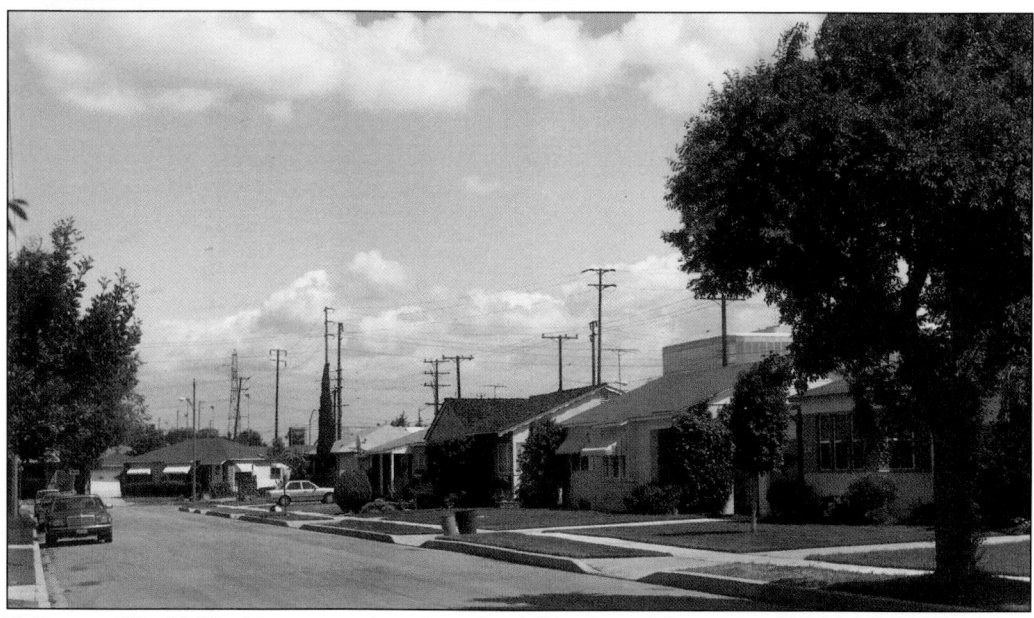

Following World War II, improved roads and vehicles brought greater growth and development to the city. In April of 1953, a special census indicated 26,315 people now resided in the city. By 1955, the city boasted of a population of 30,000. The newest home building tract consisted of 75 acres and indicated the trend toward continued development east of Sepulveda Blvd. The Liberty Village tract, named after the contractor, began in 1950 with 400 homes, shattering the city's previous number of building permits and setting a new record.

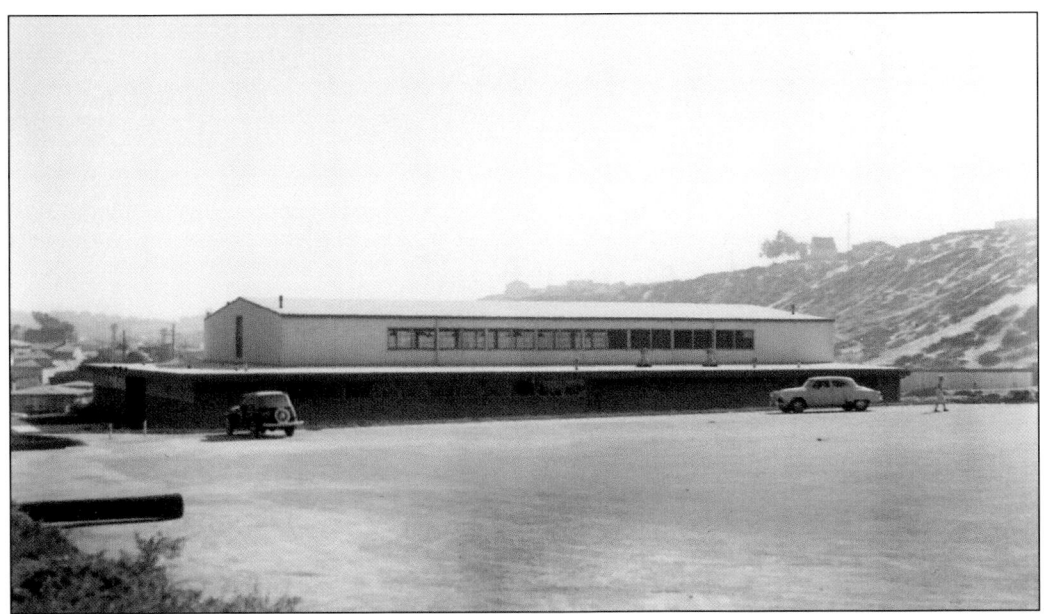

After two years of competition against other cities and a battle with the United States Government, the city of Manhattan Beach was awarded a California National Guard Armory unit. Built on eight acres at the corner of Rosecrans and Bell Avenue, the building was officially dedicated on March 29, 1951. The armory facilities could also be used for civic and social affairs if the National Guard was not occupying the property.

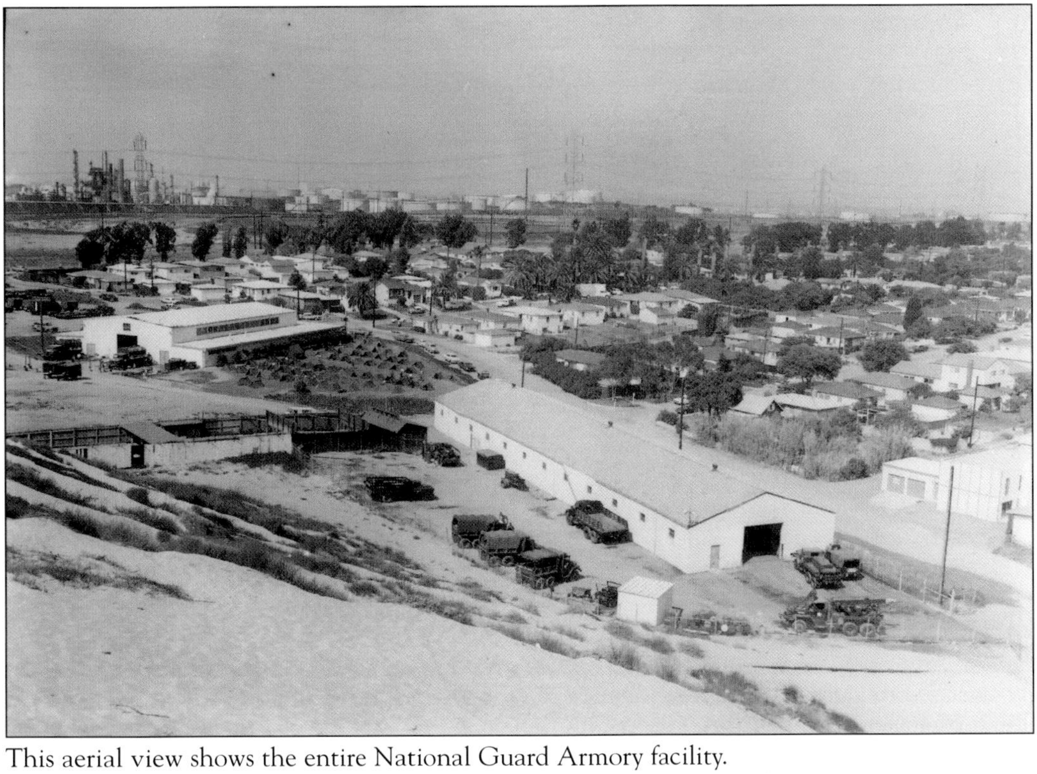

This aerial view shows the entire National Guard Armory facility.

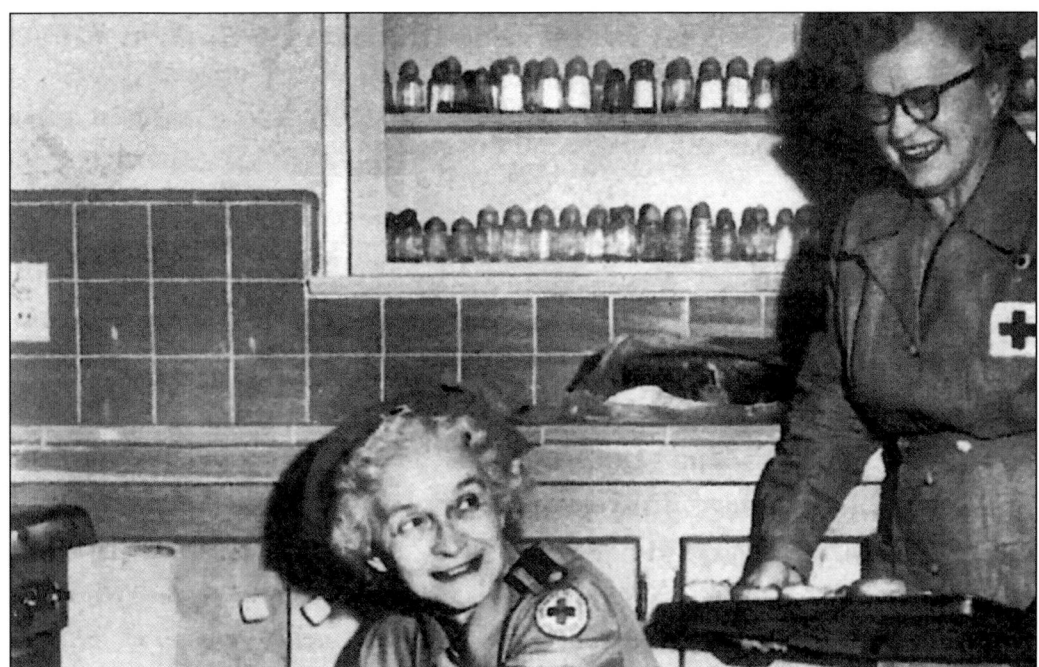
Red Cross and canteen work was an activity carried out by Neptunian Woman's Club members for more than 50 years. Here, Mrs. Charles E. Hall and Mrs. R.B. Stitzer prepare food for doctors and nurses working during a blood drive.

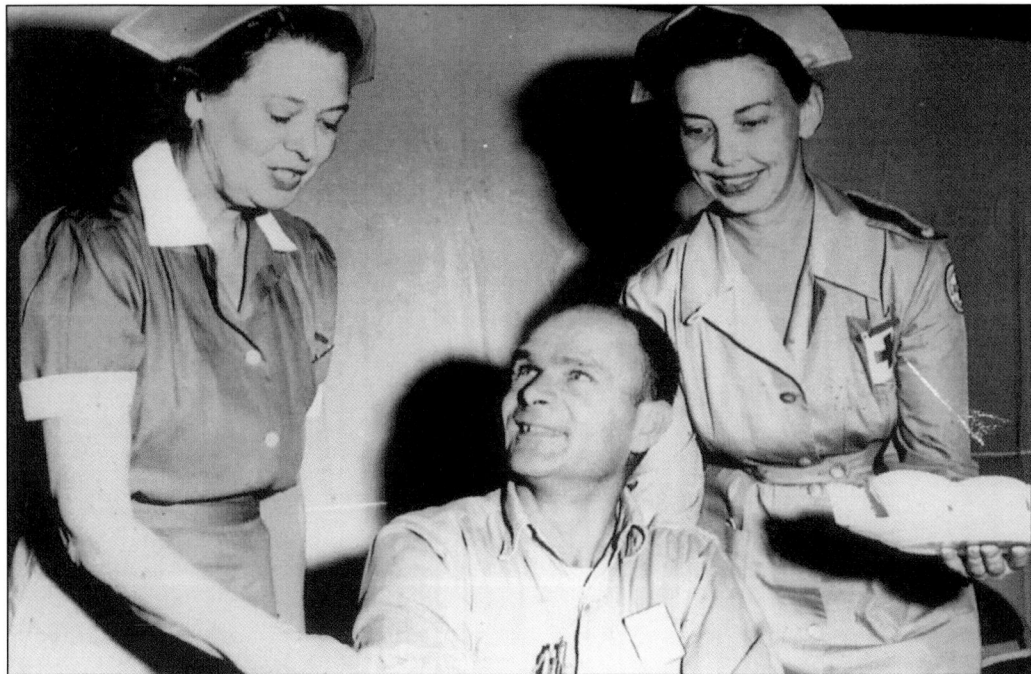
When the President of the United States, Harry S. Truman, ordered troops into South Korea, the ladies of the community mobilized by scheduling first aid classes, conducting blood drives, and door-to-door fund raising campaigns for the Red Cross.

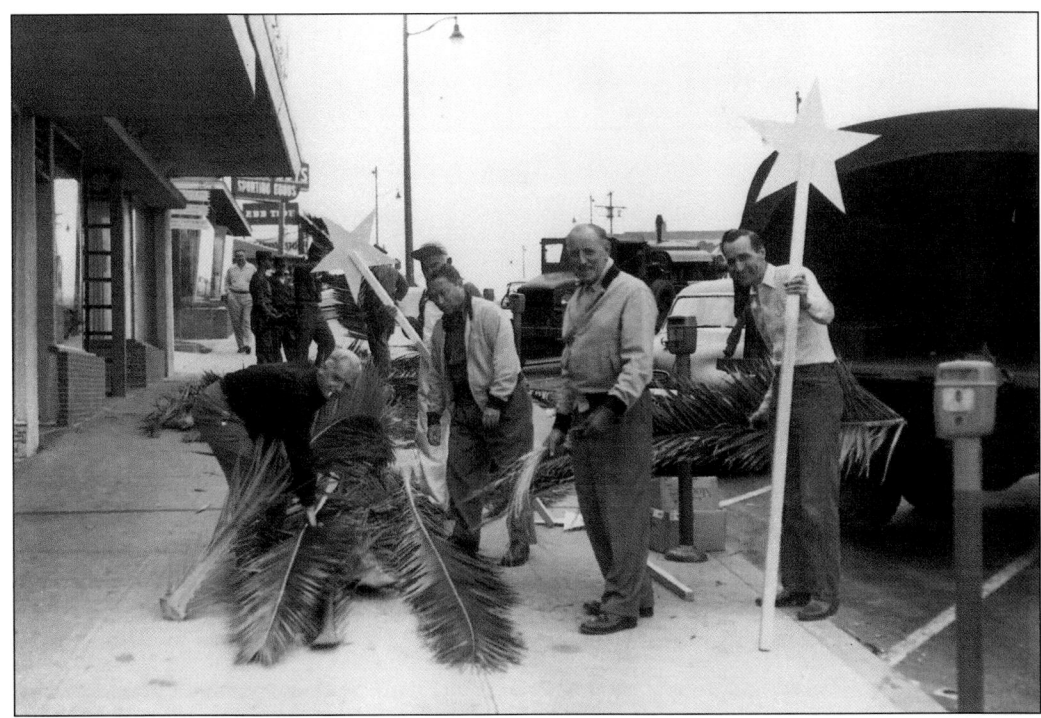

The young service men from the armory contributed to civic activities, such as helping businessmen decorate the downtown area at Christmas and helping to deliver and plant "ice plant" along the railroad tracks.

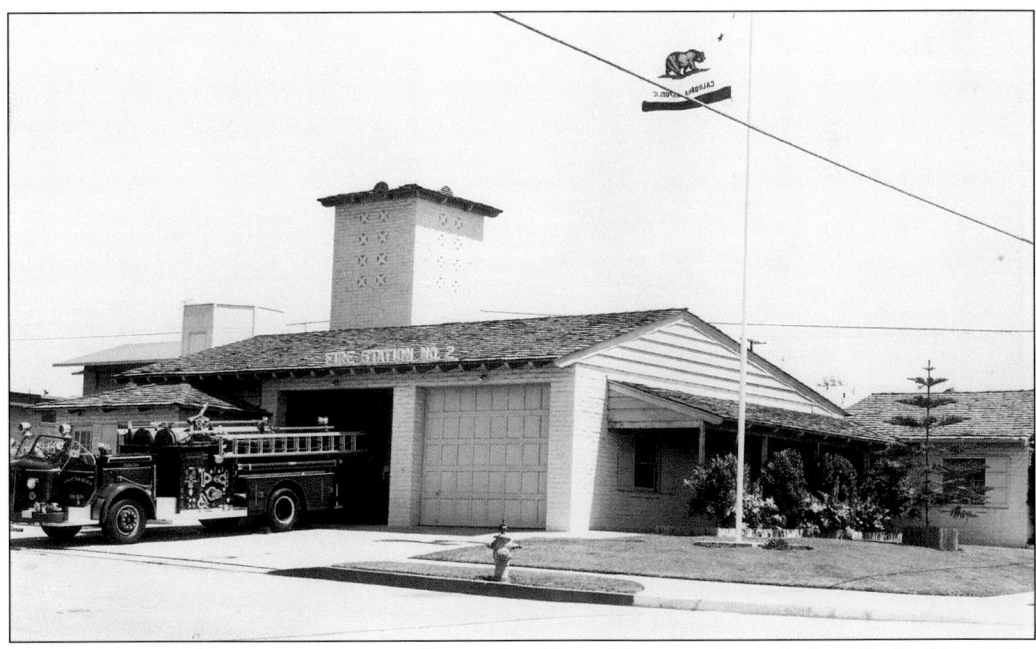

Development in the community created a vast backlog of desperately needed public facilities. The police department kept pace with the steady population growth by increasing the staff and officers of the department, while the fire department added another fire station, dedicated in 1954.

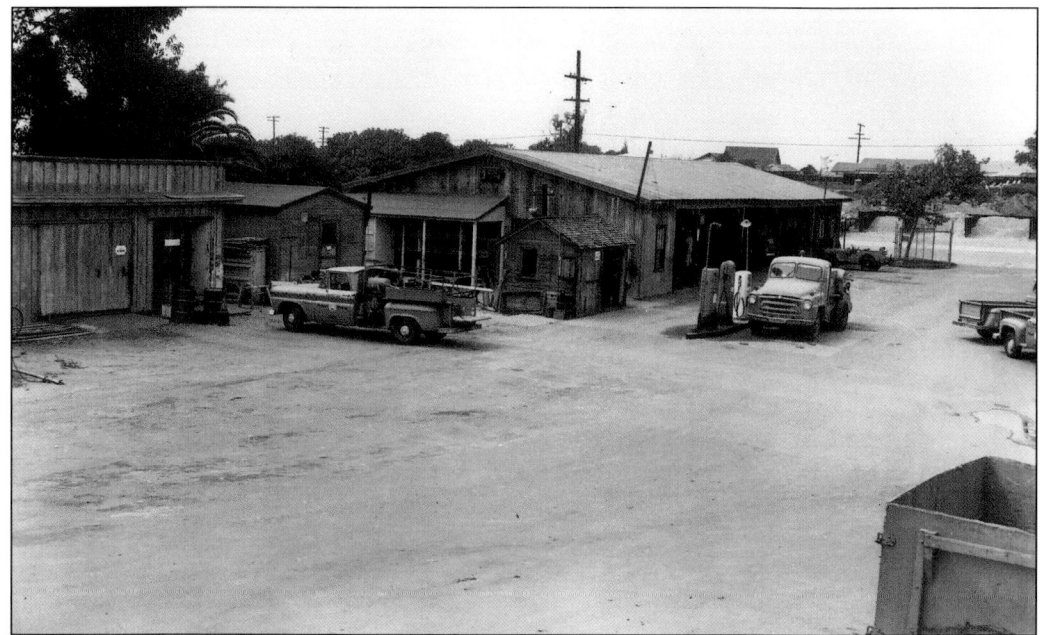
The public works department was created early in 1957, placing all public works related activities under one director, John T. Schulte. The city yard was located between 6th and 8th Street on Sepulevda Boulevard.

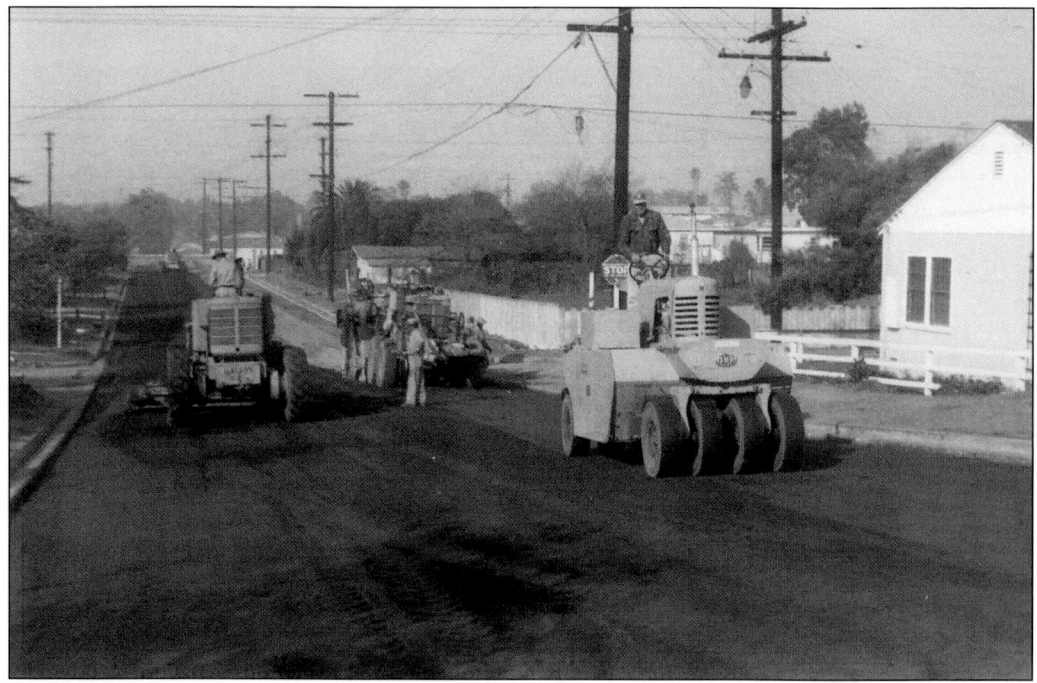
One of the major improvements undertaken by the public works department was the development of the road system. Widening, grading, curbing, and resurfacing all took place during the late 1950s. This photo looks north on Dianthus and 11th Street.

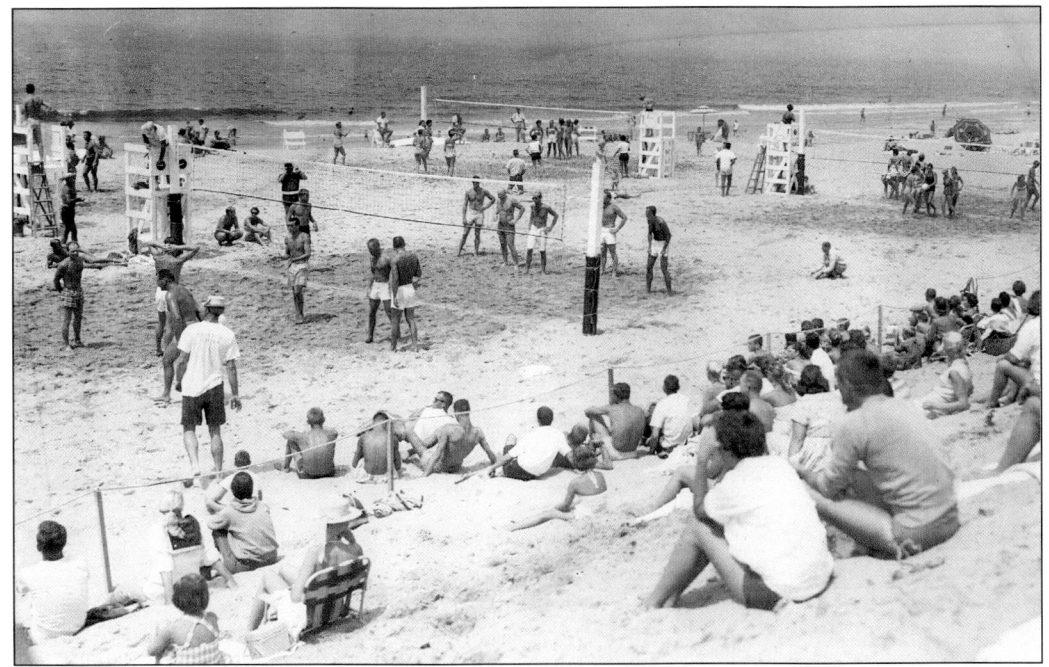

Volleyball continued to be the favorite recreational beach sport, a sport that has now risen to Olympic status. On any given weekend there would be a tournament in progress. The parks and recreation department, along with the Southern California Municipal Athletic Association (ASSOC), sponsored the beach volleyball tournament, which became part of the paddleboard festival in 1957.

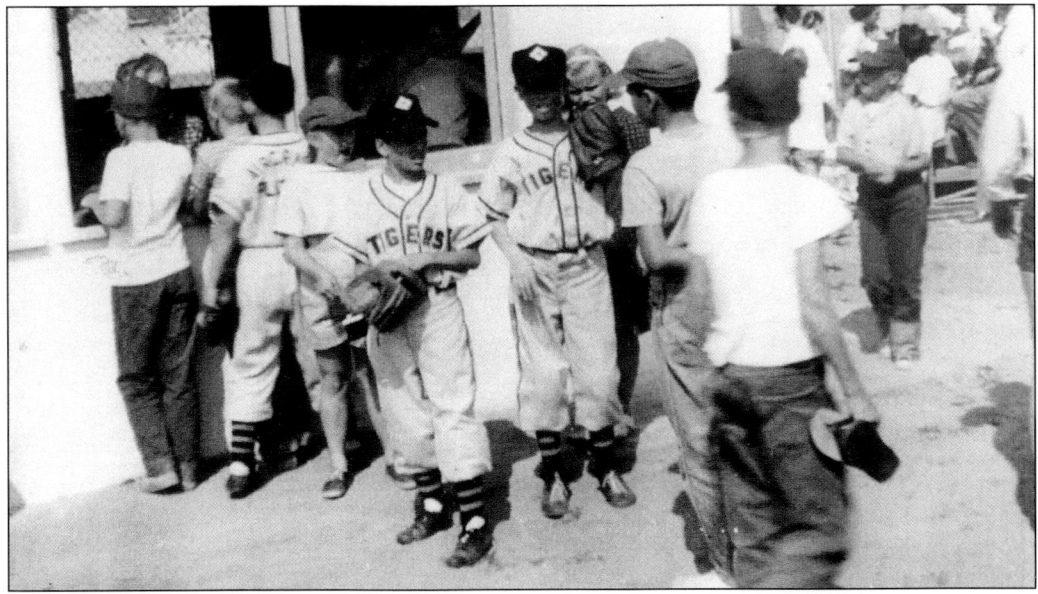

The city's infrastructure was improving and new homes continued to be built, giving citizens a chance to enjoy community recreational programs. In 1954, Premier Little League was the first baseball organization to be established for young boys. The Mira Costa League and Manhattan Little League were soon to follow.

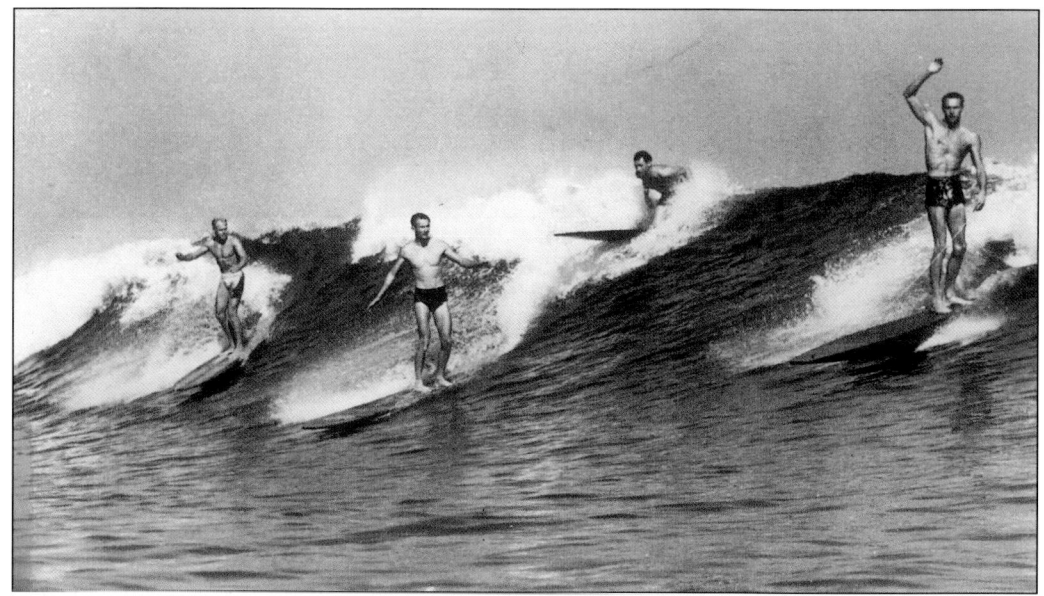

The sport of surf riding grew rapidly with the advent of boards much lighter than their old Hawaiian counterparts. Manhattan Beach became one of the important centers of this popular activity practiced year round.

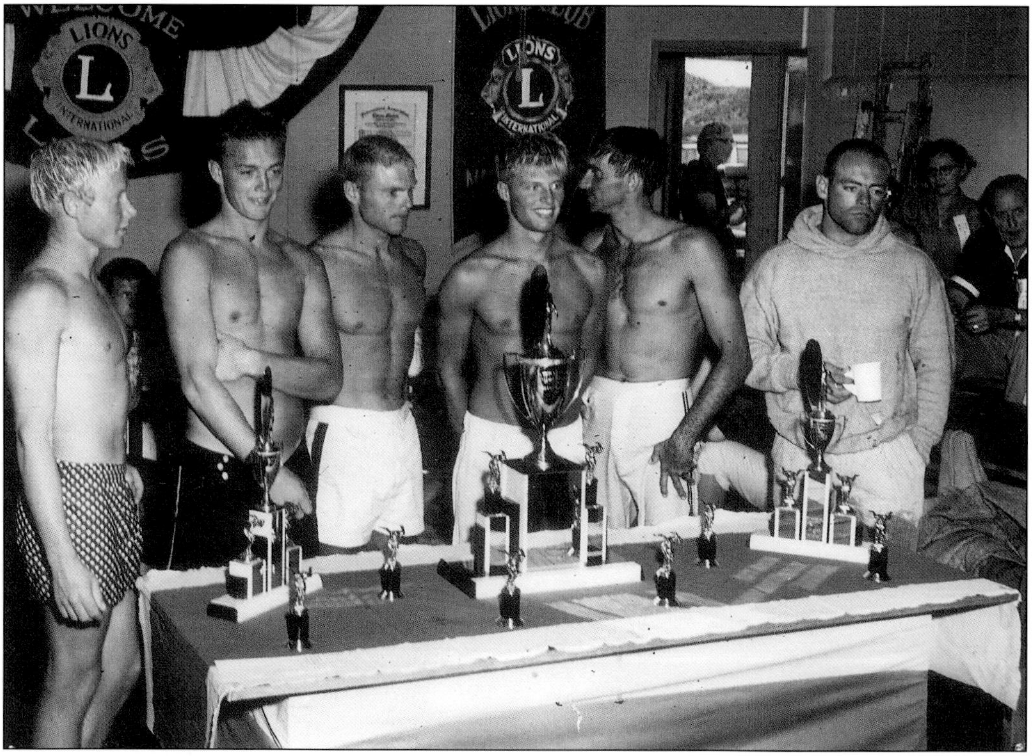

In September 1955, the first six men to finish the Catalina to Manhattan Beach Paddleboard Race were (left to right) Charles Reimers, Gregg Noll, Tom Zahn, Rickie Griggs, George Downing, and Bob Hogan.

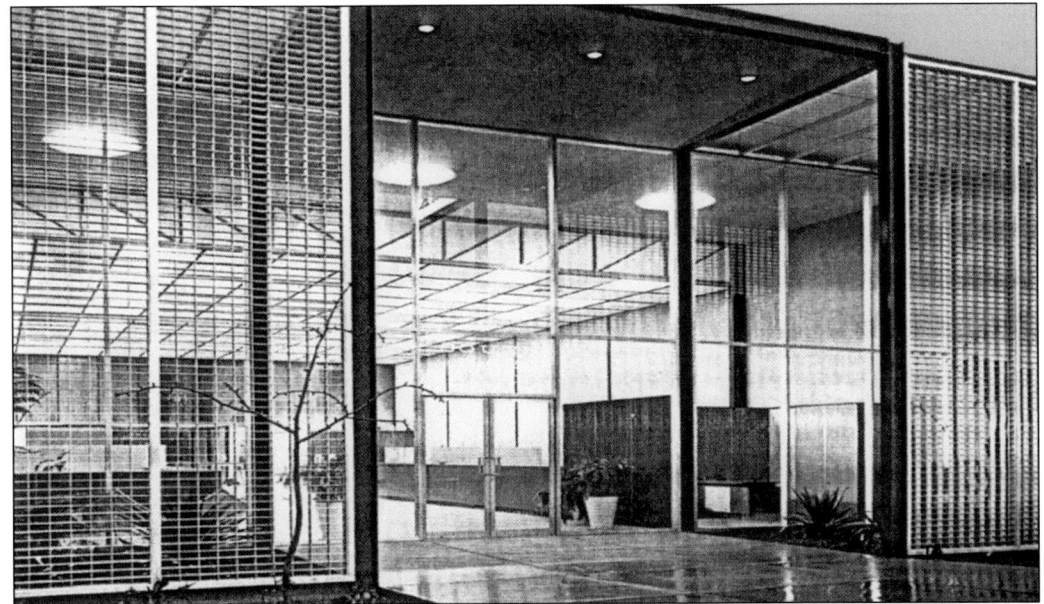

The work of architect Craig Ellwood reflects the modern style's simplicity at its best. Ellwood's trademark was his fluency in the language of steel, aluminum, and glass. This bold and innovative architectural style appeared in Manhattan Beach in 1957 with the construction of the South Bay Bank building at the corner of 18th Street and Sepulveda Boulevard.

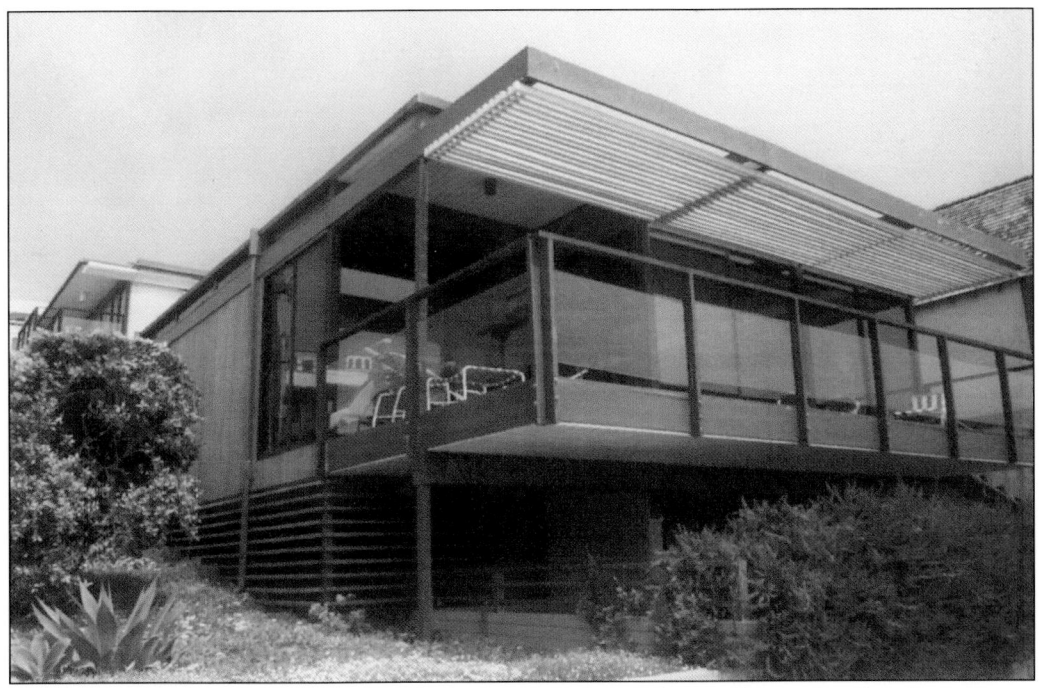

The beach cottages along the Strand were giving way to the modern style of architecture as seen in this spacious, award-winning residential design by Edward H. Fickett, built by Austin Blankenship in 1959.

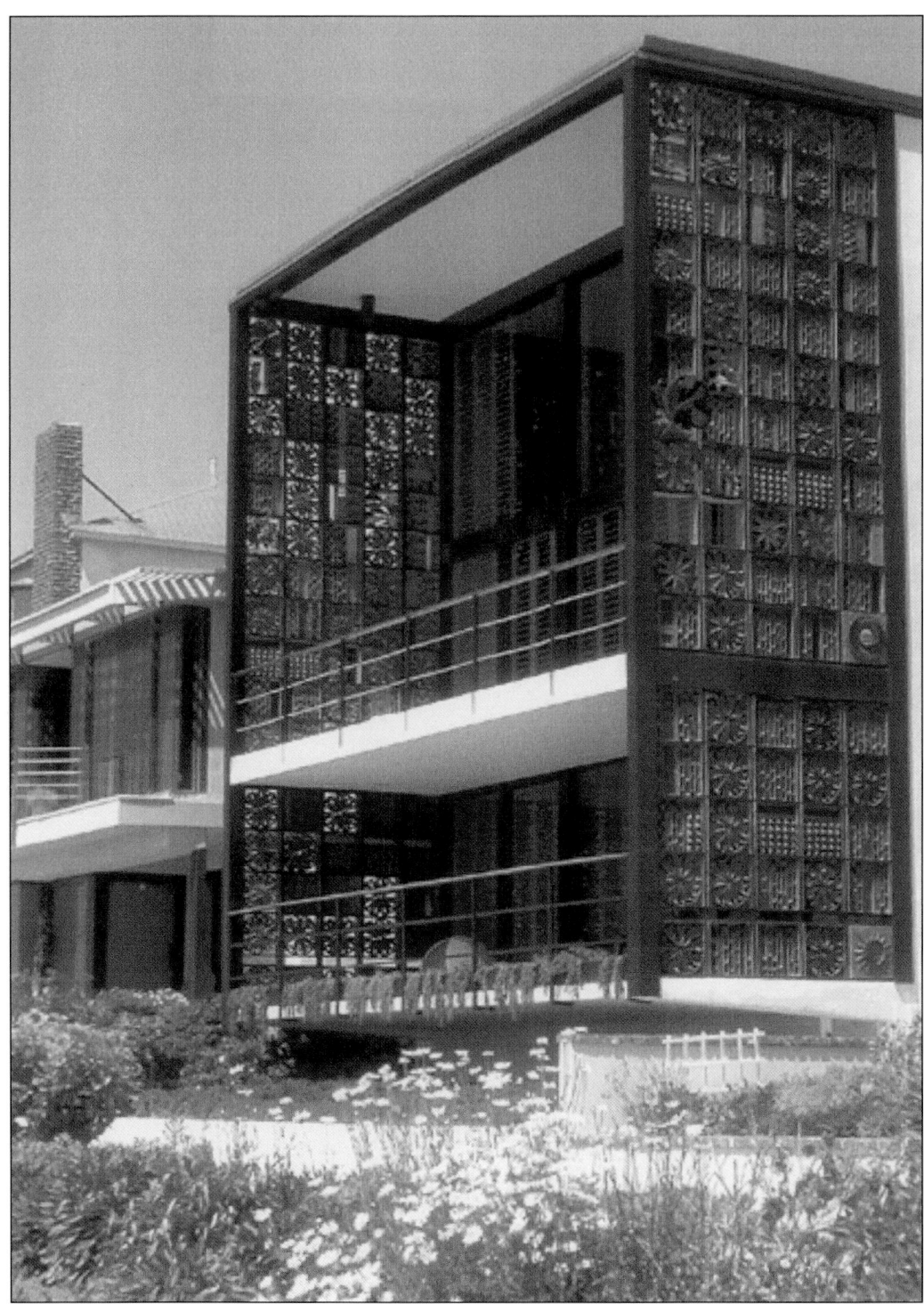

Although the traditional home of lath and plaster was still being built, innovative and dramatic materials were creating the showcase structures of the 1960s. The home of Mr. and Mrs. John Scott, located on the Strand, was the first steel-framed home constructed in Manhattan Beach.

Six
PRESERVING CHARACTER

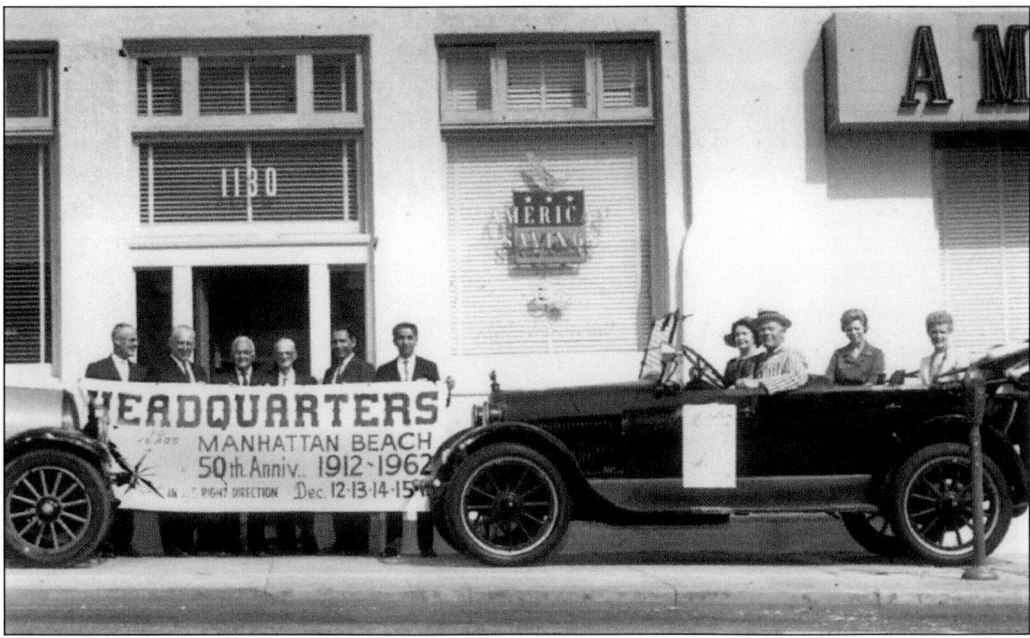

Throughout the remaining decades the community celebrated anniversaries, enjoyed beach activities, and took on a more relaxed atmosphere. The basic work had been completed: streets were in, water and utilities had been installed, and the city's tax base was in good shape. It was time to refine the special character of this seaside resort community. When financing became more available, many landowners requested variances to split their lots, due to the lack of land expansion, the increase in population, and the demand for new housing. The board of zoning adjustment was being increasingly pressed for precedent setting decisions affecting congestion and density concerns. Though we see much of the past being razed, the development of the barren sand dunes has become one of the finest residential communities in Los Angeles County. Manhattan Beach continues the task of preserving its innate charm and uniqueness with an appreciation of the past and sound judgment for the future.

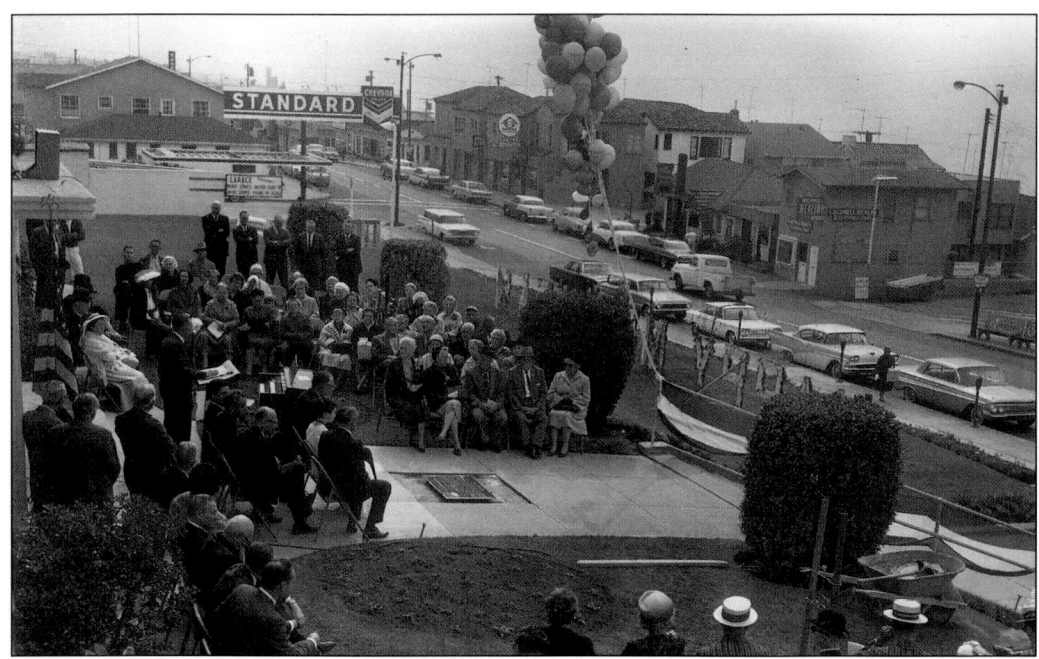

To celebrate the 50th Anniversary of the city's incorporation, a five-day calendar of events was held. On December 12, 1962, a commemorative ceremony took place on the steps of City Hall. A plaque marking the city's 50th year was embedded into the cement walk in front of City Hall. It read: "Manhattan Beach has provided its citizenry the appealing surroundings of a resort area with the leisurely simplicity of small city living."

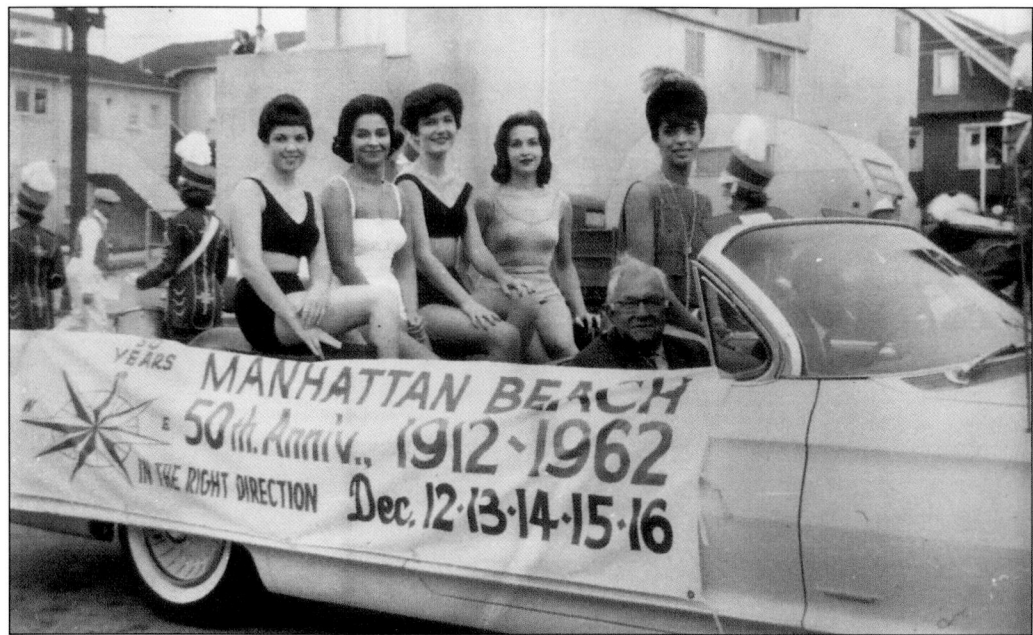

On Saturday of that eventful weekend, a surfing contest was held near the Manhattan Beach pier and a mid-morning holiday parade with "Old Time Christmas" as its theme was held. All of this was followed by a box lunch at Live Oak Park.

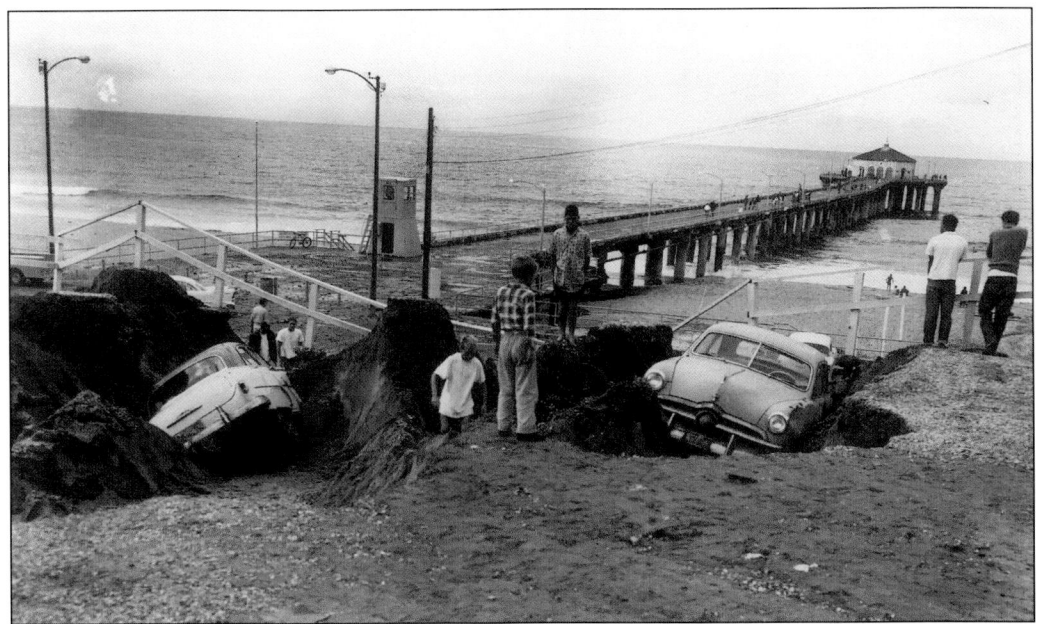

Even in an area of year-round fine weather, Mother Nature could occasionally surprise. Looking west, young boys investigate the damage done by an early 1962 February storm, which caused a cave-in of the parking lot above the Strand at Manhattan Beach Blvd.

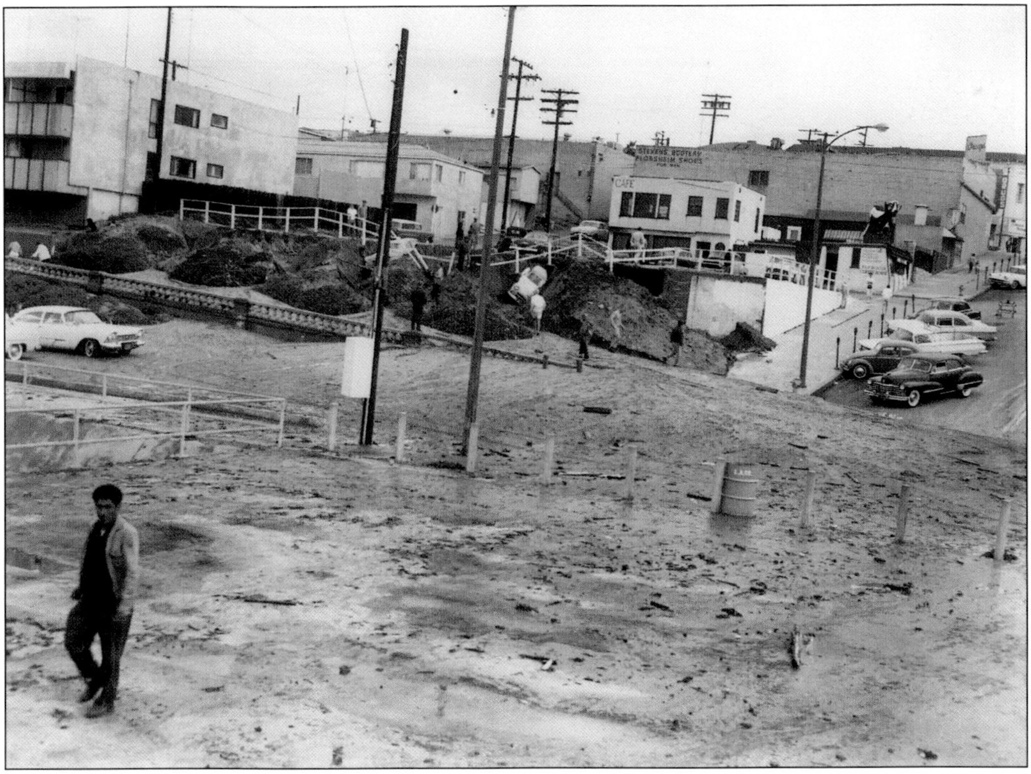

Looking east, the destruction can be seen with dirt covering the entry to the pier.

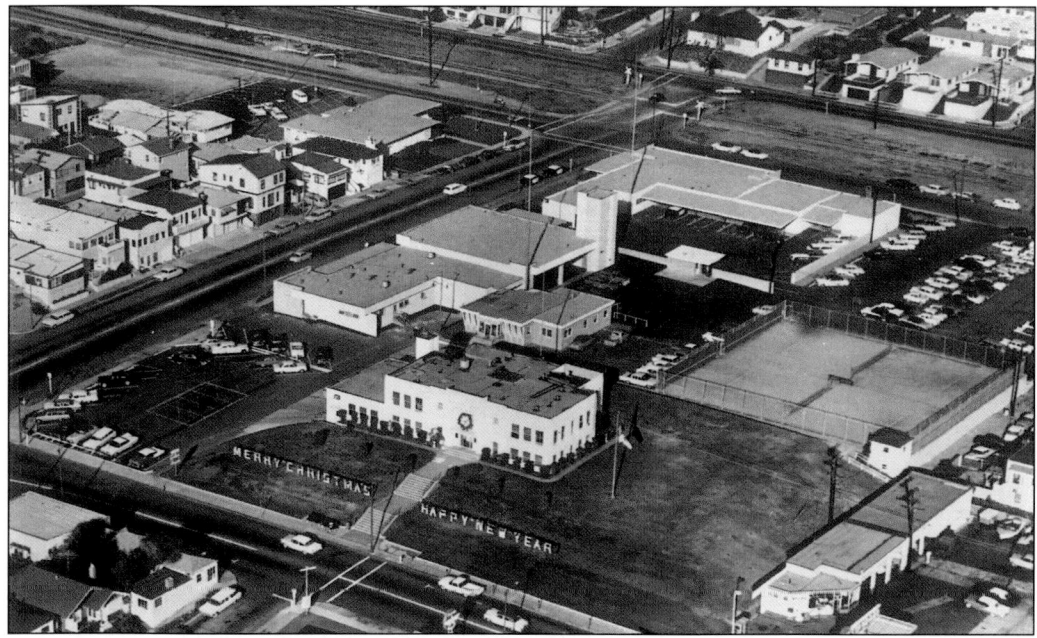

By 1962, the civic center had a new police station and a new fire station with more changes for the downtown area in the planning stages. The barren land to the north of the civic center was to be the location of a multipurpose community facility, Joslyn Center, built in 1965.

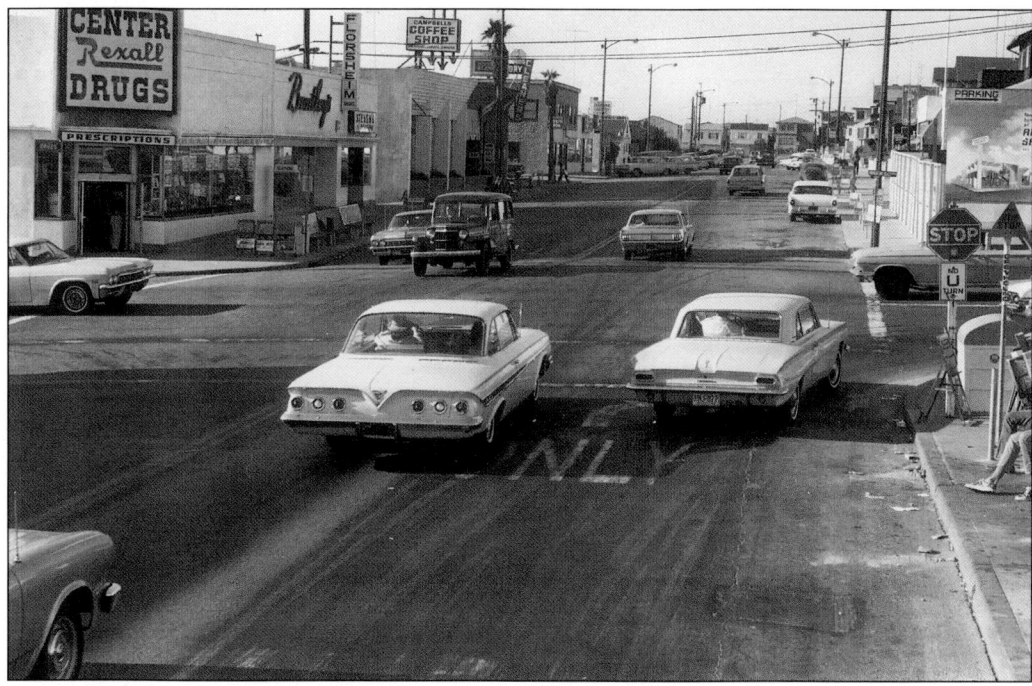

In the downtown area, the old hotel and general store, located on the northeast corner of Manhattan Avenue, was demolished and replaced by the American Savings Bank. This photo, taken in 1966 looking north, is the intersection of Manhattan Beach Blvd. and Manhattan Avenue, the birthplace of the community.

The 1915 City Hall served the community well. Irreparable damage sustained in the February 9, 1971, earthquake had sealed the building's fate for demolition that same year. On August 30th a ceremony was held at the site to bid the old landmark farewell. As the honorary mayor of Manhattan Beach, Hal Peary, well known for his radio role as "The Great Guildersleeve," gave the eulogy.

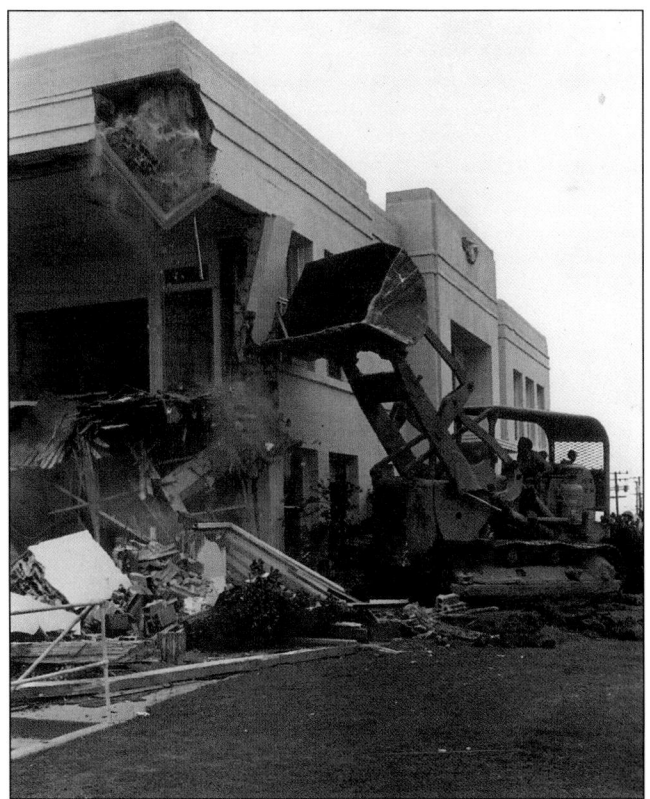

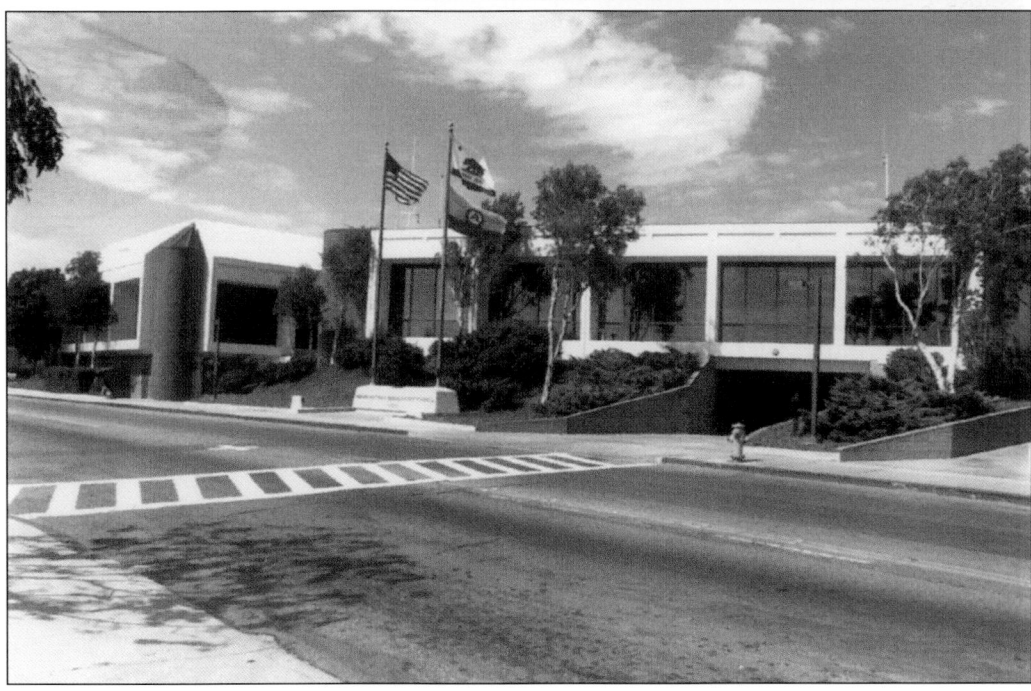

The new and present City Hall complex was built at the same location as the old City Hall and was dedicated on November 1, 1975.

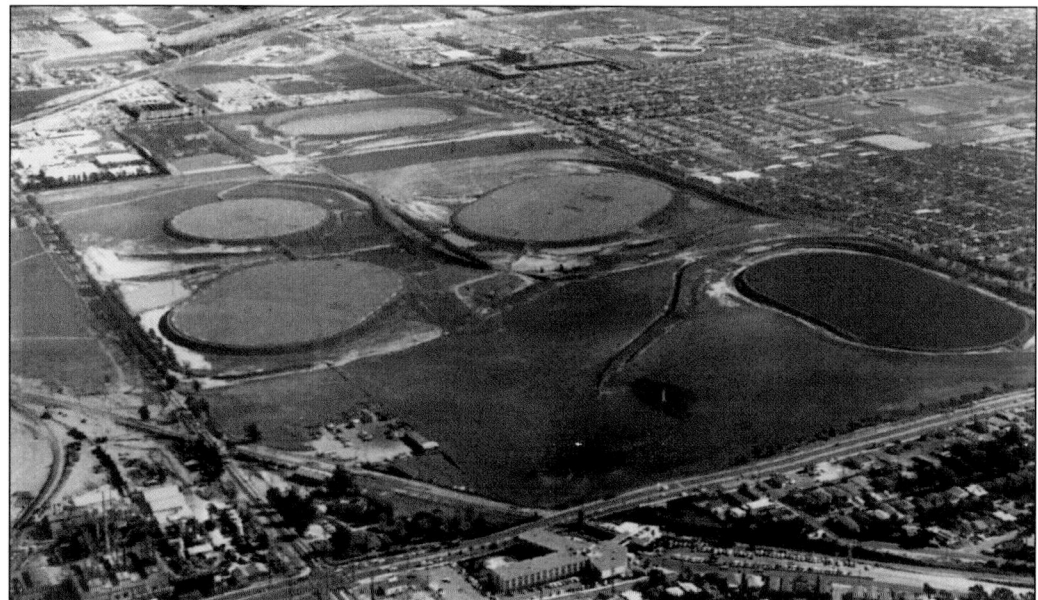

In 1967, the Standard Oil tank farm, a large expanse of 187 acres in the community, remained undeveloped. The site encompassed five oil tanks used for storage by the Standard Oil Co. (located in the neighboring town of El Segundo adjacent to Manhattan Beach's northern boundary). This portion represented 12 percent of Manhattan Beach's landmass. After many meetings and suggestions, it was determined that the property would be developed into a golf course, shopping center, residential housing, and open space, accommodating a soccer field and business park. A hotel, tennis club, and senior housing were added later.

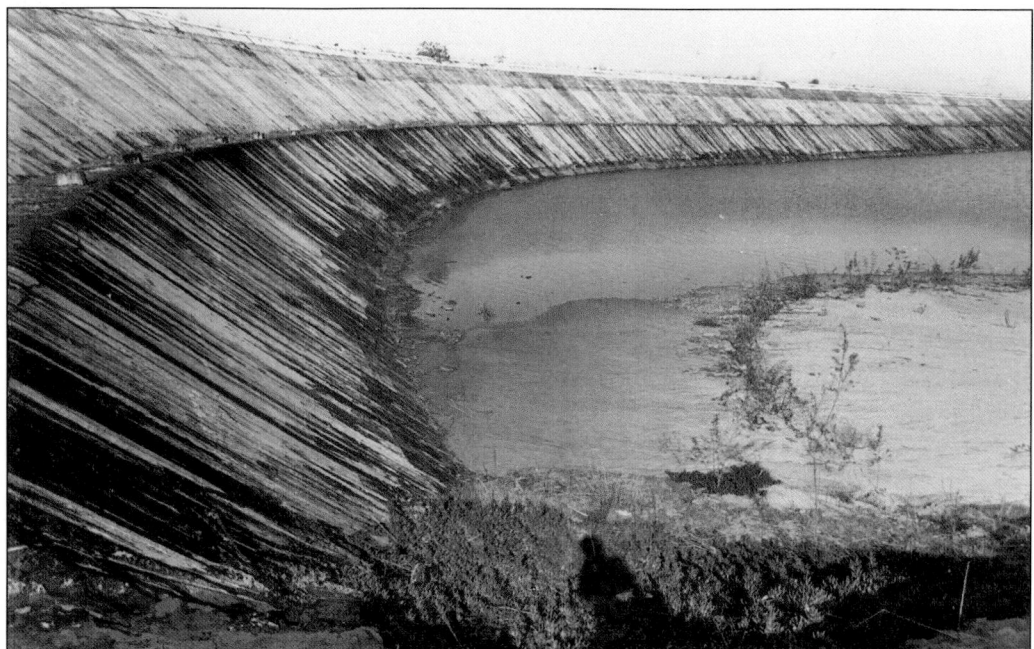

The first phase began by filling in the underground storage tanks and grading 40 acres for the shopping center.

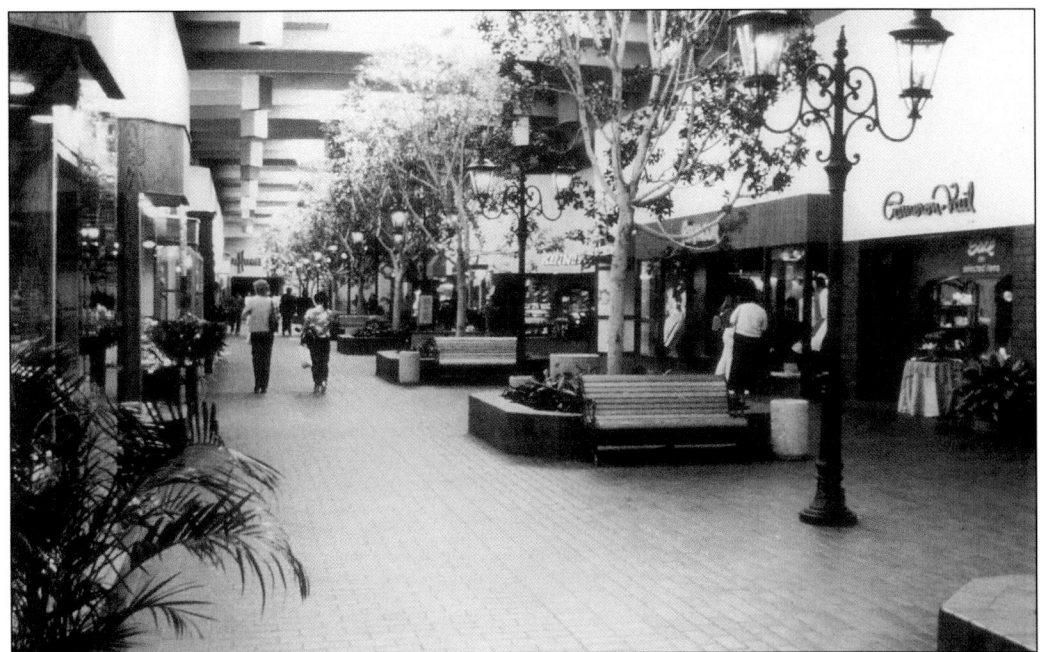

In 1981, a 450,000-squarefoot commercial shopping center complex opened. The Manhattan Village Shopping Center, developed by Haagen Land and Development Company, included an enclosed mall. The exterior of the center maintained a Spanish architecture with a warm and invitingly designed interior promenade.

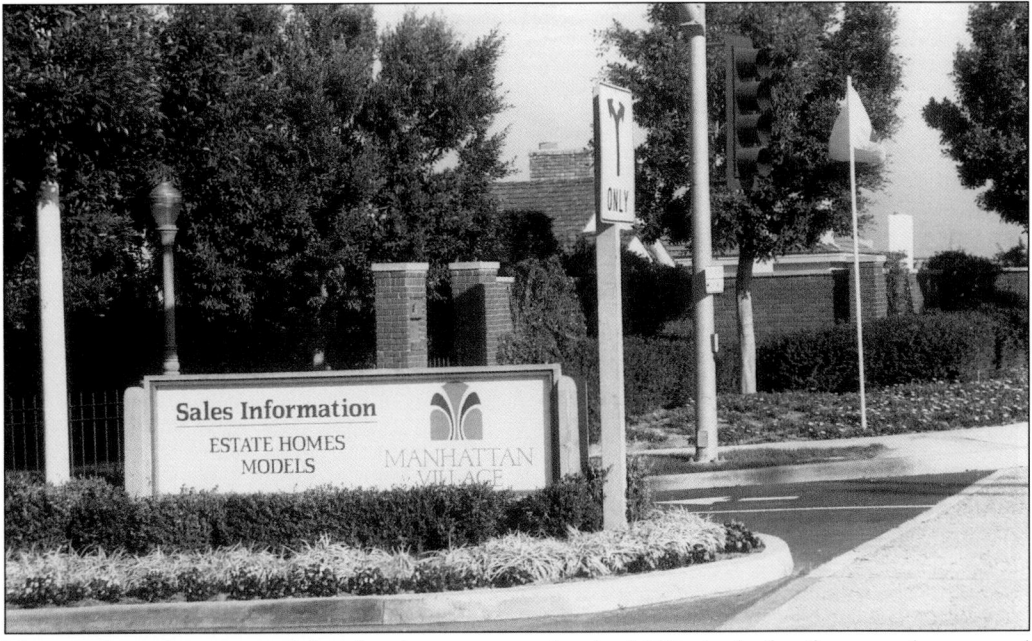

The residential portion of the development consisted of 122 single-family estate homes and approximately 400 town and court homes. By September of 1987, 468 units had received certificates of occupancy and there were 60 units under construction with 48 more units having permits issued.

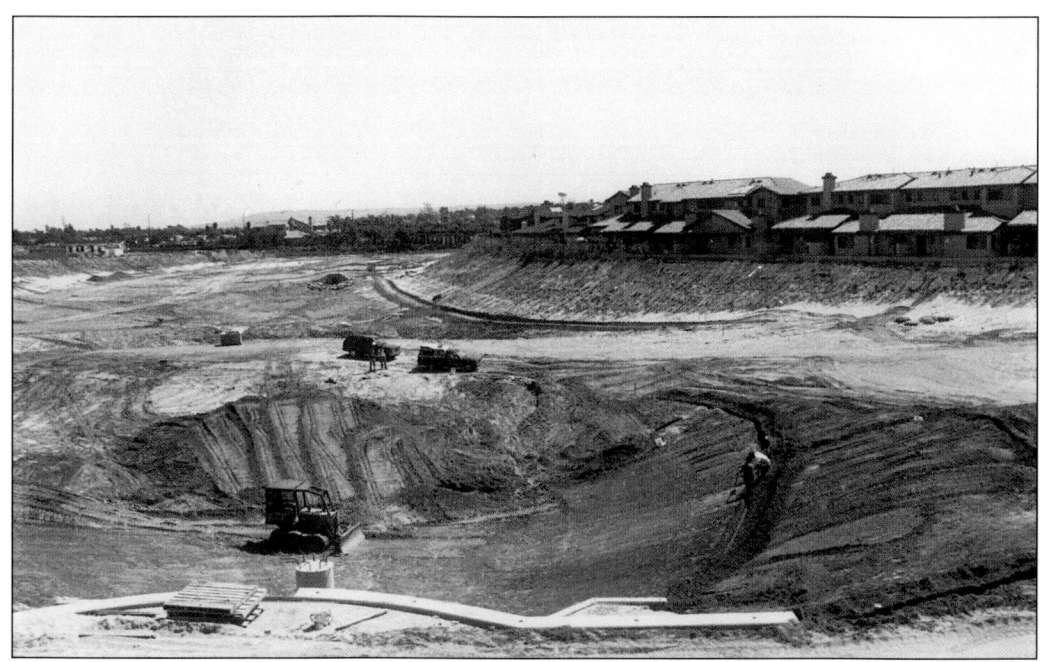

While the residential phase of the Tank Farm development was being completed, the grading for the golf course began. The later would serve also as a collector of runoff rainwater. The course became a gracious setting for the hotel.

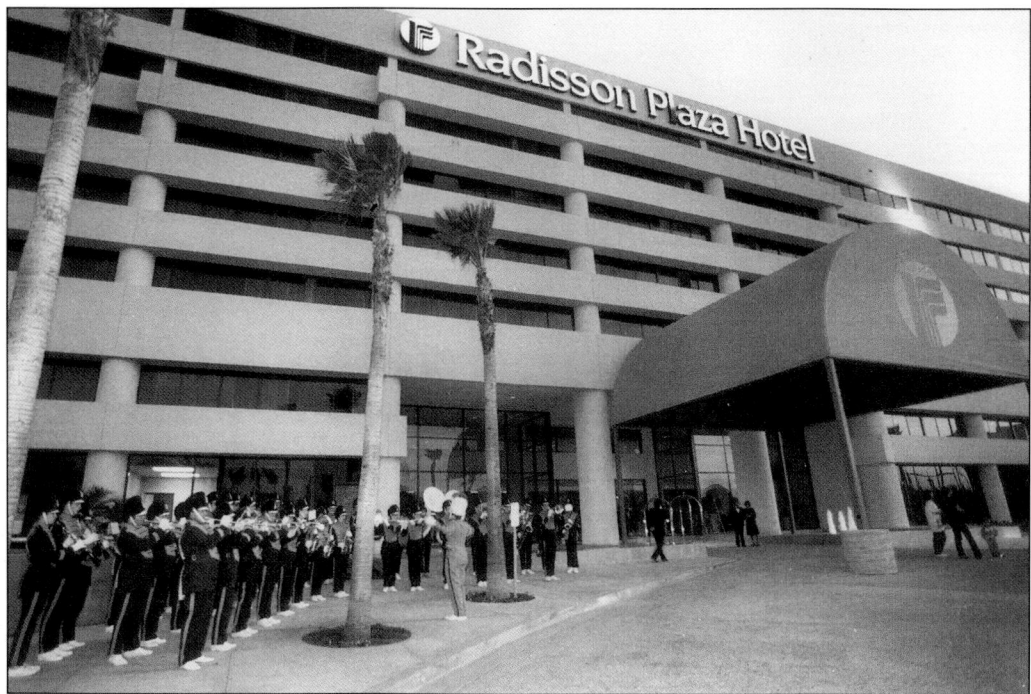

On September 20, 1986, the Radisson Plaza Hotel and Golf Course, later changed to the Manhattan Beach Marriott, celebrated its grand opening. The Mira Costa High School Marching Band saluted the arrival of over 800 quests and dignitaries.

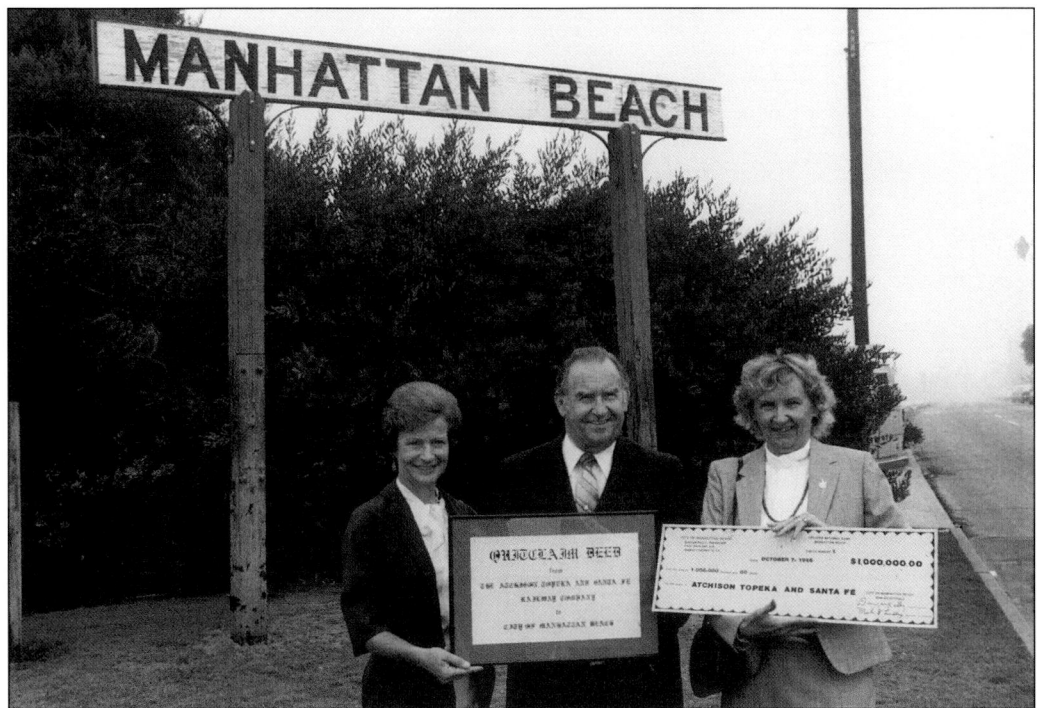

On October 7, 1986, at 9:00 a.m., Santa Fe Railway deeded 21.2 acres of abandoned railroad right-of-way to the city of Manhattan Beach. It was purchased at a price of $4.2 million to be paid over the next four years. Santa Fe retained 2.1 acres for future development. Left to right are: Connie Sieber, councilwoman; William Bentley, ATSF manager real estate and contracts; and Jan Dennis, mayor of Manhattan Beach.

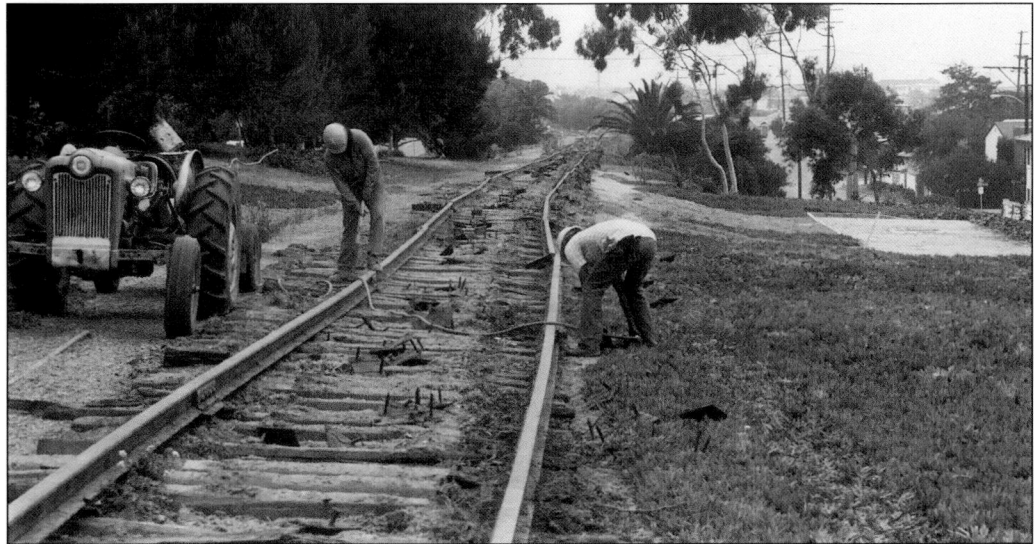

The Atchison, Topeka, and Santa Fe tracks, which had been laid in 1888, were sold to Valley Railroad Ties, an independent contractor. The dismantling of the tracks in 1986 closed an era and allowed the city to change the right-of-way into a landscaped open space that runs the width of the town from north to south.

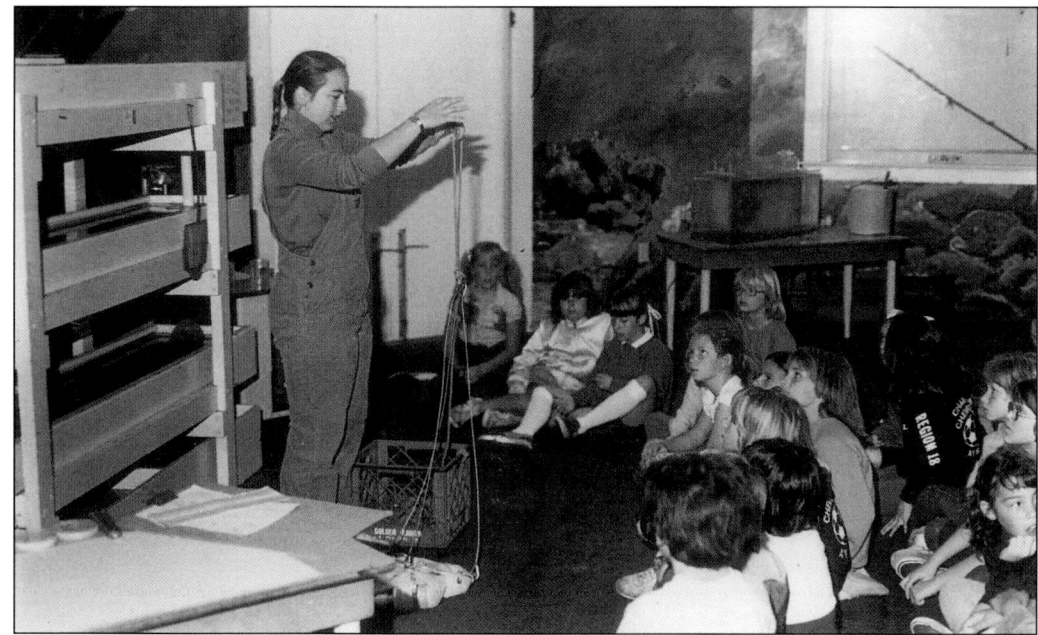

Started in 1981, the Oceanographic Teaching Station (OTS) has been a wonderful source of marine life information to young and old alike. The roundhouse at the end of the municipal pier is leased to this nonprofit organization. Here, in 1983, Wendy Gault instructs students at the OTS Roundhouse Marine Studies Lab.

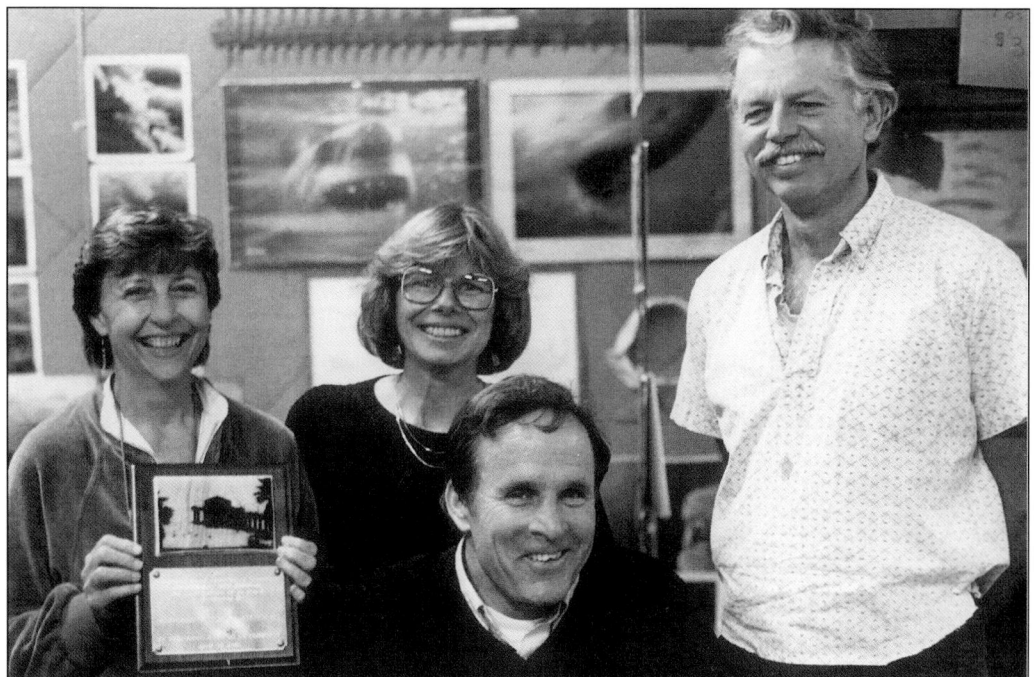

In 1985, the OTS organization received the Community Commendation Award from the Chamber of Commerce for their outstanding work with youth in the area. Left to right are: E. Hannah, C. Marsh, J. Babbitt, and F. Armistead.

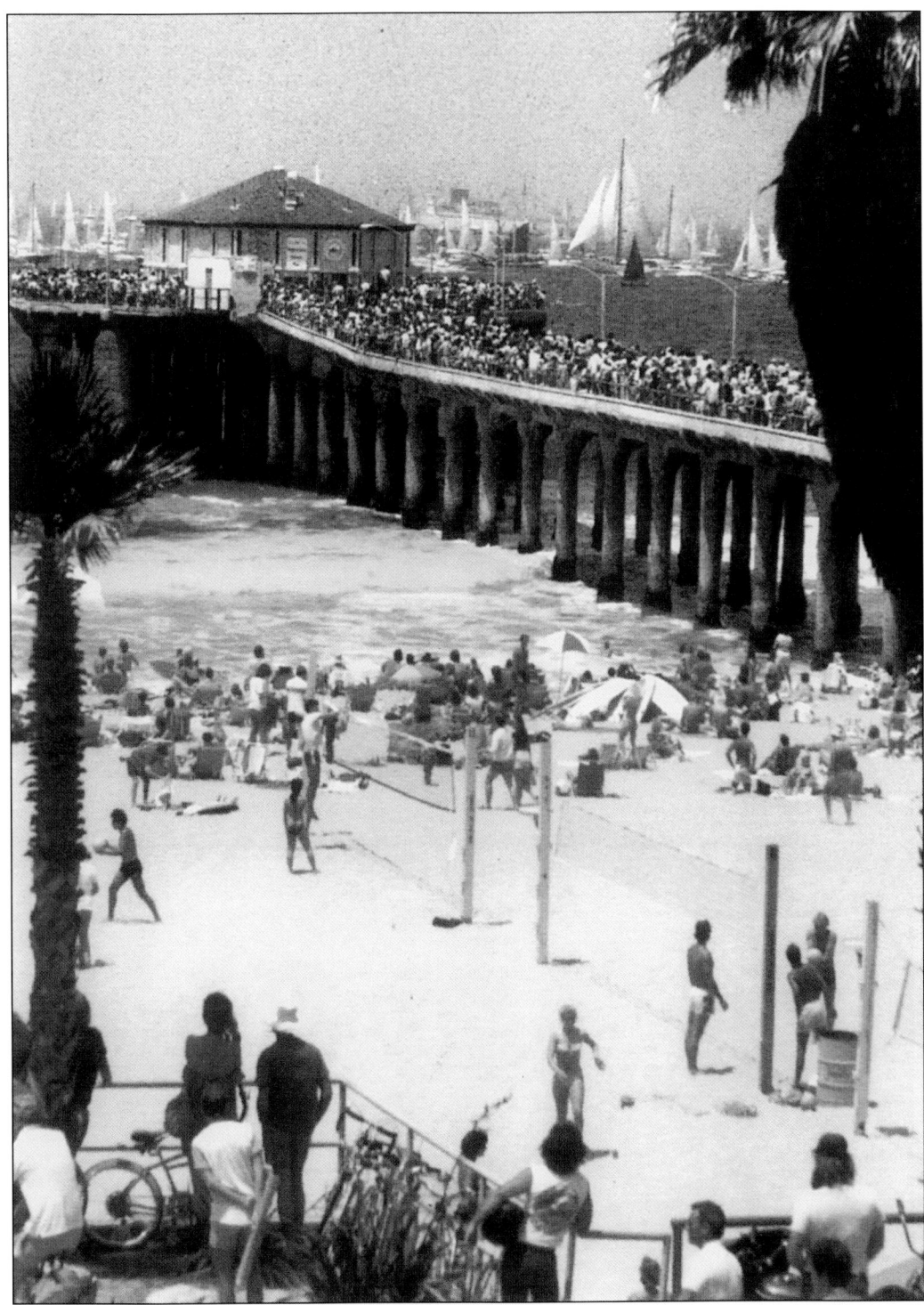
The Los Angeles Olympic Arts Festival and the Summer Olympic Games of 1984 brought thousands of visitors and residents to the beach on July 4th to catch a glimpse of the tall ships just off shore.

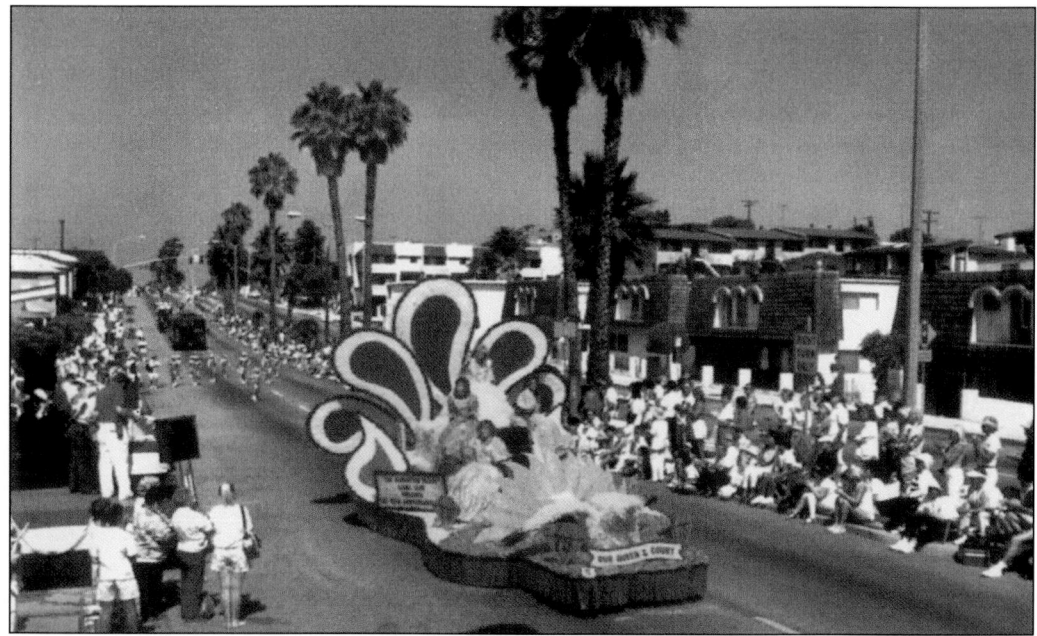

The 75th year of the city's incorporation was celebrated in 1987 with a year of social events. The weekend of July 25 and 26 brought a grand parade on Saturday and a daylong community picnic on Sunday. There were more then 120 entries in this Diamond Anniversary parade, including many floats and marching bands. Along with the 75th Queen and Her Court were representatives of local organizations.

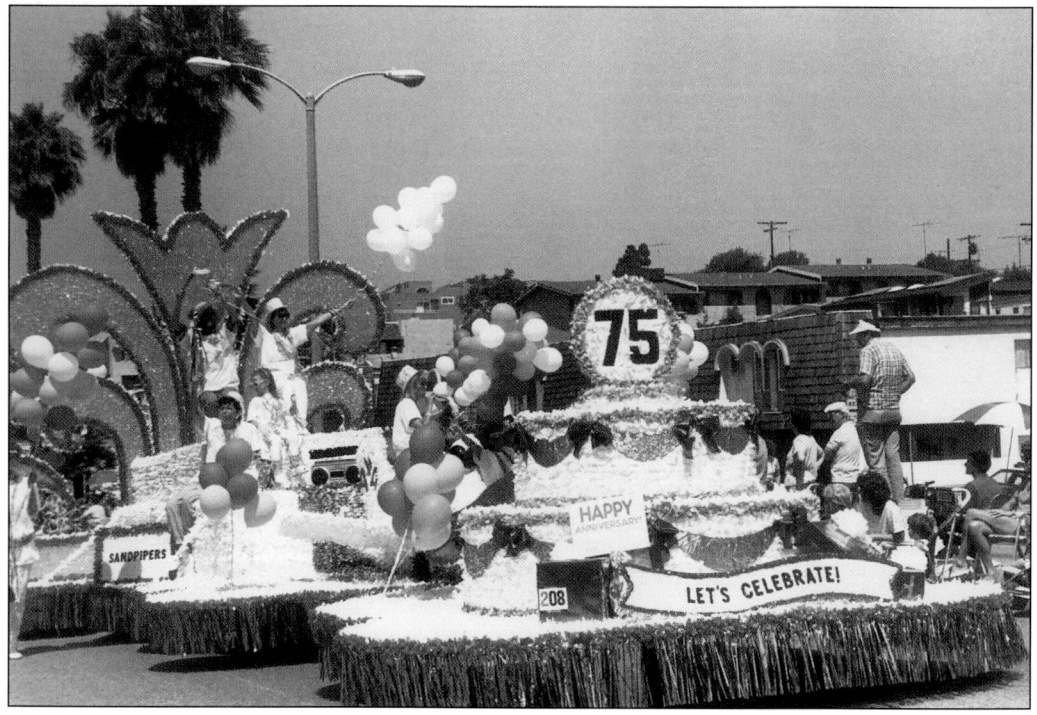

Sandpipers Inc. sponsored another large float with the slogan "Let's Celebrate."

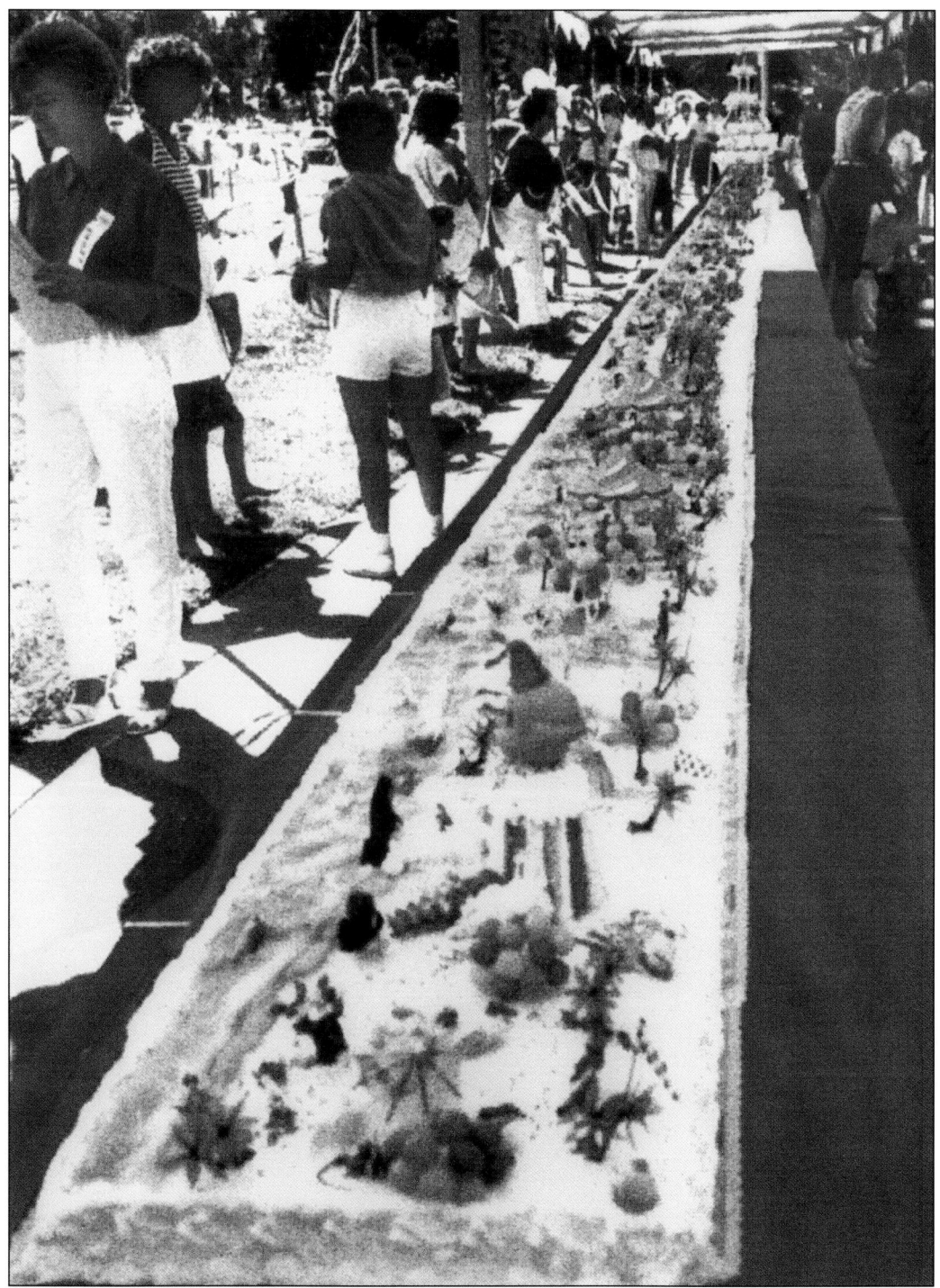
One of the outstanding features of the 75th Anniversary picnic was the 111-foot birthday cake. Made by the neighboring El Segundo Bakery, the city's cake was decorated with various scenes from the community. Members of the Neptunian Woman's Club served 5,000 pieces of cake that day.

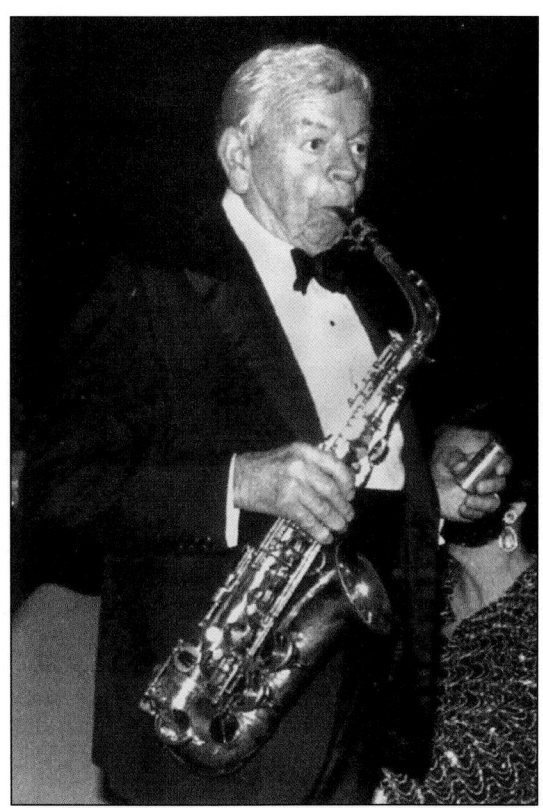

The 1987 black-tie Diamond Anniversary Ball gave glitter and glamour to the yearlong celebration. The finale came on December 12th with Les Brown and his "Band of Renown" providing the dance music for the gala event held at the Radisson Plaza Hotel (later renamed the Manhattan Beach Marriott Hotel).

These members of the rotary club served as the ball committee and worked together for over a year alongside the anniversary chairperson, Mayor Jan Dennis, seated here at the piano. Left to right, these men are: Donn Ennis, Nelson Gray, Bob Stephenson, Jim Hallett, Bill Becker, and Scott Dannison. The club received excellent support from the community and hosted 460 guests in grand style.

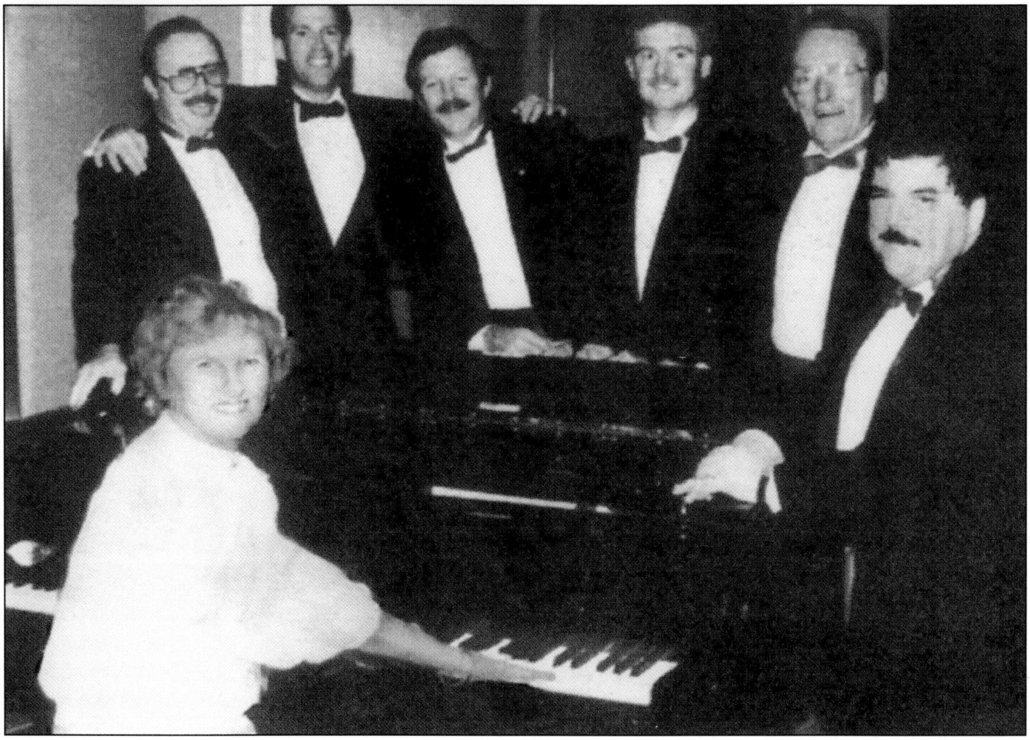

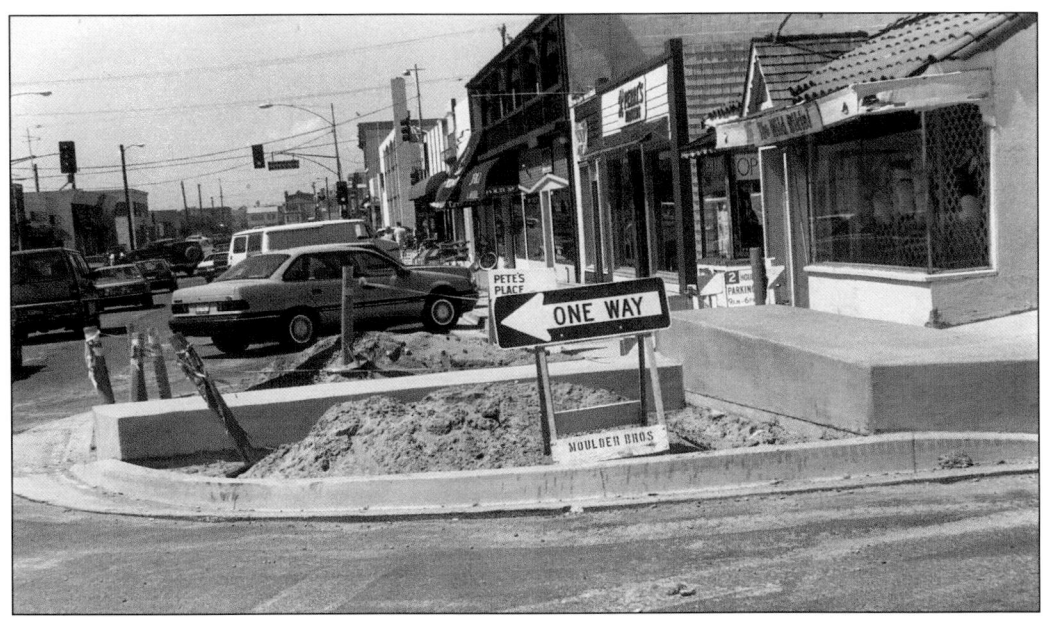

The city council, in June of 1985, adopted the downtown streetscape design after a year of much discussion and exchange of ideas. Lasting three years, the city endured blocked streets, construction workers' trucks, orange cones, and mounds of dirt seemingly piled on every street corner. Yellow tape limiting pedestrian access became commonplace decor. The project was finished in 1988.

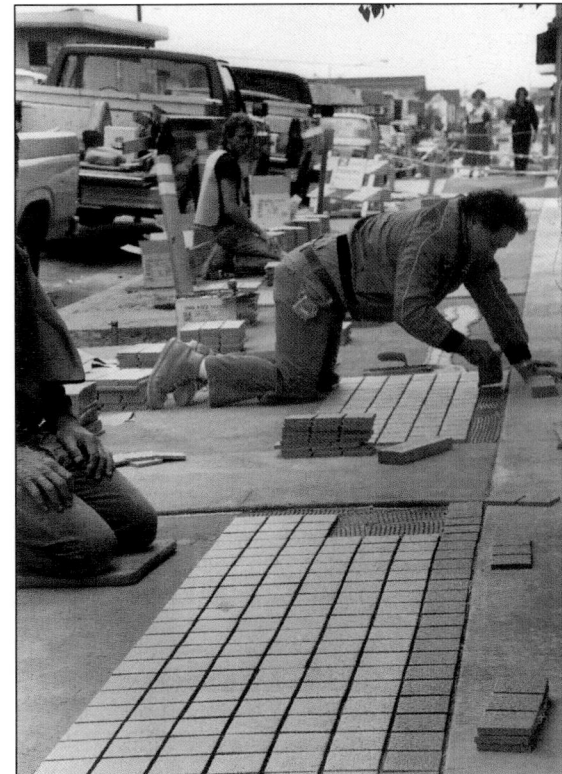

Tile setters working on Highland Avenue marked the first phase of the beautification project known as the "Downtown Streetscape." Light blue tile with a row of darker tile was set by hand, streets were redesigned, trees were planted, and parallel parking was added to the west side of Manhattan Avenue.

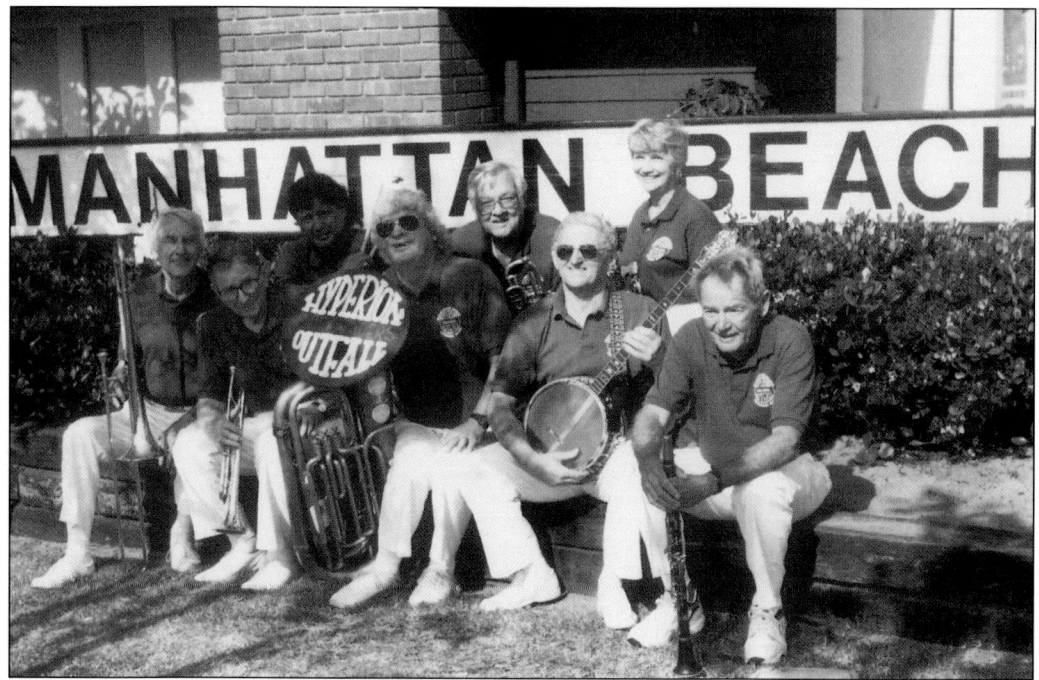

Formed in 1969, the Hyperion Outfall Serenaders became the official band of the city by a city council proclamation in 1975. The group plays at numerous South Bay and city functions such as the Hometown Fair, Chamber of Commerce Ribbon Cutting, and private parties. Seated here at the side of the historical society are band members Jack Freeman, Jules Radinsky, Luis Paster, Dave Freeman, Bob White, Jimmy Green, Fran Freeman, and Sid Pattison.

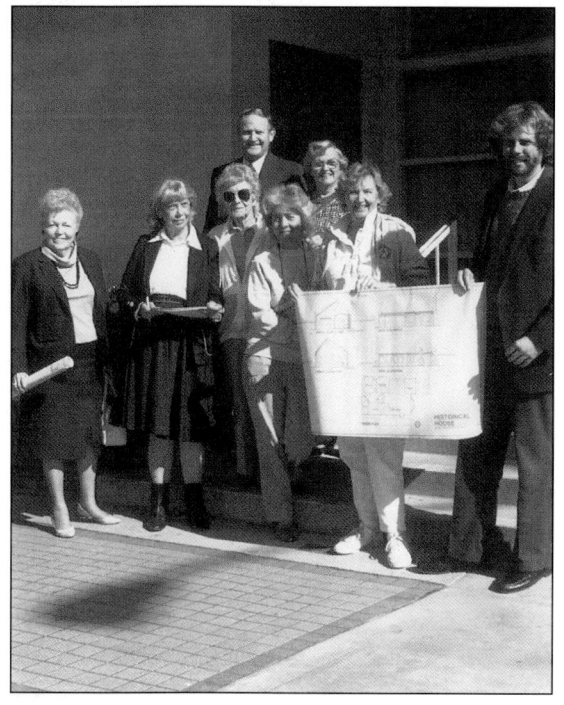

In 1988, members from the Neptunian Woman's Club, city staff, and the historical society worked together on plans for a city museum. Left to right, the members here are Mary Weaver, Mary Brandvig, Charlotte Cravello, Jim Stecklein, Phyllis Eddy, Marilyn Owen, Jan Dennis, and Keith Robinson. The historical museum officially opened May 12, 1990.

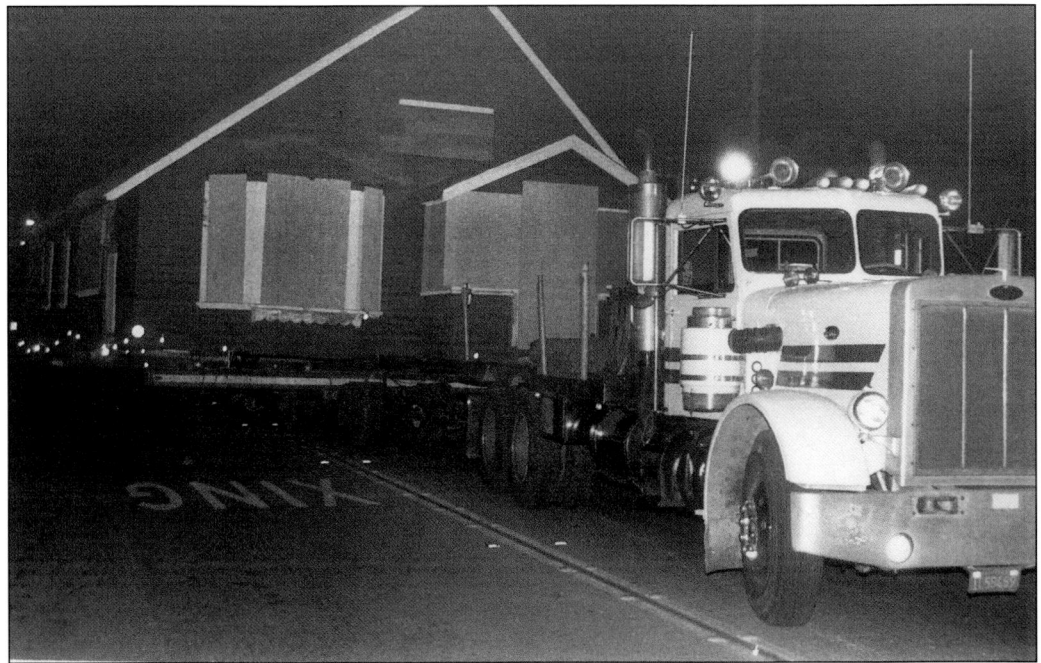

Scheduled for demolition, the city saved this classic example of a 1905 beach cottage. After its purchase from the owner for $1.00 it was moved to Polliwog Park, to land owned by the Manhattan Beach School District. Most of the early beach cottages along the Strand had already been replaced by large three story homes.

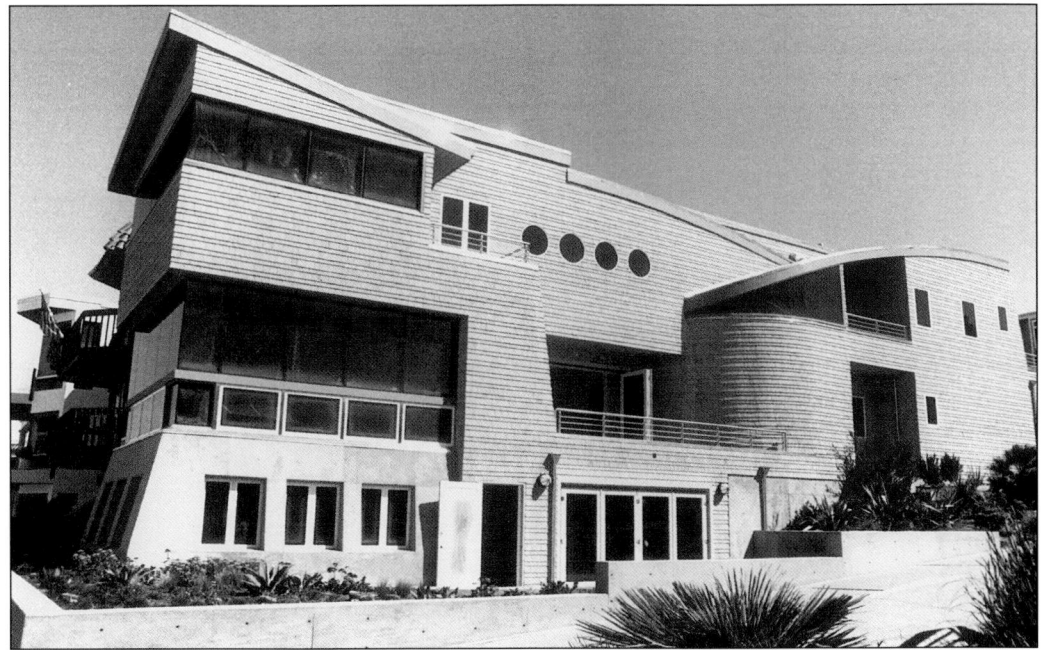

In the 1990s and through the end of the decade, the leading concern facing many of the residents of the city was the expansion of large homes built to the limits of their lot. Architects Killefer, Falmmang, and Purtill built this international style home in 1997.

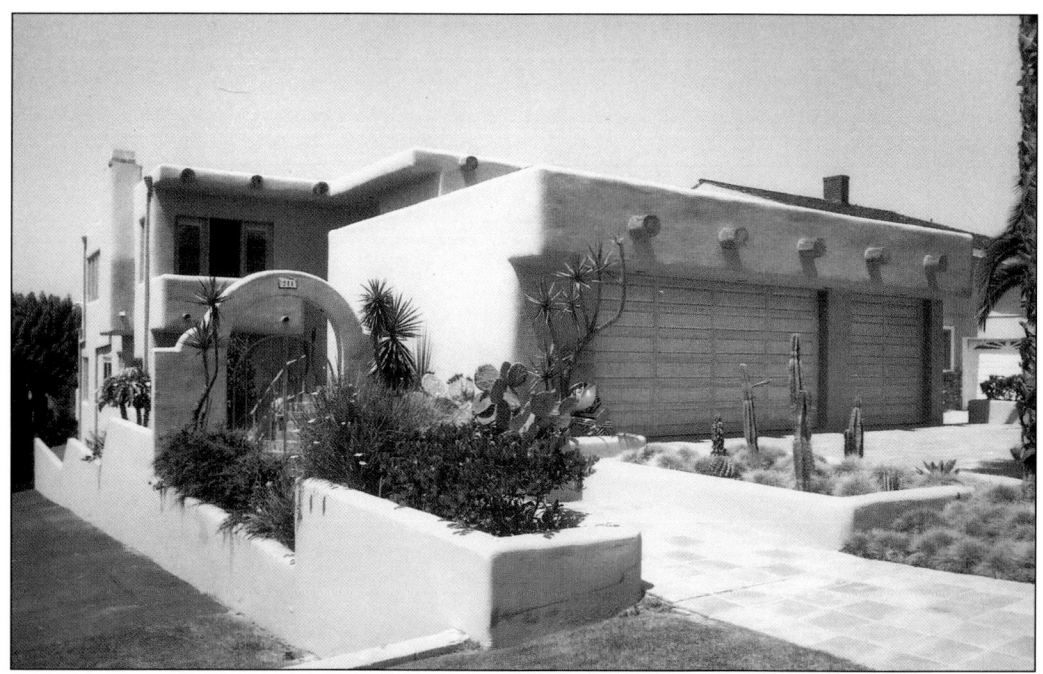

The Pueblo revival style is being seen more and more in Manhattan Beach. Inspired by the Spanish colonial and Native American pueblos, the elements of this deign are easily identified.

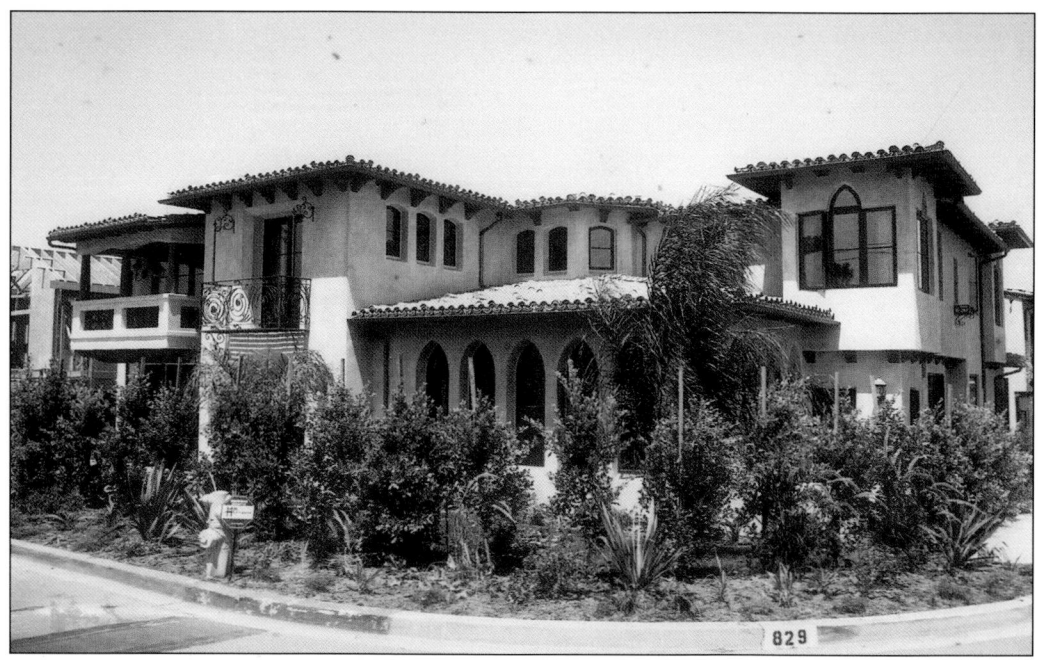

Situated high in the Hill Section, this modern Spanish-Moorish style home, designed by Dave Olin, characterizes the size of most of the new homes being built today. The shadows have changed and Manhattan Beach has come of age. The town is no longer a settlement of scattered beach cottages on shifting sand, but a multi-million-dollar jewel in the crown of Los Angeles County's South Bay section.